Adam's Wish

Adam's Wish

Unknown Poetry of Ṭáhirih

John S. Hatcher

and

Amrollah Hemmat

Bahá'í Publishing

Wilmette, Illinois

Bahá'í Publishing
415 Linden Avenue, Wilmette, Illinois 60091-2844

Printed in the United States of America on acid-free paper ∞

16 15 14 13 12 4 3 2

Library of Congress Cataloging-in-Publication Data

Qurrat al-'Ayn, 1817 or 18-1852.
[Poems. English. Selections]
Adam's wish : Tahirih's unknown poems / translated and edited by John S. Hatcher & Amrollah Hemmat.
p. cm.
Translated from Persian.
Includes bibliographical references and index.
ISBN-13: 978-1-931847-61-2 (pbk. : alk. paper)
ISBN-10: 1-931847-61-4 (pbk. : alk. paper) 1. Qurrat al-'Ayn, 1817 or 18-1852—Translations into English. I. Hatcher, John, Dr. II. Hemmat, Amrollah. III. Title.
PK6528.U77A2 2008
891'.5512—dc22

2008036372

Book design by Patrick J. Falso
Cover design by Robert A. Reddy

Contents

Foreword

It is common to capitalize the Deity and pronouns alluding to God. In Bahá'í scripture and authoritative texts, as well as in many works written by Bahá'ís about the Bahá'í Faith, it is customary to capitalize all pronouns referring to the Manifestations of God (the Prophets) as a sign of reverence for what Bahá'ís believe to be Their exalted station. Since Ṭáhirih is almost always writing about the Manifestations, both of the ancient past (Adam, Noah, Abraham, and Moses in particular) and of more recent religious history (Muḥammad, the Báb, and Bahá'u'lláh), we have opted to follow this tradition when translating her poetry, even though there is no capitalization in the original Persian and Arabic of her verse. This is a poetic license we have exercised to render her work as accurately and faithfully as we can, knowing that she herself would doubtless have done the same had she been writing in English.

In our introductions, commentaries, and footnotes in this text, we have decided to maintain this same procedure so as to be consistent throughout. Likewise, we have capitalized *Manifestation, Prophet,* and other terms that specifically allude to what the Bahá'í Faith considers to be beings who have been explicitly ordained as emissaries from the divine world sent by God to advance human civilization. Finally, the reader should note that words and phrases that we have italicized in the poems themselves indicate that the original is in Arabic. Ṭáhirih often employs Arabic terms, most particularly when she is citing a tradition or, even more commonly, when she is alluding to some well-known passage from the Qur'án. In such instances, she will often cite only a word or two from the complete verse because she expects the reader to be familiar with these passages. With most of these verses translated from the Arabic, we have indicated in footnotes the source of the allusion and the probable bearing it has on what Ṭáhirih is saying.

Note from Ṭáhirih

O people of God, God willing, pages (write ups, texts) on (about) obligatory deeds and supplications will be sent (will be issued). Strive to make progress and value these pages,[1] for the day of the great martyrdom is close at hand, and after the martyrdom of the Point, there will be no repose for anyone. Praised be God, the Lord of the Worlds.

(This was completed on Thursday, the twentieth of the month of the honored Sh'bán in the year 1267 [June 20, 1851].)

Note from the Transcriber

The lowly and annihilated Abu'l-ḥasan Neyrízí transcribed this in the first day of month of Shavval in the year 1341 [Thursday, May 17, 1923] from the Hegira (emigration) of the prophethood (the Prophet Muḥammad), the Chosen One; thousands of thousands of salutations and praise and glory and light and honor and veneration be upon the One who made that emigration.

1. *Varaqát* (ورقات): "pages." In Mohammadhoseini's version this word is *awqát* (اوقات), meaning "time," as in "treasure this special time."

Introduction

Whose life is worth recounting? Whose life's work merits study and reflection? Whomever among our contemporaries we may presently admire, time itself will in due course reveal whose lives and works have made an impact on the progress of humankind. For playwrights, historians, and women's rights activists, the life of the nineteenth-century poetess Ṭáhirih—Fáṭimih Umm-i-Salmih (1817–1852)—has proven well worth recounting. Even today in her native Persia (Iran), her dauntless courage, dramatic life story, and impassioned lyric poems have currency, most especially among those contemporary Iranian women who believe the constraints imposed on them by Shí'ih Islam are archaic and baseless.

While biographies and plays have paid tribute to Ṭáhirih's heroic life, most of her poetry was thought to be lost to the ages. Indeed, we struggled mightily to assemble her better known lyric poems in our first volume of her work, *The Poetry of Ṭáhirih* (2002). Now we have been fortunate to have obtained and reproduce herein, both in the original calligraphy and translated into English, the first of two rich manuscripts containing unpublished and largely unknown poems that are among some of Ṭáhirih's more industrious and serious works.

Unlike the shorter and more passionate lyrics of the first volume, the poems in this collection are considerably longer and more complex. Some portions of these works have the tenor of a treatise as she examines, often in great detail, the foundation for her most cherished theological and philosophical perspectives. In a future volume, it is our hope to give a similar treatment to the poems from another unpublished manuscript of her poetry.

For those who may be unfamiliar with the early history of the Bahá'í Faith or, more especially, with the important role that Ṭáhirih played in that heroic age of this religion, we provide here an introduction to the Bahá'í religion and to the social and historical context that formed the backdrop against which the dramatic story of Ṭáhirih's life and art played out.

1. Ṭáhirih and the Bahá'í Faith

The Bahá'í Faith began May 23, 1844, when Siyyid 'Alí-Muḥammad—known as "the Báb" (the "Gate")—revealed that He was the Promised One Whose mission was to herald the advent of a turning point in human history. According to His own writings, the sole mission of the Báb and His religion (the Bábí Faith) was to proclaim and prepare people for the advent of another Prophet of God Who would soon appear to bring about world unity and global peace. The Báb alluded to this Prophet as "Him Whom God shall make manifest" and asserted that He would appear in the year nine of the Bábí dispensation, or 1853.

The Báb first revealed His identity to Mullá Ḥusayn-i-Bus͟hrú'í, a student who had been searching for the promised Qá'im of S͟hí'ih Islam, but the Báb admonished this first follower to tell no one else until seventeen other individuals had also discovered the Báb's identity through independent search. These first eighteen disciples the Báb titled "Letters of the Living," and He charged each of them to undertake a specific mission to teach others about the fulfillment of this promised Day of Resurrection, as it is called in the Qur'án.

Among the most prominent of these stalwart souls was Fáṭimih Umm-i-Salmih (1817–1852), the only female among these eighteen individuals, a woman who would later be titled *Ṭáhirih* ("the Pure One"). Interestingly, Ṭáhirih was never able to meet the Báb in person, yet she became one of the most notable teachers of His religion and played a crucial role in the revealing of the Bábí religion as an independent revelation from God and not merely as a sect or reform movement within Islam.

Described in *Memorials of the Faithful* as a "woman chaste and holy, a sign and token of surpassing beauty, a burning brand of the love of God, a lamp of His bestowal" ('Abdu'l-Bahá, no. 69.1), Ṭáhirih was regarded by both her coreligionists and by the most learned of her male contemporaries as erudite, heroic, and a poet of unsurpassed talent. A telling tribute to her character from a Bahá'í perspective appears in *God Passes By,* where Shoghi Effendi states that she was "regarded from childhood, by her fellow-townsmen, as a prodigy, alike in her intelligence and beauty," that she was "highly esteemed even by some of the most haughty and learned 'ulamá of her country," that prior to her conversion to the Bábí Faith she was renowned "for the brilliancy and novelty of the views she propounded," and that she was "acclaimed as 'Qurrat-i-'Ayní (solace of my eyes) by her admiring teacher, Siyyid Káẓim." Shoghi Effendi goes on to note that "she had, through a dream . . . established her first contact with a Faith which she continued to propagate to her last breath, and in its hour of greatest peril, with all the ardor of her unsubduable spirit" (73).

Such lofty praise can be translated into more contemporary terms when we learn that though Ṭáhirih lived under the rigid constraints against women that existed in mid-nineteenth-century Persia (Iran, as it is called today), she declared in her final words before she was executed in August of 1852, "You can kill me as soon as you like, but you cannot stop the emancipation of women" (quoted in Shoghi Effendi, *God Passes By,* 75). She was then strangled and thrown into an abandoned well.

This rudimentary information about her life is hardly incidental to her poetry. Knowledge about the rapid spread of the Bábí Faith and the equally vehement and virulent treatment of the new converts to the religion is crucial in understanding many of the topical religious and historical allusions in her poetry. We have attempted to include and elucidate much of this vast information in footnotes and introductions because it is essential to comprehending her poetry. The complexity of some of this information also helps to underscore the depth and breadth of Ṭáhirih's knowledge of theology, philosophy, and some of the more esoteric traditions of Islam, Gnosticism, Ṣúfísm, and most especially the works of her teacher, Siyyid Káẓim-i-Ra<u>sh</u>tí—a precursor of the Báb who taught that the Day of Resurrection foretold in the Qur'án was at hand.

A. THE BÁBÍ AND BAHÁ'Í RELIGIONS: "TWIN REVELATIONS"

The Bahá'í Faith, second only to Christianity in its diffusion of believers worldwide, is comprised of more than five million believers who reside in over two hundred countries and territories. Because this religion appeared in the midst of the <u>Sh</u>í'ih Islamic culture of mid-nineteenth-century Persia, the Bahá'í Faith is sometimes portrayed as an offshoot or sect of Islam. Actually, it is an independent world religion whose relationship to Islam somewhat parallels the relationship between Christianity and Judaism. Even as the early Jewish converts to Christianity believed Christ to be the promised Messiah of Judaism, so the first followers of the Bahá'í Faith were Muslims who believed the Báb to be the Promised Qá'im. The vast majority of these believers subsequently accepted Bahá'u'lláh[1] as the Prophet prophesied by the Báb.

1. "The Glory of God," a title bestowed on Mírzá Ḥusayn-'Alí by the Báb. He assumed the title *Bahá'u'lláh* after the Conference of Bada<u>sh</u>t in the summer of 1848. At the same gathering, the title *Ṭáhirih* ("The Pure One") was bestowed on Fáṭimih Umm-i-Salmih.

Another informative parallel to Christian history is that even as John the Baptist appeared as the herald and forerunner of Christ, Whom he later anointed as the Messiah, so the Báb declared that as Qá'im He was the "Gate," or the path to the revelation of another Prophet—what Bahá'ís call a "Manifestation of God." These specialized souls both describe the nature of spiritual attributes and exemplify these same virtues in Their own person and conduct. According to the Báb, "Him Whom God shall make manifest" would appear in the year nine (that is, nine years after the Báb's declaration of His mission, which was 1853) and would begin a revelation that would usher in world peace and the unity of humankind as foretold and anticipated by virtually all the previous Prophets of God from the time of Adam.

A careful study of the history and texts of the Bábí and Bahá'í religions leads one to the conclusion that the Báb (1819–1850) and Bahá'u'lláh (1817–1892) were intimately aware of each other's station and were in constant communication, though They never met in person. They concealed this relationship from the generality of Their believers, but it is apparent in Their writings that They considered Their religions to constitute twin revelations that inaugurated a milestone in human history—the point of confluence of two critical religious cycles. Their advent signaled the end of the Adamic or Prophetic Cycle, for which Muḥammad was the final Prophet, and the beginning of the Bahá'í Era, a cycle of human advancement that, according to Bahá'í texts, is destined to endure no less than five thousand centuries.

The Báb and Bahá'u'lláh declared that this new era in human history will be characterized by the collective understanding on the part of humanity of the spiritual purpose underlying creation and the essential unity underlying all the successive world religions revealed throughout human history. In short, They asserted, as does Muḥammad in the Qur'án, that all the successive revealed religions are actually one religion, the religion of God, revealed in progressive stages of human enlightenment and advancement.

Before His execution by government firing squad in 1850 in the town square of Tabríz, the Báb clearly implied that Bahá'u'lláh, Himself a well-known leader of the Bábí religion, was the world redeemer whose advent the Báb had foretold. Two important indications of this acknowledgment were, (1) the composition of several weighty tablets addressed to Bahá'u'lláh, and (2) the fact that immediately before being executed, the Báb bequeathed to Bahá'u'lláh His pen and His seal rings.

Also particularly relevant to the unity of Their revelations is that in His writings the Báb cautioned His own followers time and again not to treat "Him

Whom God shall make manifest" [Bahá'u'lláh] as He and His own followers had been treated by the religious leaders of Islam in Persia:

> When the Daystar of Bahá [Bahá'u'lláh] will shine resplendent above the horizon of eternity it is incumbent upon you to present yourselves before His Throne. Beware lest ye be seated in His presence or ask questions without His leave. Fear ye God, O concourse of the Mirrors[2] (*Selections from the Writings of the Báb,* 6.14.1).

Even more to the point, the Báb stated that "Him Whom God shall make manifest" [Bahá'u'lláh] would appear in the year nine:

> "In the year nine," He, referring to the date of the advent of the promised Revelation, has explicitly written, "ye shall attain unto all good." "In the year nine, ye will attain unto the presence of God." And again: "After Ḥín (68) a Cause shall be given unto you which ye shall come to know." "Ere nine will have elapsed from the inception of this Cause," He more particularly has stated, "the realities of the created things will not be made manifest. All that thou hast as yet seen is but the stage from the moist germ until We clothed it with flesh. Be patient, until thou beholdest a new creation. Say: 'Blessed, therefore, be God, the most excellent of Makers!'" (Shoghi Effendi, *God Passes By,* 29)

It was in 1853 (year 1269 of the Islamic calendar and the year nine of the Bábí dispensation) that Bahá'u'lláh received the first intimations of His revelation while He was imprisoned in the dungeon of the *Síyáh-Chál* (the Black Pit) because He was a well-known leader of the Bábí Faith.

Knowing that He Himself would be executed and that the persecution which would occur as a result of the spread of the Bábí Faith would deprive the religion of its major teachers, the Báb in "A Second Tablet Addressed to 'Him Who Will be Made Manifest'" requested that Bahá'u'lláh forestall revealing His station until the year nineteen: "do Thou grant a respite of nineteen years as a token of Thy favor so that those who have embraced this Cause may be graciously rewarded by Thee" (*Selections from the Writings of the Báb,* 1.2.4). The Báb was thus alluding to

---

2. As we will note in the poetry of Ṭáhirih, the term *mirrors* is used as a metaphorical or symbolic epithet for the earliest believers of the Prophet—those who reflect His power and attributes.

the year 1863 (1844 + 19 = 1863), the year when Bahá'u'lláh formally announced to His followers assembled in the Garden of Riḍván outside Baghdad that He was indeed "Him Whom God shall make manifest," the world-redeeming Prophet for Whom the Báb was the herald.

In the years that followed, Bahá'u'lláh was exiled to Adrianople (1864–68), during which period He made this same announcement to the world at large through a series of remarkable epistles to many of the major world religious and political leaders of that time.[3] But during the interval between Bahá'u'lláh's exile to Baghdad in the winter of 1853 and His further exile to Adrianople in 1863, He inspired and rejuvenated the Bábí community in Baghdad.

When Bahá'u'lláh arrived in Baghdad, the Bábí Faith was in disarray. The Báb had been executed in 1850, and more than twenty thousand of His staunchest followers had been tortured and executed between 1848 and 1852. Virtually all of the major Bábí leaders and teachers, except for Bahá'u'lláh, had likewise been killed. So it was that Bahá'u'lláh took it upon Himself to transcribe the writings of the Báb and to teach the small community of Bábís, particularly those in Baghdad, much of what the Báb Himself would have taught them had He lived. The end result of this period of study and teaching on the part of the Bábís under the tutelage of Bahá'u'lláh in Baghdad was that they became renowned for their dignity, spirituality, and exemplary conduct as citizens, so much so that they won the esteem of the governor himself.

The final exile of Bahá'u'lláh was to the prison city of 'Akká, where the officials of the Ottoman Empire assumed He would perish and the Bahá'í Faith would dissipate and vanish. But from 1868 until His passing in 1892, Bahá'u'lláh wrote some of His most prominent works and gradually explained to 'Abdu'l-Bahá, His eldest son and appointed successor, how the world center of the Bahá'í Faith would be established on Mount Carmel. Bahá'u'lláh even went so far as to mark the spot where the Shrine of the Báb would be erected and the Báb's remains entombed.

Today, the buildings that constitute the Bahá'í World Center have been constructed in the environs of the Shrine of the Báb. The Shrine of Bahá'u'lláh is a modest building situated in the midst of beautiful gardens at the mansion of Bahjí, a few miles outside the city of 'Akká. Bahá'ís worldwide regard this spot as the *Qiblih,* "the Point of Adoration" toward which they turn when they pray, even as the Kaaba in Mecca is the *Qiblih* for Muslims.

3. See Shoghi Effendi, *The Promised Day Is Come,* for an account of how these epistles were received, and see Bahá'u'lláh, *The Summons of the Lord of Hosts,* to study the letters themselves.

B. THE ROLE OF ṬÁHIRIH

To understand the crucial role Ṭáhirih plays in the whirlwind of events that caused such an incredible stir throughout Persia among the clerics, government authorities, and general population, we must examine some of the critical events that set in motion the initial stage in the history of the Bahá'í Faith, a period known as the "Heroic Age" of the Bahá'í religion.

As we have mentioned, the Bahá'í Faith dates its beginning from May 23, 1844—the day the Báb declared His station to Mullá Ḥusayn-i-Bus͟hrú'í, the first follower to recognize Him as the promised "Qá'im" (He who shall arise) of S͟hí'ih Islam. Mullá Ḥusayn had been a prominent student of Siyyid Káẓim-i-Ras͟htí, and when Siyyid Káẓim sensed that his death was near, he bade his disciples scatter throughout Persia and the Ottoman Empire in search of the Qá'im.

Mullá Ḥusayn felt particularly drawn to the city of Shiraz in southern Persia, and the very afternoon when he arrived and entered the city gate, He was greeted by the Báb, Who invited him to take tea in the upper chamber of His modest dwelling. That evening, the Báb mysteriously fulfilled the final test that Mullá Ḥusayn had secretly reserved in his own mind should he meet someone who fulfilled the known requisites that would characterize the Qá'im. Unasked and having no earthly means at His disposal to know what Mullá Ḥusayn had decided, the Báb began revealing a commentary on the Súra of Joseph, a most challenging súra of the Qur'án that alludes to events that would occur in the life of Bahá'u'lláh.[4]

Now thoroughly convinced of the authenticity of the Báb's identity as the Qá'im, Mullá Ḥusayn expressed his eagerness to inform everyone he knew of what he had discovered, but the Báb told him that His identity should remain concealed until seventeen other souls independently sought Him out and recognized His station. It did not take long before this prerequisite was accomplished, and among these eighteen Letters of the Living was Ṭáhirih, the only woman among these first and foremost disciples.

Like Mullá Ḥusayn, she had been a student of Siyyid Káẓim-i-Ras͟htí, though early in her life, even as a child, Ṭáhirih had demonstrated an inherent capacity to decipher some of the most enigmatic passages from the Qur'án and various *ḥadít͟h* (traditions attributed to Muḥammad or His successors) regarding the imminent appearance of the Qá'im.

4. One parallel was that Bahá'u'lláh's own brother, Mírzá Yaḥyá, would attempt to take His life even as the brothers of Joseph tried to kill him.

Outspoken, defiant, undaunted by tradition or the station of cleric or king, Ṭáhirih could converse with anyone on equal footing and surpassed the reputed scholars of her day in both her specific learning and her rhetorical prowess. Through independent study she discovered the writings of Shaykh Aḥmad-i-Aḥsá'í and his student, Siyyid Káẓim-i-Rashtí. Then in a dream she saw the Báb reciting verses, and when she awoke, she wrote down one of the verses. Later, when she had access to His writing, she found this very same verse. This was an important sign for Ṭáhirih that the Báb was indeed the promised Qá'im, and she immediately recognized His station even though she was never to meet Him in person.

From that point on, her life was never the same. She devoted herself entirely to teaching everyone she encountered about the Báb and the Cause He had revealed. But even before this fulfillment of her search for the Promised One, she could not countenance pretentiousness in any form, and brazenly defied any attempts to suppress her thirst for knowledge, in spite of her father's high position and virulent antipathy toward these new teachings. She also defied her husband's equally vehement and ruthless condemnation of what he regarded as her inappropriate and unseemly pursuit of spiritual and intellectual matters.

When she was allowed no alternative to being faithful to her calling, she was forced to abandon her home, her husband, and her three children, but she never looked back. She was well aware that in due time the only certain fate awaiting her would be her own martyrdom, something about which she had no fear or concern. Indeed, in her verse and in her actions, she revealed an inner longing, an ecstatic desire to attain the presence of the "Beloved" by transcending what she regarded as the limitations of her earthly existence. She blatantly rejected any attempts by clerics and authorities to placate her, even rejecting marriage to the king, Náṣiri'd-Dín Sháh, who promised that were she to agree to be one of his wives, she could save herself from execution.

After brazenly refusing the sháh's offer and after an extensive period of imprisonment, she was executed in August of 1852. But in many of the poems she penned, even while under strict confinement, she revealed her devotion both to the Báb (Who had already Himself been executed by firing squad in Tabríz in 1850) and to Bahá'u'lláh, Whom she had met in 1848 and in Whose home she had stayed after He helped to free her from house arrest in Qazvín. Her verses indicate that she was already well aware that Bahá'u'lláh was "Him Whom God shall make manifest," the Manifestation Whose advent the Báb had heralded.

Besides being a noted poet, Ṭáhirih also took part in one of the major events that helped transform the Bábí religion from a group of religious reformers to a unified body of believers who recognized the Báb as possessing a status equal to that of Muḥammad. She helped define the Bábí Faith as a new revelation, not merely an attempt to reform Islam. This event was the famous Conference of Badasht, which took place in the summer of 1848. At this conference, in collusion with Bahá'u'lláh and Quddús, Ṭáhirih removed her veil in defiance of what she regarded as an outmoded law, announced that the Day of Resurrection foretold in the Qur'án had occurred, and that she was the trumpet sounding the advent of that Day.

2. The Manuscript

Unlike the poems collected, translated, and published in *The Poetry of Ṭáhirih*, most of the verse in this volume is not as focused on Ṭáhirih's earlier personal experiences or on allusions to her ecstatic longing to attain a state of spiritual transcendence. Instead, these poems reveal her insight into the process by which God empowers His Messengers to educate humankind. They further examine how the Prophets of the past established the foundation for all that has followed. She was firmly convinced that she was living in the "Day of Resurrection" foretold in the Qur'án, that the Báb was the long-awaited Qá'im, and that what the Báb refers to as "the Latter Resurrection" would soon occur with the Revelation of Bahá'u'lláh.

While her primary theme is her explication of the theme of Adam's "wish," the broader discourse in these pieces concerns the early stages of the Adamic or Prophetic Cycle, a period of religious history that begins with the dispensation of Adam and ends with the dispensation of Muḥammad. Consequently, there is so much remarkable intellectual matter in some of these poems that portions of them have the tenor of a religious or philosophical treatise rather than the passionate lyric quality of some of her best known shorter poems.

What is more, the tone of conviction and authority that we find in some parts of these works seems to confirm the inference by some Bahá'ís that Ṭáhirih may well be a special figure in religious history. One senses that she possessed a knowledge, capacity, and station that set her above even some of the more astute and dedicated followers of the Bábí movement. Indeed, some passages possess something of the dynamic tone and power usually associated with the utterances of the Prophets themselves.

A. THE SOURCE

The handwritten manuscript translated in this volume consists of eleven poems. Nine of them are attributed to Ṭáhirih, and two short poems (poems 4 and

6) may have been written by Karím Khan-i-Máfí, whose title was *Bihjat* (meaning "joy," "grace," "excellence," or "exaltation"). Bihjat was a follower of the Báb from the city of Qazvín, the hometown of Ṭáhirih. He had corresponded with her through exchanges of poetry while she was imprisoned at the house of the *kalántar* (the governor) of Tehran before her dramatic execution.

Four of the poems in this volume (poems 3, 8, 9, and 10), together with small portions of some of the other poems, have been previously published, both in the original language and as translations in English. The rest of the verses, which constitute the bulk of this volume, have never been viewed by the public before, let alone published in Persian or translated into any other language.

There has been some scholarly debate as to whether or not poems 8, 9, and 10 were composed by Ṭáhirih. It is believed by some that because these poems were either copied in her handwriting or recited by her, they were simply verses she found appealing. However, our opinion after studying her work with careful attention to style, vocabulary, and themes is that there is no convincing evidence that these poems were not composed by Ṭáhirih herself.[5]

There is no disputing that the rest of the poems of this manuscript were composed by Ṭáhirih, except for the two poems already mentioned that may have been composed by Bihjat. Neither the style nor the language of these poems would lead one to think of them as belonging to other poets, nor have they been included in the collections attributed to any other poets, as some of her best known poems have been.

Scholar Dhuká'í Bayḍá'í, who originally submitted this volume to the Bahá'í archives of Iran, endorses the belief that these poems are in fact written by Ṭáhirih. Indeed, we are grateful to his son Bijan Bayḍá'í for providing us with a copy of the manuscript, a facsimile of which is printed in this volume. These eight previously unknown poems were probably written during the last year or two of her life, sometime shortly before she was executed in 1852 by the Persian government.

Ṭáhirih, together with Bahá'u'lláh and Quddús, was one of the most prominent Bábí leaders, even though she was imprisoned and confined virtually the entirety of her life as a Bábí (from 1844–52). Consequently, most of her exquisite verse

5. Refer to Mohammadhoseini, pp. 350 and 364, regarding the authenticity of poems 8 and 10 and to footnote 403 on page 200 of Hatcher and Hemmat, *The Poetry of Ṭáhirih,* regarding poem 9.

and erudite discourses were conveyed to her followers through Bihjat, who functioned as an intermediary between her and them. While much of her work has been lost to posterity, what survives vindicates the rather astounding reputation she garnered as a poet and scholar, both among the Bábí community and within Persian culture at large. Even today, her name is invoked by learned Iranians as an icon of brilliance and as a standard-bearer of indefatigable defiance against outworn traditions and most especially against the oppression of women.

B. THEMES IN HISTORICAL CONTEXT

As a whole, these previously unknown pieces constitute a remarkable discourse on the concept of the succession of Prophets. Similar to the portrayal of the concept and station of an "Apostle" in the Qur'án, the Bahá'í texts characterize the Prophets, especially those Who instigate a new revelation and religion, as emissaries from the divine realm, not merely as inspired human beings. Put succinctly, these beings are of a more exalted ontological station or order. As a result of Their station, these intermediaries are capable of manifesting perfectly all the attributes of God, as opposed to highly spiritual but ordinary human beings who might become inspired and who might manifest the attributes of God to a greater or lesser degree. Consequently, the authoritative Bahá'í texts refer to these specialized beings as Manifestations of God because They not only teach about the relationship between physical and spiritual reality but also manifest perfectly the same spiritual attributes, whether in Their character, Their comportment, or Their courageous response to rejection and persecution by religious and secular authorities who erroneously perceive Them as a threat to their own position and power.

Emanating from the same divine source and functioning with identical capacity, the Manifestations of God thus serve as the link between the will of God and the progress and well-being of humankind. Furthermore, it is the belief of the Bábí and Bahá'í Faiths that these divinely ordained teachers are fully aware of each other and are coordinated in Their successive dispensations. What is more, this divine educational process is considered to have as its abiding goal the provision of humankind with two categories of guidance: the unfolding of an ever more complete description of reality and the revealing of ever more advanced methodologies by which humankind can apply this knowledge to ever more comprehensive social relationships and social programs.

Understood in this light, the Manifestations appear as ordinary human beings but with extraordinary capacity. They are careful to conceal Their station and full powers, choosing instead to attract followers by Their spiritual character and

Their innovative teachings. Consequently, because Their utterance is often veiled in poetic language—parable, symbol, and metaphor—the first followers are often the meek and the lowly who are oblivious to the sometimes legalistic standards of assessment common among the learned and the powerful, whose own knowledge and station may veil them from the subtle truths about reality.

However, such was not entirely the case with the first followers of the Báb. As we have noted, His first followers, whom He designated as "Letters of the Living," were eighteen individuals of widely recognized intellectual capacity, among whom was Ṭáhirih herself. Because she was a Bábí and a woman who rebelled against the constraints imposed on women of nineteenth-century Persia, she was perceived by authorities to be a source of mischief and rebellion against religious orthodoxy.

Whether because of this historical context or because she chose to veil her thoughts in sometimes obscure and abstruse allusions, her poetry is extremely difficult, whether studied in the original Persian and Arabic or in translation. Nevertheless, her verses contain a storehouse of insights about the principal axioms that dictate the relationship among the Prophets and, in particular, the wisdom in the incremental nature by which humankind must be gradually instructed in the process of bringing forth an ever-advancing civilization based on principles of spiritual attributes.

It is in this vein that these poems establish the divine process by which God has educated and guided humankind despite the rejection of the Prophets by the very people who, one might think, would most eagerly await Their appearance—the clerics and followers of the religion founded by the previous Manifestation of God. In these poems Ṭáhirih thus examines the ministries and dispensations of Adam, Noah, Abraham, and Moses to elucidate a number of subtle points about how each Manifestation receives essentially the same power and inspiration, even though each appears in the guise of a distinct persona or personality and fashions His teachings to befit the social and historical exigencies of the age and place in which He appears.

Interwoven within this foundational concept is Ṭáhirih's exultation in the anticipated appearance of the One for Whom the Báb had sacrificed His life and to Whom the Báb devoted the entirety of His voluminous texts. Even though it was not until 1863 that Bahá'u'lláh openly declared His station, Ṭáhirih indicates quite clearly in her poems and other writings that she was well aware of Bahá'u'lláh's station early on. As we have noted, she was in close communication with Bahá'u'lláh, and, after being rescued by Him from Qazvín, she, along with Bahá'u'lláh and Quddús, played a crucial role in directing the Conference of

Bada<u>sh</u>t in the summer of 1848. Indeed, the climactic episode of this twenty-two day meeting occurred when Ṭáhirih removed her veil as she proclaimed that a new dispensation had begun. "The Trumpet is sounding!" she announced. "The great Trump is blown! The universal Advent is now proclaimed!"[6] (quoted in 'Abdu'l-Bahá, *Memorials of the Faithful,* 198–99).

The reader must be particularly attentive to this strategic historical perspective from which Ṭáhirih is writing in order to extract the concepts essential to this work. The language and content of the poems support the belief that Ṭáhirih is well aware of the immediacy of the revelation that will follow that of the Báb, that Bahá'u'lláh is the One to Whom the Báb alluded as "Him Whom God shall make manifest,"[7] and that she will not live to see the time when that revelation will be made manifest. At the same time, she rejoices in what she knows is about to occur.

We presume it is from her last imprisonment that she pens some of these works in which she exhorts Bihjat to understand the unparalleled impact of this turning point in human history—the coming of age of the human race. She constantly exhorts him to convey her teaching to her followers, and in the last poem in this volume she bids him convey her work to those who are unable to attain her presence or to hear her articulate this wondrous news of the impending advent of the transformation of humankind.

These are the two main themes of these poems—the process by which God has fashioned civilization throughout human history by means of His chosen Prophets and the fact that the Prophetic stage of that process has now culminated in the long-awaited Day of Resurrection. The sub-themes or motifs that underlie these two ideas are such concepts as the nature and station of the Prophets of God, the necessary gradualness by which the Prophets educate humankind, the concept of free will as it relates to the dangers of hubris and defiance on the part of those who await the advent of the Day of Resurrection, the symbolic nature of the story of Noah and the Ark as representing the covenant of God carried forth by each Prophet, and, finally, the pronouncement that though the fulfill-

---

6. Cf. Qur'án 74:8 and 6:73. Also Isaiah 27:13 and Zechariah 9:14.

7. *Selections from the Writings of the Báb,* 1:2:4.

ment of the Báb's promise of a world-redeeming Manifestation has occurred, this news must remain concealed until it is timely for the Bábís to receive this information.

C. THE DAY OF RESURRECTION AND REFORMATION

Ṭáhirih's allusion to Bahá'u'lláh, as she portrayed Him to Bihjat, is described as parallel to the appearance of Noah and to the fulfillment of what Adam began. In this sense, the appearance of the Báb is portrayed as the confluence of two vast cycles in human history. On the one hand, the appearance of the Báb is the culmination of time, the often prophesied "time of the end"—the completion of the Prophetic or Adamic Cycle for which Muḥammad was the last Manifestation and thus the "seal" of the Prophets.

At the same time, as the "Primal Point," the Báb inaugurates and instigates the beginning of what Bahá'u'lláh would designate in His own writings as the "Bahá'í Era"—a period that will witness the beginning of the maturation of humankind. Bahá'u'lláh goes on in His own works to explain that this period of maturation would be signaled by the capacity of humankind to fashion a global community based on spiritual principles of governance and a shared vision of human reality and purpose. This global "economy," Bahá'u'lláh asserts, will be a world commonwealth secured by principles of universal suffrage and collective security.

3. The Scholarly Context

These poems were penned in the religious and philosophical language of the time. More specifically, the works of Ṭáhirih are replete with references to philosophers and mystics of the past and, in particular, to Greek and Islamic philosophers and thinkers. Therefore the translation we offer here, though not definitive or authoritative, is supported by intensive study of Bahá'í theology and scripture, Islamic thought and scholarship, mystical philosophy, and major Shaykhí and Bábí texts. Consequently, a brief explanation of some key Islamic philosophical concepts may help the reader comprehend our translation of various passages as well as the footnotes in which we attempt to explain some of the less obvious allusions.

A. ADAM'S DESIRE

Like the creation myth in Judeo-Christian religious beliefs, the creation story in Islamic culture employs the story of Adam. Rather than accepting the story at face value or as literal truth, however, Islamic thinkers have developed sophisticated and sometimes complicated interpretations of the story of Adam's sin, of His partaking of the forbidden tree, and of His fall. Adam, the tree, the serpent, paradise, earth, Satan, angels, and other elements in the myth have been carefully interpreted and conjoined to create a comprehensive doctrine about the spiritual nature of creation on earth. A review of some of these concepts should prove useful in understanding the allusions to these ideas in Ṭáhirih's poems.

A key term in the poems is Adam's "desire" (*árizú,* آرزو), a Persian word that can mean "wish," "will," "resolution," "intention," "inclination," "affection," "love," "appetite," "concupiscence," "hope," or "want" (Steingass 2000). The word has negative and sensual connotations, but it can also have the positive implication of being resolute, of possessing a strong will. 'Abdu'l-Bahá in His interpretation of Qur'ánic verses that allude to Adam's sin employs the Arabic word (*muná,* مُنى) meaning "wishes," "aspirations," and "desires." In this same tablet 'Abdu'l-Bahá writes, "Adam wished for and desired the manifestation of God's perfection and Divine characteristics, a fulfillment that was conditioned on the appearance of the Master of Existence" (*Siyyidu'l-Vujúd,* سيدالوجود).[8]

"The Master of Existence" alludes to "His Holiness Muḥammad" (*Ríáz-ul-Lughát*). In other words, from the beginning of time, Adam longed for the appearance of the attributes that would be manifested at the completion of the Adamic Cycle—that is, after the appearance of Muḥammad. Therefore, the longing of Adam can be interpreted to mean that the potential and capacity for the perfection achieved at the end of the Adamic Cycle was implicit and inherent in creation from its inception. Thus Adam was aware of both the potential and the inherent destiny latent in the spiritual progress of humankind. Therefore He wished or longed for the instant realization of a process that would necessarily require thousands of years to accomplish.

B. THE FALL OF ADAM

The gradual realization of this potential is possible only through material means since in the world of the spirit such attributes are apparent and fulfilled without limit or need for concealment or "gradualness"—time and space are properties of the physical aspect of reality, not the metaphysical realm. Therefore Adam's desire for the instant fulfillment of this fruition brought about His fall from the

8. Provisional translation from *Min Makátib 'Abdu'l-Bahá,* Editorial Bahá'í Brazil, Rio de Janeiro, 1982, 1:76.

spiritual realm and His descent into the physical world (His separation from His divine origin), where He could experience firsthand the need for this indirect and progressive methodology and where, as an emissary from the spiritual world, He could help instigate and participate in the process.

In one of her letters, which is superbly penned and well deserving of translation and detailed study itself, Ṭáhirih refers to this concept of "separation" as the plight of all humankind. She states that on some level we all wish to take flight and return to the original paradise of purity and holiness in which we were created and from which we emanated.[9] In poetic language she compares the separation of human beings from their divine origin, and she relates this feeling to her own sense of longing and to the creation of Adam and His fall from "paradise": "I know who has made me to descend and what the purpose of my descent is. He wants to test me . . ." (Mohammadhoseini, i 458).

She goes on to introduce a more generalized analogy between this separation and the process of the creation of the universe as set forth in the Islamic *ḥadíth* (tradition)[10] regarding the seven stages of creation, a ḥadíth that the Báb also employs in His own writings. She also uses this same ḥadíth to allude to the appearance of the Báb and Bahá'u'lláh as the fulfillment of creation taking place in this very age, a stage of human advancement in which the manifestation of divine attributes latent in all reality will become revealed, as will the nature, station, and purpose of humankind:[11]

> O God, with this broken wing I desire to fly to the Divine clouds (*'amá'*, عماء) and with this weary heart recount the story of the world of paradise and purity. But of course there is none except You to be my helper and none except You worthy to be my support.
>
> O Thou Who created me sanctified from all extraneous conditions, Who fashioned me without trivial affections, Who performed what no one other than You could do, and Who commanded what no one other than You

9. As the Bahá'í authoritative texts explicitly affirm, this is not an allusion to a belief in preexistence per se (i.e., that we have an identity prior to our origin at conception) but rather the idea that as emanations from God, we are essentially spiritual in our origin and that we are created with an inherent love of God even though we must be educated to recognize the source of that attraction.

10. This ḥadíth, which is from Imám Ja'far Ṣádiq, can be found in *Uṣúl-i-Káfí.* Siyyid Káẓim-i-Rashtí quotes this ḥadíth in *Risálih-i-Uṣúl-i-'Aqáyid*, pp. 114–15.

11. From Mohammadhoseini, p. 459. Capitalization of terms, the paragraph structure, and some of the punctuation do not exist in the original text.

could command; You brought into being what was naught except Your own Lordship and You manifested a mystery that nothing other than Your own Grandeur could make manifest.

O God, Your first new creation, Adam, existed the first time[12] in that same light and ascended to that same station, and upon Him was bestowed this same grace, and He was manifested in that same safeguarded station, and He was drunk from this same wine, and He also recounted the attributes of this same divine beauty. O God, You made him descend solely by the exigency of your Will (*mas͟híyyat*, مشيّت), and He was lassoed solely by the lariat of Your Determination (*irádih*, اراده), and from the station of Measure (*qadar*, قدر). He was formed solely by You in the world of Decree (*qaḍá'*, قضاء) to proclaim: "I am the Mirror of purity and the Sign of *Bahá*," the One whom, after the Term (*ajal*, اجل) has transpired by Your Permission (*id͟hn*, اذن), of [You] the Supreme God, You desire to recite from the written account of Genesis (*kitáb*, كتاب) the Tablet that has already been transcribed within the atoms of existence, created by the First Cause to enlighten material realities with the illumination of the Light and the Eternal Beauty.

O God, I bear witness that the Term has transpired and that the mystery of the promise is emerging, and the promised Sign and the Beauty of the Truth has dawned from the Supreme Station, and the Great Countenance has proclaimed: "I am indeed God! There is no beloved except Me, the Exalted, the Great!"[13]

In this poetic letter there are multiple levels of meaning regarding the creation myth, the concept of paradise, and the meaning of Adam's fall from grace. One interpretation is related to the unfortunate condition of humankind in the physical world in comparison to the original purity and delight in the spiritual paradise from which humankind emanates. The inherent desire of humankind is to partake of the fruits of that lost state of innocence and its former proximity to the presence of God.

12. In the Islamic literature and the writings of the Báb there are references to many "Adams," and in fact to an infinite number of Adams (see *Bayán-i-Fársí,* p. 95 and Kitáb-i-Íqán, ¶172 and 179) as well as the Adam newly created for the first time, *Ádam-i-badí'-i-fiṭrat-i-avval*: آدم بديع فطرت اوّل (*Bayán-i-Fársí,* 95). This concept is an allusion to the unity of station and purpose of all the Prophets of God.

13. Translated by Hatcher and Hemmat.

However, this "reunion" can be achieved only when Adam successfully completes the course of His physical life. Consequently, partaking of the fruit of the tree in paradise is accompanied by the descent to the physical realm where one can refine one's spiritual essence only through the tests and difficulties of physical experience. Of course, implicit in such an interpretation when it is applied to ordinary human beings is the concept of preexistence, a concept explicitly contrary to what Ṭáhirih intends inasmuch as "preexistence" is in the Bábí and Bahá'í teachings applicable only to the Manifestations of God. According to these same teachings, ordinary human life begins at conception when the soul simultaneously emanates from God and assumes its associative relationship with the physical temple.

Another level of interpretation is related to the station of Prophethood and the concept of progressive revelation. According to Islamic, Bábí, and Bahá'í theology, God is portrayed as educating humankind by degrees through Emissaries or divinely empowered Teachers—"Prophets" in the Judeo-Christian tradition, "Apostles" (*rasúl*, رسول) in the Islamic-Arabic tradition, and "Manifestations of God" in the Bábí and Bahá'í tradition. These Educators are not perceived as ordinary human beings who have been chosen and endowed with power, but as Messengers or Teachers from the realm of the spirit Who have been selected for the task of educating humankind for a specific duration of time—a "dispensation" or, poetically, a "Day."

Spiritually, these Beings appear with the same essential truth inasmuch as each is describing the same reality, though in ever more complete and complex terms. However, as inherently wise teachers, They reveal only that which is meet and appropriate to the capacity, circumstances, and conditions of the civilization where They become manifest.

This progression of revelation thus accords with the exigencies of the human race at a given point in history when the Manifestation "descends" to the material plane of existence in the form and guise of an ordinary human being. However, the appearance of the Manifestation causes civilization to advance, both as a direct result of the new information They impart about reality and as the indirect result of the impetus loosed upon creation as a result of Their infusion of spiritual and intellectual energy into the physical realm.

While the literal nature of Adam's appearance is ambiguous at best in the Pentateuch of the Old Testament, Adam in the Qur'án is presented as a Prophet or Manifestation of God. In the Qur'ánic version of the story, Adam is ordained by God to go to earth and to have dominance over physical creation. Eblis, a djinn, a spiritual being of fire, resents the idea of a mere mortal—a being whose essence will be expressed through physical limitations—possessing a spiritual station higher than his own, and he refuses to humble himself before Adam.

Adam's mission in this "descent" to the physical realm is, among other things, to advance human understanding of the essentially spiritual nature of creation and its function as a teaching device created to introduce humankind to spiritual attributes. In this sense, physical reality becomes a classroom for newly created souls. Therefore, to instruct humankind in the spiritual meaning inherent in all created things, Adam reveals or unveils the attributes of each creation by ordaining it with a "name."

Obviously the "names" of things have great power because they allude to some spiritual significance. These are the "names of God," "virtues," or "attributes" that are made manifest through physical reality, even as Bahá'u'lláh notes that

> Every created thing is a sign of the revelation of God. Each, according to its capacity, is, and will ever remain, a token of the Almighty. Inasmuch as He, the sovereign Lord of all, hath willed to reveal His sovereignty in the kingdom of names and attributes, each and every created thing hath, through the act of the Divine Will, been made a sign of His glory. So pervasive and general is this revelation that nothing whatsoever in the whole universe can be discovered that doth not reflect His splendor (*Gleanings,* no. 93.1).

C. REVELATION AS PROCESS, NOT A SINGLE EVENT

As many other Manifestations observe, the individual Prophet restrains Himself from revealing all that He knows because the capacity for human understanding evolves gradually. Thus in an often cited farewell to His disciples, Christ states, "I have yet many things to say unto you, but ye cannot bear them now. Howbeit when he, the Spirit of truth, is come, he will guide you into all truth: for he shall not speak of himself; but whatsoever he shall hear, that shall he speak: and he will show you things to come" (John 16:12–13).[14] Likewise, Bahá'u'lláh, in His renowned Tablet of Wisdom, reveals to Nabíl-i-Qá'iní a number of axioms about the nature of acquired learning when He suddenly halts the work with this passage: "When the discourse reached this stage, the dawn of divine mysteries

14. This and all other citations from the Holy Bible are from the King James version.

appeared and the light of utterance was quenched. May His glory rest upon the people of wisdom as bidden by One Who is the Almighty, the All-Praised" (*Tablets of Bahá'u'lláh,* 151). Similarly, in the Hidden Words, Bahá'u'lláh implies the same sort of constraints on what He can reveal at this particular time in history, even though this is a time of fulfillment and the maturation of humankind:

> Then summoned to return I beheld, and lo! certain doves of holiness were sore tried within the claws of the dogs of earth. Thereupon the Maid of heaven hastened forth unveiled and resplendent from Her mystic mansion, and asked of their names, and all were told but one. And when urged, the first letter thereof was uttered, whereupon the dwellers of the celestial chambers rushed forth out of their habitation of glory. And whilst the second letter was pronounced they fell down, one and all, upon the dust. At that moment a voice was heard from the inmost shrine: "Thus far and no farther" (from the Persian, no. 77).

Reflecting on the limitations imposed on each Manifestation of God by the relative progress of humankind, Shoghi Effendi, the great-grandson of Bahá'u'lláh and appointed Guardian of the Bahá'í Faith, interprets this verse as confirmation that Bahá'u'lláh, too, is limited by the present condition of human advancement and that more enlightenment and advancement is forthcoming in future revelations:

> "The Revelation of which I am the bearer," Bahá'u'lláh explicitly declares, "is adapted to humanity's spiritual receptiveness and capacity; otherwise, the Light that shines within me can neither wax nor wane. Whatever I manifest is nothing more nor less than the measure of the Divine glory which God has bidden me reveal" (quoted in Shoghi Effendi, *World Order of Bahá'u'lláh,* 60).

Another allusion by Bahá'u'lláh to this same verity is asserted in the Most Holy Book in the following words:

> By the one true God! We read the Tablet ere it was revealed, while ye were unaware, and We had perfect knowledge of the Book when ye were yet unborn. These words are to your measure, not to God's. To this testifieth that which is enshrined within His knowledge, if ye be of them that comprehend; and to this the tongue of the Almighty doth bear witness, if ye be

> of those who understand. I swear by God, were We to lift the veil, ye would be dumbfounded (¶176).

In another comment on this same axiom, Shoghi Effendi makes an even more detailed observation about the continuity of revelation. It is an observation that, especially in the light of the commonly held belief by many Muslims that there would be no Prophet after Muḥammad, has immense importance in terms of contemporary religious and political history:

> In a more explicit language Bahá'u'lláh testifies to this truth in one of His Tablets revealed in Adrianople: "Know verily that the veil hiding Our countenance hath not been completely lifted. We have revealed Our Self to a degree corresponding to the capacity of the people of Our age. Should the Ancient Beauty be unveiled in the fullness of His glory mortal eyes would be blinded by the dazzling intensity of His revelation."
>
> In the Súriy-i-Ṣabr, revealed as far back as the year 1863, on the very first day of His arrival in the garden of Riḍván, He thus affirms: "God hath sent down His Messengers to succeed to Moses and Jesus, and He will continue to do so till 'the end that hath no end'; so that His grace may, from the heaven of Divine bounty, be continually vouchsafed to mankind."
>
> "I am not apprehensive for My own self," Bahá'u'lláh still more explicitly declares, "My fears are for Him Who will be sent down unto you after Me—Him Who will be invested with great sovereignty and mighty dominion." And again He writes in the Súratu'l-Haykal: "By those words which I have revealed, Myself is not intended, but rather He Who will come after Me. To it is witness God, the All-Knowing." "Deal not with Him," He adds, "as ye have dealt with Me" (*World Order of Bahá'u'lláh*, 116–17).

Of course, there is also in Shoghi Effendi's account of the life of Bahá'u'lláh in *God Passes By* the remarkable account of how Bahá'u'lláh ordered His amanuensis Mírzá Áqá Ján to destroy hundreds of thousands of revealed verses because humankind would not be ready to receive them during this dispensation:

> No less an authority than Mírzá Áqá Ján, Bahá'u'lláh's amanuensis, affirms, as reported by Nabíl, that by the express order of Bahá'u'lláh, hundreds of thousands of verses, mostly written by His own hand, were obliterated and cast into the river. "Finding me reluctant to execute His orders," Mírzá Áqá Ján has related to Nabíl, "Bahá'u'lláh would reassure me saying: 'None is to

> be found at this time worthy to hear these melodies.' . . . Not once, or twice, but innumerable times, was I commanded to repeat this act" (138).

The principle underlying these statements and actions is unmistakably clear. We presently stand at a major turning point in human history—the emergence of the maturation of humankind as signalized by the gradual unfolding of a global commonwealth—but neither the individual nor humankind collectively ever achieves some final or complete stage of development. The spiritual evolution of humanity, like that of the individual, is constantly becoming an ever more refined expression of divine principles. These principles are then reflected in familial, community, and global structures.

This precise matter of the gradualness of human advancement is what so frustrated Adam in the mythic treatment of His "sin": since He could see the "end" in the "beginning" (i.e., the end result of this organic process), He wanted everything to become transformed instantly. So it is that while the Manifestations of God are doubtless anxious to inform humankind of all there is to know and desire to expedite the spiritualization of the planet, each Manifestation must confront the limitations of what can be accomplished during a given period in human enlightenment. Bahá'u'lláh relates this idea to a well-known tradition about time and timeliness for advancement in the physical realm:

> How manifold are the truths which must remain unuttered until the appointed time is come! Even as it hath been said: "Not everything that a man knoweth can be disclosed, nor can everything that he can disclose be regarded as timely, nor can every timely utterance be considered as suited to the capacity of those who hear it" (*Gleanings,* no. 89.3).

4. Symbolic Meanings of Adam's Sin

The figure of Adam in this volume has both mythic and historical significance. From the point of view of Adam as the first Manifestation of God in what is termed the "Adamic" or "Prophetic" Cycle, Adam inaugurates a religious-historical cycle of about six thousand years, a cycle that is completed with the termination of the Islamic dispensation when the Qá'im appears—that is, with the advent of the Báb in 1844. As a poetic or fictional character in religious tradition and in some of these poems, we encounter Adam as a figure longing to bring into reality His vision of what humankind would become, as opposed to that relatively slight degree of advancement that might occur solely during His own dispensation.

A. THE LONGING FOR INSTANT TRANSFORMATION OF HUMANKIND

Adam's "sin" in one sense is His desire that the enlightenment and subsequent transformation of humankind occur immediately. What Adam must learn is to counter this insistence with the realization that humankind must proceed by degrees and that He alone cannot instantly usher in human enlightenment in one fell swoop. His "wish" can only be fulfilled after the completion of the Adamic Cycle, and even then the maturation of human understanding will be only relatively advanced.

From the standpoint of Bábí and Bahá'í theological beliefs, Adam's "wish" or "sin" as historical fact is baseless. Each Manifestation of God is well aware of the bounds and limitations within which He must play His part in the ongoing spiritual education of the planet. Therefore, the myth of Adam's selfishness, His desire to partake of the forbidden tree to initiate such development and growth in the world of existence, is a symbolic or metaphorical representation of the Prophet's desire to propel human progress. This tradition may also constitute an allusion to a similar wish on the part of His followers who, having received the gift of comprehending the essentially spiritual significance underlying physical reality, think themselves in possession of, or capable of acquiring, all the knowledge that exists, the same sort of hubris that afflicted much of the scientific community at the end of the nineteenth century.

Another noteworthy observation should be kept in mind as we study Ṭáhirih's allusions to Adam's "sin," hubris, or presumption. In discussing the representation of Manifestations of God or Prophets in the scriptures of past religions, 'Abdu'l-Bahá in *Some Answered Questions* responds to the enigma of how a Being Who is by nature "stainless" or "flawless" could be condemned as having committed a "sin" or as misunderstanding the process by which He must carry out the Will of God. For example, Moses is portrayed as being deprived of the opportunity to enter the Promised Land because He became impatient with God.[15] 'Abdu'l-Bahá's explanation for such scriptural allusions is that when the Mani-

15. See Numbers 20:12, where Moses is "impatient" with God by striking the rock twice instead of once to call forth water.

festations are described as having erred, these criticisms or condemnations are to be attributed to the erroneous actions of the followers and not to the Prophets Themselves:

> All the divine discourses containing reproof, though apparently addressed to the Prophets, in reality are directed to the people, through a wisdom which is absolute mercy, in order that the people may not be discouraged and disheartened. They, therefore, appear to be addressed to the Prophets; but though outwardly for the Prophets, they are in truth for the people and not for the Prophets (167).

Likewise, in Their own prayers when the Manifestations confess Their limitations or transgressions, They are in fact training Their followers and not suggesting that They Themselves have committed some wrong:

> How often the Prophets of God and His supreme Manifestations in Their prayers confess Their sins and faults! This is only to teach other men, to encourage and incite them to humility and meekness, and to induce them to confess their sins and faults. For these Holy Souls are pure from every sin and sanctified from faults ('Abdu'l-Bahá, *Some Answered Questions,* 170).

It is clear, then, that whatever Ṭáhirih means by "Adam's wish," "Adam's sin," or "Adam's fall," she is not alluding to some sinful or prideful act perpetrated by the historical Adam Who was a Manifestation of God. Obviously some symbolic or mythic meaning must be applied to these allusions, both as they occur in scripture and as they are employed by Ṭáhirih.

B. ADAM'S SELFISHNESS

In light of the foregoing, the concept of Adam's selfishness (*anáníyyat,* آنانيّت) could be understood as the sense of pride or presumption on the part of Adam's followers who, once having attained a sense of their own intellect, might understandably perceive themselves as capable of autonomous ascent into the realms of knowledge. Indeed, several times in her poems, the concept of being "self-centered" as opposed to being "God-centered" is key to the overall philosophical theme of Ṭáhirih's works. Prior to the expression of this desire, Adam (the human spirit) was in paradise—in a station of preincarnate purity—existing in the ecstasy of the divine presence.

Ṭáhirih seems to have related this station to the station of "He is Myself" from the ḥadí<u>th</u> in which Muḥammad proclaims regarding His relationship with God, "I am He, Himself, and He is I, Myself, except that I am that I am, and He is that He is."[16] Thus *"He is I, Myself"* is the condition in which there is no separation or distinction between God and the Manifestations of God. It refers to the station of "essential unity" derived from the fact that the Prophets are like flawless mirrors reflecting the attributes of the divine. Whereas *"I am that I am"* and *"He is that He is"* denote the station of distinction of the Manifestations of God. In this station, They are individual spiritual beings distinct from God and separate from the original paradisiacal divine unity They experience prior to Their descent to earth in the form of a distinct personality:

> We have already in the foregoing pages assigned two stations unto each of the Luminaries arising from the Daysprings of eternal holiness. One of these stations, the station of essential unity, We have already explained. "No distinction do We make between any of them" [Qur'án 2:136]. The other is the station of distinction, and pertaineth to the world of creation and to the limitations thereof. In this respect, each Manifestation of God hath a distinct individuality, a definitely prescribed mission, a predestined Revelation, and specially designated limitations. Each one of them is known by a different name, is characterized by a special attribute, fulfills a definite Mission, and is entrusted with a particular Revelation (Bahá'u'lláh, *Kitáb-i-Íqán,* ¶191).

Another interpretation of this symbolism relates to the stations of the Manifestations of God before and after proclaiming Their mission. Unlike ordinary human beings, the Manifestations are preexistent and willfully accede to the Will of God—They become incarnate in the world of being in the guise of ordinary human beings, but They still possess extraordinary powers and capacities. As we

16. This ḥadí<u>th</u> is quoted in many Bahá'í texts such as *Gems of Divine Mysteries* (p. 30) and 'Abdu'l-Bahá's commentary on the ḥadí<u>th</u> of the Hidden Treasure (*Makátíb-i-Ḥaḍrat-i-'Abdu'l-Bahá,* 2:21). A similar ḥadí<u>th</u> is attributed to Imám Ja'far Ṣádiq, which is quoted in the Báb's commentary on the Súra of the Cow (see *A<u>th</u>ráru'l-Á<u>th</u>ár,* 1:11).

have already noted, They carefully conceal this station that They might be recognized for Their spiritual attributes and wise guidance rather than for Their special powers—Their ability to perform what humans would regard as spectacular or miraculous feats.

Therefore, when a Manifestation of God becomes incarnate in a human persona and then proclaims His mission, He has uttered His "selfishness" by proclaiming His unique identity as a messenger separate and distinct from the Prophets of the past. "Selfishness" in this regard alludes to the revelation of God in the world of existence through a specific personality, what Bahá'u'lláh in the Book of Certitude refers to as the "station of distinction" (Bahá'u'lláh, *Kitáb-i-Íqán,* ¶191).

In the Adamic Cycle, this process is initiated by Adam and repeated by successive Manifestations of God such as Noah, Abraham, Moses, Christ, and Muḥammad, even though there were, according to Bábí and Bahá'í belief, many cycles of Manifestations prior to the Adamic Cycle. In Ṭáhirih's tropes, the figure of Adam will often allude to these successive Manifestations Who return time and time again, always wishing to manifest God's names and attributes in the world of existence.

But as soon as Adam expresses this desire or wish, He has ontologically separated Himself from the original Divine station, to which Bahá'u'lláh alludes in the Book of Certitude as the station of "essential unity," by assuming a distinct personality and by descending (metaphorically) to the world of creation in order to make this wish possible.

5. Other Major Symbols

While the poems in this volume focus on the figure of Adam and the other early Prophets in the Adamic Cycle (Noah, Abraham, and Moses), the abiding theme of the work as a whole is the divine process by which God educates humankind. Consequently, there are several major symbols Ṭáhirih employs that apply equally well to the appearance of every Prophet. A fundamental introduction to the source and persistence of these images will assist the reader in coming to appreciate the layers of meaning Ṭáhirih has infused into her work.

A. THE ROOTED TREE

The Manifestations of God, though distinct in personality, are all descended from the same divine origin. In her poems Ṭáhirih sometimes refers to the Manifestations of God as "branches" of the "root-tree," (*shjari-i-aṣlíyyih,* شجره اصليه), the "forbidden tree" in paradise as portrayed in scripture. The metaphors of the rooted-tree (see Qur'án 14:24),[17] the "forbidden tree of knowledge of good and evil and the tree of life" in paradise in Genesis 2:9, and in Bahá'í imagery the "Tree beyond which there is no passing" (Shoghi Effendi, *God Passes By,* 94) (*sadratu'l-muntahá,* سدرة المنتهى), and the "Divine" or "Sacred Lote Tree" all allude to this same figurative meaning, though sometimes these symbols may also be employed to allude to God Himself, and at other times to the successive Manifestations of God.

In some references, the Manifestations of God partake of this tree, and Their mission is portrayed as being inspired by the tree. 'Abdu'l-Bahá interprets "the forbidden tree" in paradise as alluding to the station of the "Master of Existence," Muḥammad. This station is thus the reality of Muḥammad, but in Ṭáhirih's verse it is also an allusion to "the Mohammedan Light"—the spiritual power that emanates from this tree as the sacred source and origin of all the Manifestations of God.

In sum, all the Prophets or Manifestations are thus "rooted from" this selfsame source. On another occasion 'Abdu'l-Bahá interprets this tree to symbolize "the position of Christ," which in comparison to the embryonic condition of Adam's revelation, indicated "the condition of maturity and the age of reason" (*Some Answered Questions,* 124).

B. THE "WORLD OF LIMITATIONS"

As we have already observed, the outcome of Adam's selfishness is His descent into the world of materiality, a reality wherein spiritual essence can only be understood indirectly through material or composite analogues and only to a limited degree. Furthermore, a physical being manifesting divine attributes or "names" can never *become* the spiritual essence it reflects.

Even so, 'Abdu'l-Bahá does note that this limitation does not imply that physical reality is a negative or unspiritual aspect of reality. Rather, physical reality is the outer or visible expression of metaphysical reality. In this sense, these two aspects of reality possess and take part in a reciprocal or counterpart relationship: "The spiritual world is like unto the phenomenal world. They are the exact counterpart of each other. Whatever objects appear in this world of existence are the outer pictures of the world of heaven" (*Promulgation of Universal Peace,* 12).

---

17. "Seest thou not how Alláh sets forth a parable of a good word as a good tree, whose root is firm and whose branches are high."

However, because the physical symbol or analogue can only allude to a spiritual reality and can never become that reality, the composite, physical, or metaphorical expression of reality is sometimes alluded to as "the world of limitations" or as "the kingdom of names." While these are not intended as pejorative appellations, they do clearly indicate that physical reality has as its sole function the representation of the loftier and, ultimately, more accurate expression of reality that is the metaphysical realm. Accordingly, physical reality is clearly subordinate in station or rank to metaphysical reality.

To indicate this concept of limitation, Ṭáhirih in poem 7 applies various forms of the word *ḥadd* (حدّ), meaning "limit": for example, *ḥadd* (□حد), *maḥdúd* (محدود), and *ḥaddíyyat* (حدّيت). These words seem to refer to the station of distinction of the Manifestations of God or, in a more poetic sense, Their sense of separation, however temporary, from Their original divine unity wherein all knowledge and reality is apparent—the "world of vision," as spiritual reality is sometimes characterized in Bahá'í scripture.

In the stage of essential unity (*aḥadíyyat*, احديّت) there is no limitation or distinction among the Manifestations, even as Bahá'u'lláh notes in the Book of Certitude:

> These Manifestations of God have each a twofold station. One is the station of pure abstraction and essential unity. In this respect, if thou callest them all by one name, and dost ascribe to them the same attribute, thou hast not erred from the truth. Even as He hath revealed: "No distinction do We make between any of His Messengers!" For they one and all summon the people of the earth to acknowledge the Unity of God, and herald unto them the Kaw<u>th</u>ar of an infinite grace and bounty. They are all invested with the robe of Prophethood, and honored with the mantle of glory. Thus hath Muḥammad, the Point of the Qur'án, revealed: "I am all the Prophets." Likewise, He saith: "I am the first Adam, Noah, Moses, and Jesus." Similar statements have been made by 'Alí. Sayings such as this, which indicate the essential unity of those Exponents of Oneness, have also emanated from the Channels of God's immortal utterance, and the Treasuries of the gems of divine knowledge, and have been recorded in the scriptures. These Countenances are the recipients of the Divine Command, and the daysprings of His Revelation. This Revelation is exalted above the veils of plurality and the exigencies of number. Thus He saith: "Our Cause is but one." Inasmuch as the Cause is one and the same, the Exponents thereof also must needs be one and the same. Likewise, the Imáms of the

> Muḥammadan Faith, those lamps of certitude, have said: "Muḥammad is our first, Muḥammad our last, Muḥammad our all." (¶161)

Though in the station of Emissary the Manifestations are immaculate reflections of God's names and attributes, in the physical realm of time and place (*vaḥidíyyat,* واحديّت) They are necessarily constrained by laws and ordinances that must change and evolve over time.

C. THE THEME OF *QADAR*

Related importantly both to the concept of "limitation" in Ṭáhirih's treatment of the Adamic myth and to the concept of free will, so much a part of this entire mythic tradition, is the concept of *qadar* (قدر) or "measure."[18] On the personal level, the term has to do with the fact that not all individuals are created with the same capacities, talents, skills, or abilities, even though all may be "spiritually" equal in the sight of God.

We discover this same axiomatic observation as parents. We may recognize that each of our children possesses distinctly different abilities, talents, personalities, and potentialities; yet we are capable of loving them all equally. We recognize that the inherent capacity with which they have been endowed is beyond their control. Furthermore, if we are wise parents, we will be primarily concerned with what they do with their free will in developing and applying the capacities they possess, with their willful development of their own character.

Bahá'u'lláh observes that each individual is endowed with a preordained "measure" or "capacity" that is inherent when a soul emanates from the world of the spirit. However, in this same discussion Bahá'u'lláh explains that this ostensible "inequality" has no bearing on the worth, value, or status of the individual:

> Show forbearance and benevolence and love to one another. Should anyone among you be incapable of grasping a certain truth, or be striving to comprehend it, show forth, when conversing with him, a spirit of extreme kindliness and goodwill. Help him to see and recognize the truth, without esteeming yourself to be, in the least, superior to him, or to be possessed of greater endowments.
>
> The whole duty of man in this Day is to attain that share of the flood of grace which God poureth forth for him. Let none, therefore, consider

18. See references to the concept of *qadar* in Qur'án 54:49 and 42:27.

> the largeness or smallness of the receptacle. The portion of some might lie in the palm of a man's hand, the portion of others might fill a cup, and of others even a gallon-measure (*Gleanings,* no. 5.3–4).

The importance of this passage is beyond calculation, asserting as it does that those qualities traditionally deemed to cause one individual to be valued above another are beyond our willful control and, therefore, are not important distinctions spiritually. Indeed, these gifts, these expressions of *qadar,* are truly valuable only when appropriately developed and exercised in service to the Cause of God.

Bahá'u'lláh notes as much when He asserts that, regardless of the measure or capacity with which we may be endowed, each of us is judged according to how well and persistently we apply these gifts to the inherent goal of spiritual development:

> And now, concerning thy question regarding the creation of man. Know thou that all men have been created in the nature made by God, the Guardian, the Self-Subsisting. Unto each one hath been prescribed a preordained measure, as decreed in God's mighty and guarded Tablets. All that which ye potentially possess can, however, be manifested only as a result of *your own volition* [emphasis added]. Your own acts testify to this truth (*Gleanings,* no. 77.1).

In this context the term *qadar* in Ṭáhirih's verse not only alludes to our "measure" or "capacity," but also to the level of freedom and responsibility bestowed on everyone to perfect those abilities by seizing the available opportunities for this purpose.

In one of his own poems, Rúmí likewise uses the term *qadar,* as it is at times used to mean "free will," and he points out the enigmatic nature of this gift:

> In my ode there is both *jabr* (predestination) and *qadar* (free will), but ignore both
>
> since there would be no outcome from this subject except tumult and dispute.[19]

19. Translated by Hatcher and Hemmat.

In another verse, Rúmí alludes to this age-old debate in the following couplet:

> O my son, between the people of predestination (*jabr*) and those of the free will (*qadar*),
>
> the dispute will continue till the raising of the dead (the Day of Resurrection).[20]

D. THE CONCEPT OF THE "POINT" IN RELATION TO CREATION

Yet another extremely important symbol and theme of the poems in this volume is the concept of the Point. As we have already noted, it is clear in these poems that the Point represents the source from which emanates the spiritual force that animates and empowers the Manifestations. One way to think of it is as the appearance of the power of the Holy Spirit coming through the Manifestations of God at Their advent. Ṭáhirih sometimes employs the term "fiery point" or the "point in the breast of the Manifestation," but there is a depth of meaning in this implied chain of causality that is not readily apparent.

To begin with, if all creation emanates from God, then what is "the Point"? 'Abdu'l-Bahá states that the first emanation from God is the Will or Wish of God:

> Therefore, all creatures emanate from God—that is to say, it is by God that all things are realized, and by Him that all beings have attained to existence. The first thing which emanated from God is that universal reality, which the ancient philosophers termed the "First Mind," and which the people of Bahá call the "First Will." This emanation, in that which concerns its action in the world of God, is not limited by time or place; it is without beginning or end—beginning and end in relation to God are one (*Some Answered Questions,* 203).

Obviously, then, the Point is representative of the source of this emanation, even as this same passage describes the "Will" as the source of all action and creation

20. Translated by Hatcher and Hemmat.

in the world of being. In addition, Bahá'í texts also state that the Manifestations are the means by which God effects creation:

> Without the bounty of the splendor and the instructions of these Holy Beings the world of souls and thoughts would be opaque darkness. Without the irrefutable teachings of those sources of mysteries the human world would become the pasture of animal appetites and qualities, the existence of everything would be unreal, and there would be no true life. That is why it is said in the Gospel: "In the beginning was the Word," meaning that it became the cause of all life" ('Abdu'l-Bahá, *Some Answered Questions,* 162–63).

The Point, then, would represent the concept of a chain of causality through which God guides humanity, a creative process that is a continuum—a reality that has no beginning or end. And yet, this constant and ongoing process does have points of beginning *relative* to particular aspects of creation. For example, there are points of beginning with regard to the formation of a galaxy, or a planetary system, or, in terms of the evolution of our planet, to a dispensation instigated by the appearance of a new Prophet in the evolution of the human body politic.

In this sense *point*—the Arabic term *nuqṭah* (نقطه)—is a word that, in the context of Bahá'í and mystic philosophy, is replete with meanings. For example, if we take the concept of the "word" as the source of creation, as the "beginning" of articulating the wish or will of God, as expressed memorably in John 1:1 ("In the beginning was the word . . ."), the Point represents the beginning of a letter of that word, the point where the pen first touches the page. In Ṭáhirih's poem that we have titled *Adam's Wish,* the Point often represents the sense of intense enlightenment the Manifestation experiences when the Wish or Will of God inspires in Him the ability to utter the "Word of God." For even though the Manifestation is, according to 'Abdu'l-Bahá, well aware of His station from the beginning of His conscious existence in this world, Bahá'u'lláh describes the actual event of receiving the revelation in powerfully poetic and sensual terms:

> During the days I lay in the prison of Ṭihrán, though the galling weight of the chains and the stench-filled air allowed Me but little sleep, still in those infrequent moments of slumber I felt as if something flowed from the crown of My head over My breast, even as a mighty torrent that precipitateth itself upon the earth from the summit of a lofty mountain. Every limb

> of My body would, as a result, be set afire. At such moments My tongue recited what no man could bear to hear (*Epistle to the Son of the Wolf,* 22).

This passage seems very precisely to portray the event to which Ṭáhirih alludes when the power latent in Adam, Noah, or the Báb manifests itself through Their utterance and command. The Point in this context is the symbolic or metaphorical representation of the source of God's Will in the breast of the Prophet.

Ṭáhirih artfully describes this process by personifying the Point in *Adam's Wish.* The Point itself speaks and describes the historical process as It becomes the source of the power for the Prophet and, in turn, the source of all action or creation in the world of existence. In the context of these verses, Ṭáhirih has the Point represent God Himself in such a manner that this notion is neither blasphemous nor inappropriate since the Point functions in the poem as the primal source of inspiration for the Manifestations of God. Thus the Point is a source without in any way daring to represent the "Essential Reality of God," which cannot be represented in any meaningful way without trivializing or demeaning the station of God.

Finally, we should note Bahá'u'lláh's explicit allusion to "the Point" as the term applies both to the Báb as the "Primal Point" and to the Manifestations of God in general. In the following passage Bahá'u'lláh indicates that in the station of essential Unity, all the Prophets proceed from and are expressive of one and the same source or point of origin:

> In this station, were He Who is the Embodiment of the End to say: "Verily, I am the Point of the Beginning," He would indeed be speaking the truth. And were He to say: "I am other than Him," this would be equally true. Likewise, were He to proclaim: "Verily, I am the Lord of heaven and earth," or "the King of kings," or "the Lord of the realm above," or Muḥammad, or 'Ali, or their descendants, or aught else, He would indeed be proclaiming the truth of God. He, verily, ruleth over all created things and standeth supreme above all besides Him. Hast thou not heard what hath been said aforetime: "Muḥammad is our first, Muḥammad our last, Muḥammad our all?" And elsewhere: "They all proceed from the same Light?" (*Gems of Divine Mysteries,* 30–31)

Perhaps more relevant to the issue that Ṭáhirih is raising with Bihjat is the fact that when the new Manifestation appears, He becomes the new source, the new "point" of revelation toward which all must turn. Therefore, He has the power to change or abrogate any or all of the laws of the previous Manifestation, including the *Qiblih*, the "point of adoration," the direction toward which believers turn when they pray.

Furthermore, inasmuch as Ṭáhirih is well aware that Bahá'u'lláh will meet with resistance from some Bábís, she is forewarning Bihjat to be ready, to be prepared, not to fall prey to the same error, an admonition that Bahá'u'lláh expresses with vivid clarity in the following passage from His last major work, *Epistle to the Son of the Wolf:*

> Likewise, refuting certain disbelievers, He saith: "For none knoweth the time of the Revelation except God. Whenever it appeareth, all must acknowledge the Point of Truth, and render thanks unto God." They that have turned aside from Me have spoken even as the followers of John (the Baptist) spoke. For they, too, protested against Him Who was the Spirit (Jesus) saying: "The dispensation of John hath not yet ended; wherefore hast thou come?" Now, too, they that have repudiated Us, though they have never known Us and have been at all times ignorant of the fundamentals of this Cause, knowing not from Whom it proceeded or what it signifieth, have spoken that which hath made all created things to sigh and lament (157).

6. Poetics and the Mathnaví

While there are many poetic traditions at work in this collection, the principal construction of these poems is the traditional *mathnaví* (مثنوی), not so much a poetic structure as it is the rhymed couplet typical of classical Persian poetry. Though it has been employed from the third century BC to the ninth century AD for heroic or epic verse, it has also been used in works dealing with historical events or romantic stories.

While in Persian the mathnaví usually restricts the number of syllables per line in each couplet to no more than eleven, it is a broadly used style that may vary immensely according to the topic presented. Our work faithfully renders a line-for-line translation with exacting attention to the poetic sensibility of the verse, but we have not attempted to retain the rhymes or the syllabic restrictions. Indeed, it is often the case that the topic or theme of the mathnaví will dictate both style and meter.

Most commonly, the mathnaví begins with praise of God and then proceeds to set forth the theme in a symphonic arrangement of motifs that are interwoven throughout what is often a form of narrative story or discourse. The term *mathnaví* also refers to the Arabic term *muzdavaj*, which means "two by two," and, indeed, over time the form that began to be employed in Arabic mystical poetry is the rhymed couplet that constitutes the traditional mathnaví, even though the Arabic writers have not been particularly disposed to fictional narratives such as epics and romances.

We have translated these couplets into English couplets to retain the line-for-line relationship between the original and the English version. Likewise, as most of these couplets are "closed couplets" (complete sentences or statements) in the original, we have rendered the translation into closed couplets whenever appropriate to do so. And while we have not attempted to replicate the rhyme or the syllabic form because these constraints simply do not work well in English, we have attempted as best we are able to retain the poetic "feel" for the lines, whether that sensibility derives from the tonality of the original or from the primary images and allusions.

Put simply, we have attempted to avoid interpreting or translating the poetry out of the poem. We have responded to the same challenge that poets and scholars before us have likewise discovered, whether in Chapman's famous translation of the dactylic hexameters of Homer's Greek epic into unrhymed iambic pentameter of English verse, or more recently Seamus Heaney's translation of the Anglo-Saxon alliterative verse of *Beowulf,* or Coleman Barks's translations of Rúmí's works into modern free verse.

To state the matter more plainly, we feel that one cannot really translate poetry in any exact sense. One may replicate as much as possible the theme, the tone, even the imagery from a poem in one language into a poem in another language. But because each language and each culture has its own unique poetic strengths and shared referents, any attempt at translating a poem must necessarily end up creating another poem that can only hint at or give clues to the feel and meaning of the original.

Sometimes that effort is extremely successful. One might even say that on occasion the translation is equal to or even superior to the original. The point is that the "translated" poem is never really the same poem. What one does when translating well is to create a new poem because the only exact way to gain access to the original poem is to learn the language, the culture, and the historical context out of which the poem derives its meaning. Even then, reading and understanding poetry is a thoroughly subjective process.

One need only survey some of the vast interpretations of noteworthy modern poems in English to understand the difficulty of reading poems in one's own language to appreciate this fact. Consequently, to avoid imposing our own understanding of these works on the reader, we have included in this collection an abundance of explanatory notes together with the original text. In this case, we have the bounty of being able to include the original calligraphy of an early copyist. The source this transcriber used was completed prior to Ṭáhirih's death while she was imprisoned at the house of the *kalántar,* or governor, of Tehran.

Finally, we have attempted to be faithful to the original. At the same time, we realize only too well that a significant problem with making Ṭáhirih's work accessible is the depth and complexity of her intellectuality. We can attempt to make the language say what the original says, but the original is extremely allusive and elusive, even to someone well versed in Persian and Arabic. Her works are elliptical, symbolic, imagistic, and just plain hard. At the same time, her lines are bountiful whether or not we are able to penetrate the depth of meaning veiled by her pen.

Poem 1: The Announcement

"The Announcement" alludes to the promise of God inherent in the eternal covenant whereby humankind has been subtly fashioned with free will, then inexorably and unfailingly guided by the divine Emissaries Who, through Their successive appearances in human history, have come to unfold the straight path to God. More generally, "The Announcement" is about the concept of the "Point," its mysteries, and its manifestations.

The poem begins with rather cryptic references to six Manifestations of God Who appeared prior to the Báb, Who Himself is designated as the "Primal Point." Adam, Noah, Abraham, Moses, Jesus, Muḥammad, and the Báb are referred to in sequence; each in successive lines of the poem (verses 2–8). The station of Muḥammad, Who has symbolically reappeared in this new revelation, is alluded to (18–22), and the twin Manifestations of the Point in the world of existence are symbolized by the twin reflections of the sun in the Great Ocean of existence (23–25). This allusion is followed by a conversation with the Pen instigated by a question (26–38).

In verses 99–111 Ṭáhirih constructs a figurative contrast between the two aspects of remoteness (concealment and transcendence) and proximity (manifestation and immanence) of the divine. In verses 100 and 105 she makes references to the story of Moses, Whom God told "You shall never see me!" Thus, when God manifested His light on *Ṭúr* (Mount Paran), the intensity of the light rendered Moses unconscious and He "fell down in a swoon" (Qur'án 7:143). In verses 100 and 111, the sun—the figure of Muḥammad—appears from behind the clouds. Also, in verse 104 there is an allusion to a bright light hidden because of its intense illumination and referred to as "the light of avoidance" and in verse 106 as the "shimmering veil."

Ṣúfís have used letters of the alphabet to symbolize transcendence and immanence as attributes of God. The isolated letters in the Qur'án—commonly alluded to as the "disconnected letters"—appear at the beginning of some sections of the Qur'án and are to them a sign of the concealed unity of God that only Muḥammad is aware of. Bahá'u'lláh in the Book of Certitude states the following about these letters:

> In the beginning of His Book He saith: "Alif. Lám. Mím. No doubt is there about this Book: It is a guidance unto the God-fearing." In the disconnected letters of the Qur'án the mysteries of the divine Essence are enshrined, and within their shells the pearls of His Unity are treasured. For lack of space We do not dwell upon them at this moment. Outwardly they signify Muḥammad Himself, Whom God addresseth saying: "O Muḥammad, there is no doubt nor uncertainty about this Book which hath been sent down from the heaven of divine Unity. In it is guidance unto them that fear God" (¶224).

The revelation of the hidden mystery of these letters takes place through other letters (*Sharḥ-i-Iṣṭiláḥát-i-Taṣavvuf*, 4:192–93). The isolated letters in the Qur'án are also called "the illumined letters" (*ḥarf-i-núrání*, حرف نوراني) in contrast to the rest of the letters of the alphabet that are the "dark letters" (Dehkhoda, 19:454). A related Ṣúfí term is "the exalted letters" (*ḥurúf-i-'álíyát*, حروف عاليات) (*Sharḥ-i-Iṣṭiláḥát-i-Taṣavvuf*, 4:193), which is a reference to the divine and hidden potential of human souls to manifest God's attributes. By "the blazing Letter" (*ḥarf-i-náríyyih*, حرف ناريه) in verse 99 Ṭáhirih is referring to the primordial nature of the Point, the source of the world of creation, the hidden reality that has now become disclosed and manifest.

Some sections of the poem are prayers. For example, there is a prayer for the appearance of the next Manifestation of God, a prayer that the mysteries of God will be revealed through Ṭáhirih's own verse (65–78), and a prayer for the revelation of God's command to the world and for the salvation of humankind (93–98). God's response to this prayer (verses 148–99) is that the revelation has actually taken place but that humanity has denied itself God's benevolence (149–56). God then invites humanity to embrace this revelation (157–81).

The Station of Muḥammad

In describing Muḥammad's true station, Ṭáhirih alludes to the Qur'án in three lines—lines 18, 19, and 20—that allude respectively to Qur'ánic verses 29:48,

46:9, and 48:10. Taken as a whole, this section of the poem refers to the reappearance of Muḥammad in this age and to the disclosure of His true station, which was hidden in the past due to people's lack of capacity. Therefore people had either rejected Muḥammad and the verses revealed to Him or had not fully understood His station, the station of the Qur'án, and the full meaning of the verses revealed to Him.

Line 18 alludes to a verse from a section of the Súra of the Spider that deals with the "Book" (29:45–50). In verse 48 God tells Muḥammad that if He had read any of the holy books before the revelation of the Qur'án, or if He had transcribed anything with His right hand (that is, if He had been learned or erudite), then His detractors would have questioned His assertion that the Qur'án was a revelation from God: "And thou didst not recite before it any book, nor didst thou *transcribe* one with thy *right* hand, for then could the *liars* have doubted."[1] In other words, if God had wished, Muḥammad would have demonstrated His capacity to read and write. However, His eloquence would have made the detractors and disbelievers doubt that His revelation was from God—they would have assumed the Qur'án to be merely a work derived from His own creativity and His study of the works of other scholars.

Line 19 of the poem alludes to the beginning of the Súra of Sand Hills. As with the previous allusion, the first ten lines of this súra concern the "Book." Sometimes when the Qur'án was recited to people, disbelievers would say, "This is clear enchantment" (verse 7). In fact, they would say that Muḥammad had forged the lines (verse 8). In verse 9, God commands Muḥammad, "Say: I am no apostle of new doctrines: and *I know not what* will be done with me or with you. I follow naught but that which is revealed to me, and I am not but a plain warner."

In this verse Muḥammad declares that He is a normal human being in every respect except that He has the capacity to reveal the verses of God. Ṭáhirih interprets this verse as concealing the true station of Muḥammad for the sake of the people He is teaching. That is, had God clearly revealed His station, they might not have accepted the authority of His utterance as being from God. She explains that Muḥammad's station was thus hidden in the ornament of *"I know not what."*

---

1. The italicized words here and in the following citations from the Qur'án indicate the words Ṭáhirih has incorporated into her poem as an allusion to the Qur'án for those who are sufficiently knowledgeable in it to understand the reference.

Line 20 alludes to a Qur'ánic verse from the beginning of the Súra of Victory. This section of the súra deals with the station of Muḥammad in response to the events of the Treaty of Ḥudaybiyah. These verses progressively reveal the station of Muḥammad. At first, Muḥammad is depicted as an ordinary man. In verse 2 there is a reference to God's forgiveness of Muḥammad's shortcomings and sin. Verse 3 promises God's almighty help to Muḥammad, and in verses 8 and 9 God tells Muḥammad, "Surely, we have sent thee as a witness and as a bearer of good news and as a warner, that you may believe in Alláh and His Messengers and may aid Him and revere Him. And [that] you may declare His glory, morning and evening." Verse 10 hints at Muḥammad's true station, to which Ṭáhirih refers in line 20 of her poem: "Those who swear allegiance to thee do but swear allegiance to Alláh. The *hand* of Alláh is above their hands. So whoever breaks [his faith], he breaks it only to his soul's injury. And whoever fulfills his covenant with Alláh, He will grant him a mighty reward."

Ṭáhirih offers an interpretation and explanation of this verse of the Qur'án by relating the hand of God to the divine station in which there exist no opposites like those extant in the material world—such as light and darkness. In effect, in the world of vision there is no distinction between God's hand and Muḥammad's hand.

Poem 1: The Announcement

He is the Beloved Attractor manifest in every fleck of dust,
the Creator of every new reality!

1
O melodious Nightingale, return!
Sing to us of thoughts wondrous and refined.

2
Make the world entranced[2] with your warbling, wholly entranced!
Make Adam[3] serene[4] with your singing, completely serene![5]

3
Cause Noah to appear with your song of lamentation!
Sail the ark of ecstasy upon this whirling globe!

4
Bring forth the holy and fragrant Tree!
Bring forth that *fiṭríyyih*[6] melody, so original, so delightful!

5
From those Sinai drops
bring forth perfumed glass.

---

2. *Maḥv* (محو): "entranced," "charmed," or "annihilated."

3. "Adam" here and elsewhere in the poem sometimes alludes to the historical figure of the Manifestation Adam, sometimes to the myths about Adam and His "rebellion" against divine law, and sometimes to humankind in general. On occasion the allusion may represent all three.

4. *Ṣaḥv* (صحو): "becoming sober."

5. This verse alludes to Adam, verse 3 alludes to Noah, verse 4 alludes to Abraham, verse 5 alludes to Moses, verse 6 alludes to Jesus, verse 7 alludes to Muḥammad, and verse 8 alludes to the Báb.

6. *Fiṭríyyih* (فطريّه): "original" or "inherent," therefore endowed by the Creator. See Qur'án 6:79, where Abraham instinctively turns His allegiance from the power manifest in creation (e.g., the Sun) to the Creator of all the heavens and the earth, vowing, "and never shall I give Partners to God." Therefore this line of the poem is a cryptic reference to Abraham. Most of our citations from the Qur'án are from the Abdullah Yusuf Ali translation (New York: Tahrike Tarsile Aur'an, Inc. 11th edition, 2004). In some instances when further clarity is needed, we have used translations by Rodwell, by Maulana Muhammad Ali, or by ourselves.

6
Bring back the Sun from the west,
  its face beaming with a yellow hue.[7]

7
Cast the world into ecstasy and adulation
  by chanting the letters of *bismilih!*[8]

8
Recount all the mysteries of the Point![9]
  Bestow again the good news to all these bewildered lovers!

9
From attraction to the hidden mystery,
  let life's blood trickle in the veins of their hearts.

10
Make the world become filled with brightness, a land of light!
  Fill the created universe with ecstasy from one end to the other!

11
That Cause concealed in the garments of glory,
  that blessed ecstasy veiled by the robe of praise,

7. This description alludes to the traditional portrait of Christ as being crowned with a halo. "West" in Ṣúfí terminology is the physical and material world where the sun of the Holy Spirit hides in the earth of nature (Núrbakhsh, 2:288, under *gharb*). "Bring back the sun from the West" means to make the sun of the Holy Spirit, "face beaming with a yellow hue," or the reality of Jesus Christ that has disappeared, to appear again. The face of Jesus (beaming with a yellow hue) has been likened to the sun that has set. In the Báb's writings "West" symbolizes Fárs, the land from which the sun of truth has risen. There is a reference to the West in the Qur'án (28:44) as the place where God's commandments were given to Moses: "And thou wast not on the western side when We revealed to Moses the commandments."

8. *Bismilih* (بسمله) literally means "in the name of God." Every súra in the Qur'án, except for Súra 9 (*Tawbah* or *Birá'at*), begins with the phrase "In the name of God, the Most Gracious, the Most Merciful." *Bismilih* is the first word in that phrase. Therefore, this line of the poem is a cryptic reference to the dispensation of Islam or to Muḥammad.

9. The Báb has the title "The Primal Point."

12
now has dawned from the constellations of *innamá*[10]
  and has caused all covers and veils to be removed!

13
That Edifice,[11] so mightily unfolding His mystery,
  that Edifice whose Builder is Ancient

14
has emerged from the pavilions of majesty,
  has become greater still with the illumination of His beauty!

15
From the Eternal Veil have radiated
  infinite splendors of Aḥmad.[12]

16
The Hidden Mystery in the luminous veil
  has become radiant from the station of *that which was before!*

17
From the point of *bá* the countenance of *há'*[13]—
  concealed ere now in its Essence—has become entirely manifest!

---

10. *Innamá* (انّما): "indeed" or "verily." Ṭáhirih is referring to the Qur'án 48:10, where it is made clear that the Prophet is God's representative and thus speaks and acts on God's behalf: "Verily, those who were swearing allegiance to you, were indeed swearing allegiance to Alláh."

11. God's Cause.

12. With this allusion to Muḥammad, we encounter a reference to the eternal process by which God has revealed His attributes and power through the sequential appearance of the Manifestations. 'Abdu'l-Bahá, in the Lawḥ-i-Aflák, states that there are infinite Manifestations to minister to the infinite worlds of God.

13. The Point of *bá* is a reference to the point appearing under the letter *bá*, "b," the second letter of the Arabic alphabet: ب. The point is a symbol of the primordial origin of the world of being and also a symbol of the source of revelation. It represents the first manifestation of the hidden Essence of God symbolized by the letter *há'* (هاء). *Há'* is the first letter of the word *Hú* (هو) meaning "He" (God). The phrase "From the point of *bá* the countenance of *há* has become manifest" means that spiritual realities that thus far had been hidden have now been made manifest through the Primal Point (a title for the Báb). The letter *bá* is also the first letter of the word *bismilláh*, the first word in the invocation "In the name of God, the Beneficent, the Merciful" that appears at the beginning of all súras of the Qur'an except one. Explications of this invocation, the first word of it, and the first letter "*bá*," have been provided by Siyyid Káẓim-i-Ras͟htí, the Báb, and 'Abdu'l-Bahá.

18
Aḥmad was *didst not transcribe with the right hand*[14]
for the sake of protecting the "mystery" from the *doubters.*

19
He was hidden from the letters of praise,
hidden in the ornament of *I know not what.*[15]

20
Indeed, Aḥmad's hand was the hand of God
where neither light nor darkness had any other source[16]

21
but imbibed instead from the spring of His benevolence:
Even if they had been opposites, they are what they have become.

22
Even the people of that realm are veiled
from this mystery[17] churning in the depths of your beating heart.

23
Metaphorically, the Point is only a drop from this Ocean,[18]
yet visible from the loftiest and most exalted Summit,

---

14. This verse recounts a verse of the Qur'án (29:48) in which God tells Muḥammad, "And thou didst not recite before it any book, nor didst thou transcribe one with thy right hand, for then could the liars have doubted."

15. Qur'án 46:9: "I am no bringer of newfangled doctrine among the apostles, nor do I know what will be done with me or with you. I follow but that which is revealed to me by inspiration; I am but a warner, open and clear."

16. Qur'án 48:10: "Verily those who plight their fealty to thee do no less than plight their fealty to God: The Hand of God is over their hands: Then any one who violates his oath, does so to the harm of his own soul, and any one who fulfils what he has covenanted with God—God will soon grant him a great Reward."

17. The mystery of how the progressive development of the world of creation is sustained by the continuous influence of the successive revelations of God through the intermediary of the Manifestations.

18. The "similitude" Ṭáhirih alludes to here reveals her remarkable comprehension of the theological and philosophical principles that would become unveiled in the writings of Bahá'u'lláh and 'Abdu'l-Bahá. Here she is referring to the fact that while the Báb, the Primal Point, is but one Manifestation in an infinite universe of worlds and Prophets, He is, nonetheless, a perfect imprint

24
two images manifesting reflections of *ḥadd*,[19]
two suns assisted by two human temples![20]

25
Behold! The Most Great Sea has begun to stir!
The Primal Point, motionless ere now, has begun to move!

26
Ask the Pen about the mystery of endlessness[21]
to fulfill your desire that all the dry bones may become resurrected.[22]

27
O Pen, You were hidden, unconscious, and drunk!
Who awakened you, O Pen, after You concealed Yourself?[23]

---

of godliness expressed in human form. Stated another way, while the universe is infinite, there is no more lofty expression of divinity than the Prophets of God.

19. *Ḥadd* (حدّ), like *qadar,* symbolizes the portioning out of enlightenment or assistance according to the requirements and capacities of an evolving humanity. We come across this term in Mullá Sadrá's philosophy as meaning "a description of the characteristics, type, kind and attributes of each thing" (Sajjádí, 191).

20. *Haykal* (هيكل) here seems to be a reference to the two human personae assumed by the twin Manifestations of the Báb and Bahá'u'lláh as enabling the rays of the sun (divine attributes of God) to reach humankind.

21. Here the entire issue of the "Seal," Muḥammad as the last of the Prophets, and Islam as the final revelation from God is implicitly addressed. That is, the process of enlightenment never ceases but is endless and continuous.

22. This allusion works on various levels. It is obviously referring to the Day of Resurrection as affirmed in the Old and New Testaments, as well as in the Qur'án. Specifically, it is alluding to the Twin Manifestations of the Báb and Bahá'u'lláh, Who fulfill the prophecy that there will be two Trumpet Blasts. The first will render all humankind dumbfounded, bewildered, and unconscious (in a state of shock) as the greatest point of transition in the course of human history is signaled and readied. The second blast, described in the writings of the Báb as the "Latter Resurrection," is that of Bahá'u'lláh, which will awaken and revive the bewildered masses of humankind and lead them to the path of unity, reconciliation, and harmony.

23. This allusion is reminiscent of Bahá'u'lláh's description of His own experience when in His tablet to Náṣiri'd-Dín Shāh He states, "O King! I was but a man like others, asleep upon My couch, when lo, the breezes of the All-Glorious were wafted over Me, and taught Me the knowledge of all that hath been" (*Summons of the Lord of Hosts,* 1:192).

28
Your consciousness rendered creation lowly, meek, and humble.
Through Your resurrection, superstition became eradicated.

29
Indeed, superstitions were removed from understanding
so that all knowledge became illumined.

30
In the Bayán You embraced every distant path and form.
Indeed, You removed every limitation from our midst!

31
You disclosed the mystery of unity among all created things.
You expelled from the earth all discord and enmity.

32
The veils of *Jalál* have been rent asunder!
Lo, every *Jamál*[24] has now become resplendent!

33
So many lights reacting to this conflagration
were extinguished by lightning bolts of *Jamál!*

34
O Pen, the Command[25] emanated from two Commands;[26]
Indeed, after two thousand years You have prevailed:

24. According to the Muslim Gnostics, God's names are of two kinds: the names of His grandeur (*Jalál,* جلال) and the names reflecting His beauty (*Jamál,* جمال). God's names related to His grandeur characterize Him as inaccessible to human beings and therefore are like veils that hide Him from human understanding. These are names such as "Inaccessible," "Mighty," "Great," "Majestic," and "High King." In contrast, God's names related to His beauty describe attributes that are accessible to human beings, such as "Beautiful," "Merciful," "Compassionate," "Near," "Loving," "Pardoner," and so forth. (Refer to Murata 9.)

25. From the word *Amr* (امر).

26. Also from *Amr.*

35
One thousand since the appearance of Aḥmad;[27]
another thousand since the appearance of the Enlightened One.

36
Each of you[28] has been unconscious because of the mystery of *baná'*,[29]
then drunk without wine[30] at the appearance of *He willeth*.[31]

---

27. Muḥammad. Here Ṭáhirih is speaking in general terms about how Prophets appear approximately every thousand years. Thus approximately one thousand years has elapsed since the advent of Muḥammad and two thousand years since the appearance of Christ (the Enlightened or Illumined One). So it was that the Báb stated to the tribunal in Tabríz just before His execution, "I am, I am, I am the Promised One! I am the One Whose name you have for a thousand years invoked, at Whose mention you have risen, Whose advent you have longed to witness, and the hour of Whose Revelation you have prayed God to hasten. Verily, I say, it is incumbent upon the peoples of both the East and the West to obey My word, and to pledge allegiance to My person" (quoted in Shoghi Effendi, *God Passes By*, 21).

28. Ṭáhirih now shifts back to addressing the peoples of the world with "You."

29. *Baná'* (بناء): "building" or "creating" as a process or as a gradual and endless succession of ever more complete descriptions of reality, as opposed to some Muslim interpretations of the Qur'án that imply that there was no need for further revelation after Muḥammad.

30. Ṭáhirih here alludes to Súra 22:22, which observes that God's inexplicable actions cause consternation on the Day of Resurrection: "Thou shalt see mankind/ As in a drunken riot,/ Yet not drunk: but dreadful/ Will be the Wrath of God."

31. This Arabic passage, "He willeth" (*in yashá'*, إن يشاء), is a reference to Qur'án 14:19 and 35:16, in which God is described as having the capacity to do whatsoever He wills, even should the rationale of His decree be difficult to understand or cause confusion or consternation, for everything that God wills is ultimately the cause of felicity and justice. Obviously relevant to the context of Ṭáhirih's discourse on progressive revelation is the concept of equality among the Messengers or Manifestations of God. She also deals with the explicit idea of history as a continuity, as opposed to the idea of religious history ending with the appearance of Muḥammad, Who, some Muslims believe, brought the final and complete revelation from God. In the Kitáb-i-Íqán (the Book of Certitude), Bahá'u'lláh explains that the term *seal* has been misinterpreted, that when understood correctly, the term applies equally to all the Prophets inasmuch as all represent the culmination of all the revelations that have preceded Them:

> Notwithstanding the obviousness of this theme, in the eyes of those that have quaffed the wine of knowledge and certitude, yet how many are those who, through failure to understand its meaning, have allowed the term "Seal of the Prophets" to obscure their understanding, and deprive them of the grace of all His manifold bounties! . . . The mystery of this theme hath, in this Dispensation, been a sore test unto all mankind. Behold, how many are those who, clinging unto these words, have disbelieved Him Who is their true Revealer [the Báb]. What, We ask, could this people presume the terms "first" and "last"—when referring to God—glorified be His Name!—to mean? (¶172–73).

In short, the consternation of the Day of Resurrection alluded to in this line occurs with the appearance of the Qá'im (i.e., the Báb).

37
You were surprised by your separation!
Now you will be in a state of awe because of your zeal![32]

38
Our Friend is a mystery hidden from us,
though luminous with light and glory.[33]

39
Since He is manifest from the Exalted Shrine,
how can He be associated with names and attributes?[34]

40
The path to reunion lies in severing all distance from Him,
in transcending all that is separate from Him.

41
Because His benevolence is indescribable and boundless,
He became manifest through the mystery of the Eternal One.

32. "Zeal" (*ghayúríyyat*: غیوریّت). The word *ghayuríyyat* implies "jealousy" in the mystical terminology of a type of intense love that the wayfarer has for God. This love is compared to an earthly love in which the lover is jealous of anyone else having affection for the beloved. Here again Ṭáhirih alludes to the Báb as the Qá'im and to the fulfillment of the "Day of Resurrection" as discussed in the Qur'án. She is also referring to the appearance of Bahá'u'lláh as a test for the Bábís because He fulfills the promise that "Him Whom God will make Manifest" will appear in the "Latter Resurrection" (the Báb, *Selections from the Writings of the Báb,* 1.2.4).

33. While Ṭáhirih never met the Báb, she met Bahá'u'lláh and spent time with Him after He had her rescued from Qazvín. It is patently clear in all of her work that she is not only aware that Bahá'u'lláh is a Manifestation of God and "Him Whom God shall make manifest," but also that she is attempting to prepare her Bábí readers and followers for the tests that this transition will bring about.

34. It must be remembered that Ṭáhirih was executed two years after the Báb was executed and that she was well aware of her role in preparing the Bábís for the tests they would encounter in recognizing Bahá'u'lláh. She was also clearly aware that the Báb had requested that Bahá'u'lláh ("Him Whom God shall make manifest") not reveal His station to the Bábís until the year 19 (AD 1863).

42
This Point[35] was made manifest from the realm of the Eternal One
and is exalted beyond the condition of causes.[36]

43
How then, O exalted Lord,[37] can this intermediary condition[38]
provide a pathway for us to that (eternal) station?[39]

44
"You must (yearn) to comprehend all secrets and mysteries!"
"Lo, assume the virtue of servitude, which is naught but true lordship!"

45
Thus the Creator's wish[40] became a command
so that from Him *Separation* became manifest![41]

---

35. As throughout, the "Point" signalizes at once the specific Manifestation of God as the Point from which issues forth the command of God (even as the Báb is titled the "Primal Point") and the Point from which creation itself issues forth from the will or wish of God (the First Mind).

36. The "condition of causes" (*shu'únát-i-'ailal,* شئونات علل) alludes to physical reality, the realm of cause and effect.

37. "Exalted Lord": *Rabb-i-A'lá* (ربّ اعلي).

38. Again an allusion to the condition of "causes," the human "middle condition" between the emanation from God and the "return" to God—the condition in which free will is operant because reality is veiled.

39. Most probably Ṭáhirih is here alluding to the Manifestation as an intermediary between the two realities of the realm of the Creator and the realm of the created. The Manifestations act as a bridge between these realities by descending from the realm of Command and living in a human temple among humankind. This interpretation seems vindicated by the line that follows.

40. First or Primal Will.

41. This alludes to the Ṣúfí tradition that the world of creation laments its separation from the Creator and inherently longs to return to the source of its emanation or origin. In this case, the term seems to refer to the fact that in earthly existence, spiritual reality is veiled or concealed (i.e., "separated") from human perception and without the sacrificial assistance of the Manifestations, Who willingly submit Themselves to the trials and trivialities of human existence while They are, for a time, separated from the station They later reassume after Their ascent.

46
From His two Commands[42] originated the realm of Command.
From these two Commands, all order was instigated:[43]

Words of the Creator

47
"From the beginning that has no beginning to the end that has no end
you will continue to traverse the constellations endlessly

48
"until you discover the mystery of My insistent command
and find your way to My exalted and firm fashioning of creation,[44]

49
"until you eradicate all doubt in the world
by closing your eyes to 'separation' in the world of existence.[45]

50
"You would then disrobe yourself of the illusion of clothes[46]
and become drowned in the light of acquiring illumination.

---

42. Here again we have the word *command* from *amr* (امر), implying that the ultimate source of all causality is the realm of "command," itself but an expression of the Primal Will of God.

43. *Ḥukm* (حکم) or "order" refers here, most probably, to the entire theme of the two wishes of Adam—that humankind progress by being assisted in (1) knowing God and (2) loving God.

44. What Adam wished at the very beginning of His enlightenment (to achieve Godliness) can only be accomplished in the "Day of God" (the Day of Resurrection, the advent of the Twin Manifestations). This need for gradualness in the process of human advancement is symbolized here and elsewhere in the poetry of Ṭáhirih by a star traversing the constellations from the beginning of time to the "End of Time"—the period of the maturation of humankind as discussed in the Bahá'í texts (i.e., this present period of humanity's transition from adolescence to adulthood).

45. Eliminating "separation" here alludes to the awareness that the reality of all created things derives from the ability to manifest divine attributes. Hence, all creation is but one organic expression of the Creator. To realize this verity is to eliminate from our consciousness the idea that any part of creation is fundamentally separate from anything else.

46. You would realize that your human temple (or body) is but an illusion and that your true self is essentially a spiritual reality. You would then be so overwhelmed with knowledge that you would become bewildered. This image interestingly parallels Thomas Carlyle's discussion of the social status as indicated by apparel in *Sartor Restartis* (1833): i.e., if all were naked, how would we know who possesses rank, status, or power?

51
"In the downpour of glory you would wash away
all utterance, save this good news!

52
"You would dwell in the banquet hall of My unity!
You would give thanks to God, the Lord of all the Worlds!"[47]

Ṭáhirih Praises the Advent of the Prophets

53
The One who, by instantly manifesting Himself with splendor,[48]
has abolished the "separation" of *that which is separate!*[49]

54
He has removed all "separation" from among us,[50]
and in its stead has planted the seed of *"He made all things Rich."*[51]

55
Because in the Bayán all imaginings have been shattered,
now nothing can be seen in the created universe save God![52]

---

47. At this point, the voice of God ceases, and the narrator, Ṭáhirih, speaks.

48. *Bahá* (بهاء).

49. Has shown the unity of creation.

50. Separation from God.

51. Qur'án 4:130: "Alláh will provide abundance for all from His all-reaching bounty: for Alláh is He that cares for all and is Wise."

52. Thus Bahá'u'lláh cites the ḥadíth of the Imám 'Alí: "Nothing have I perceived except that I perceived God before it, God after it, or God with it" (quoted in Bahá'u'lláh 1988, *Epistle to the Son of the Wolf,* 113).

56
God's *Furqán*[53] was disclosed from the sleeve[54]
and the name *A'lá*[55] became established through the named One.[56]

57
Because the spirit of Aḥmad appeared in a human temple,[57]
worlds upon worlds became filled with the Holy Spirit through this human form.[58]

58
His station is *Rabb-i-A'ẓam* and *Rabb-i-A'lá*—the Greatest Lord on High;
He is *Rabb-i-Akbar*, the Garden of Paradise.[59]

---

53. *Furqán* (فرقان) means "distinction," what distinguishes truth from falsehood; a title for the Qur'án itself as indicated in 2:185; 3:3; and 25:1. In the Qur'án, however, this title has been mentioned two times regarding the truth given to Moses: "And when we gave Moses the Book and *Furqán* for your guidance" (2:53); "And we gave Moses and Aaron the *Furqán* and the Light and the Admonition (*dhikr*, ذکر) for the God-fearing" (21:48).

The word *Furqán* can also refer to the special station of the Báb. The Báb makes the following distinctions about Muḥammad as a Messenger of God, as a human Who only repeats what God says, and the reality of Muḥammad as *Furqán*—the Word of God. He explains that in this dispensation the reality of Furqán has appeared. As opposed to the time of Muḥammad when God's verses were revealed only at specific times, God's revelation in this age takes place continuously and without interruption (*min dún-i-zavál va lá iḍmiḥlál*, من دون زوال و لااضمحلال). See commentary on the Súra of Kawthar in an article by Nádir Sa'ídí, *Payám-i-Bahá'í*, June 1998, p. 12.

54. This is an allusion to Moses when He withdrew His hand concealed in His cloak to reveal a hand of power. See Qur'án 27:12 and elsewhere.

55. *'A'lá* (اعلى): "exalted."

56. The "kingdom of names" is a phrase designating material creation. Hence spiritual knowledge has become manifest in physical forms.

57. Here again we find Ṭáhirih alluding to the rationale for the Prophet's becoming manifest in a "human temple," the theme that Bahá'u'lláh explicates at great length in the Súriy-i-Haykal, the Súra of the Temple.

58. *Bashar* (بشر): "human being." In this line Ṭáhirih refers to verses 71–73 in Súra 38 of the Qur'án, in which God tells the angels, "I am about to create man from clay. When I have fashioned him (in due proportion) and breathed into him My spirit, fall down in obeisance unto him." Over the next twenty lines, Ṭáhirih will deal with this concept in depth—that the Manifestation, though possessing human form, is essentially distinct from the rest of the heavenly hosts (how much more from ordinary human beings) and that through this process the Holy Spirit functions through the intermediary of the Manifestation to fashion the universe and endow it with a spirit that is ever renewed.

59. *Rabb-i-A'ẓam* (ربّ اعظم), *Rabb-i-'A'lá* (ربّ اعلي), and *Rabb-i-Akbar* (ربّ اکبر) mean "the Exalted" and "the Great Lord."

59
The Garden of Paradise has come to *Raḍvá*,[60]
and the One from *Raḍvá* has come to *Iṭvá'*.[61]

60
The mystery of the Garden of Paradise has become manifest!
Like a vintner, He ceaselessly pours out cups of wine.

61
So many are the mysteries in the celestial realm!
So many are the thrones with the station of Splendor![62]

62
All the splendors of purity in paradise,
the manifestations of nearness in *Raḍvá*,

63
all with the splendors of glory
illumined from the stations with purity.

64
Crowns of utmost honor adorn Their heads
which are illumined by the sun and moon.

Ṭáhirih's Prayer for Enlightenment and Assistance in Teaching Others

65
O God, O God, Perpetual and Eternal,[63]
Omnipotent, Preexistent, Benevolent, Peerless,

---

60. *Raḍvá* (رضوى): a mountain between Mecca and Medina.

61. *Iṭvá'* (اطواء): a village in Yamamah with many date palms. After the Prophet's death, and especially after the battle of Yamamah (633), in which a great number of those who knew the Qur'án by heart had fallen, fear arose that the knowledge of the Qur'an might disappear. So it was decided to collect the revelations from all available written sources and, as Muslim tradition has it, "from the hearts [i.e., memories] of people."

62. "Splendor": *Bahá*.

63. Here Ṭáhirih begins a prayer praising God for bringing about the reality and the process she is attempting to describe for her followers.

66
Grant but a glance with your Merciful eyes
to resurrect these dry and dusty bones

67
so that I may venture out like the sun at noontide
and may disclose and proclaim Your hidden secrets.

68
Open Thou the gate of Thy benevolence before my face
so that we may make Thy essence manifest.[64]

69
I dare not allude to the plenitude of *'aksíyyat*[65]—
that would take months to explain!

70
By your own Essence, so pure and unique,
by the excellence of Thine own Self, which hath neither peer nor likeness,

71
there is no goal except You in my asking for protection,
no object of worship except the exaltation of You!

72
How long must I cycle in the sky like the sun?
Make manifest the secret of Unity![66]

---

64. *Jawharíyyat* (جوهريّت): our essential nature (the soul), as opposed to the earthly expressions of our reality. Ṭáhirih will continue to discuss the concept of "essential reality" versus the reality of "names and attributes" (i.e., specific manifestations in material terms of the placeless and eternal realm of the spirit).

65. *'aksíyyat* (عكسيّت): "reflection" i.e., how all things exist only to the extent that they reflect the attributes of God's essence and assume a place or station in creation according to this capacity.

66. How all things are but expressions of the Creator: i.e., there is no real "separation" from God because everything is unified through this common relationship.

73
How long do you wish me to remain so lonely on the earth's expanse
like a bewildered fish on a sandy hill?[67]

74
O Lover, O Love, O Beloved Bahá,
absorb this lovesick servant!

75
At Your feast of Grandeur and Unity,
establish me through your limitless and countless bounties![68]

76
O *Aḥad*,[69] from the fresh goblet of Oneness
cause me to imbibe . . . *indeed You are Ṣamad!*[70]

77
Quench my thirst with the wine of that goblet!
Bestow on me the food of Truth,

78
clouds most glorious in nature,
fruit for the eyes beyond all measure![71]

Her Prayer Is Answered: What the Future Portends

79
The mystery of His secret became disclosed!
The name of Benevolence became known in the land of Sinai!

---

67. Like a fish out of water, Ṭáhirih feels she is, in this life, remote from her true abode, the realm of the spirit.

68. "Grandeur" (*farr*, فرّ) is apparently an error in the transcription and should be *marr* (مَرّ).

69. *Aḥad* (احد) means "the One" and is an attribute of God.

70. *Ṣamad* (صمد): "the Eternal," a name of God. See Qur'án 12:2.

71. This and the following lines seem to be a vision bestowed on Ṭáhirih regarding the future of the revelation of Bahá'u'lláh, possibly as an answer to her prayer.

80
This is the Eternal Foundation which at last has become manifest!
The predestined time and the present have become enfolded in timelessness.[72]

81
From the realm of Order the concept of time was devised,
and from the Hidden Mystery ages[73] were ordained.

82
Verily, the Leaven of Exaltation has Itself become exalted!
Through the Cause, all feebleness and frailty have been removed,[74]

83
a world so lush, so magnificent with its beauteous vistas
that the Sinai flames Moses beheld are now resplendent!

84
The ruby red dome of God's heaven has become so inflamed
that the pen is abashed to allude to all that which is concealed.

85
O Pen, make the attributes of *'amá'*[75] manifest
so that all creation may become attracted through Your allusions:[76]

---

72. Here Ṭáhirih speaks about creation as an eternal process being divided into segments or dispensations for the benefit of humankind. Thus the concept of time is an illusory attribute or device whereby human beings can gradually understand relationships in the process of spiritual evolution. She also seems to be alluding to the dispensation of Bahá'u'lláh when humankind will come of age and realize the unity of the entire process of the historical or progressive enlightenment of the body politic.

73. Probably Ṭáhirih is alluding to "dispensations" here—the gradualness by which humankind is educated throughout history by the successive appearances of the Prophets.

74. All the imperfections or inadequacies have been removed from the manifestation of the Divine Will in the human condition (i.e., the kingdom of heaven made manifest in earthly conditions).

75. *'amá'* (عماء): "cloud."

76. The "allusions" that Ṭáhirih proceeds to cite are references to the holy texts.

86
Your separation derived from Moses
because He came to Sinai without *fiṭrat.*[77]

87
The mystery of the *mafṭúr*[78] from the presence of the Merciful Lord
shone forth from the person of Abraham.[79]

---

77. *Fiṭrat* (فطرة). In this verse of the poem and in the next, Ṭáhirih is contrasting Moses with Abraham. She alludes to the traditions in both the Old Testament and in the Qur'án that Moses was imperfect (e.g., reputed to be a murderer) until He went to Mt. Paran and was transformed by God; whereas Abraham manifests inherent goodness (*fiṭrat*, فطرت). Abraham, as portrayed in the Qur'án, seems to have a special station compared to Moses. While God told Moses "thou canst not see me" (Qur'án 7:143), Abraham is called the friend (*khalíl*, خليل) of God in the Qur'án (4:125): "And Alláh took Abraham for a friend." In fact, in Qur'án 16:120–23 God commands Muḥammad to follow the religion of Abraham: "Surely Abraham was a model [of virtue], upright (*ḥanífan*, حنيفا) to Alláh. . . . Follow the faith of Abraham, the upright one (*ḥanífan*, حنيفا)." According to one ḥadíth, Muḥammad says regarding the Qá'im: "He will arise to reveal the religion at the Day of the End, as I arose at the Day of the End." The day or era that Muḥammad ended has been interpreted to refer to an era that began with Abraham (Sadru'ssudúr, 70). See footnotes on the next line of the poem for further explanation of the special station of Abraham in the Islamic tradition. Also, see the introduction to poem 5.

78. *Mafṭúr* (مفطور) means "originated." Being originated and created by the Merciful Lord is a reference to the Qur'án 6:79 in which Abraham, at the final stage of His spiritual journey, recognizes God as the Creator of the heavens and earth.

79. *Birr-i-hím* (برّهيم) is a combination of two words: *birr* (برّ), meaning "obedience to God," "accepting the duty of pilgrimage," and "benevolence"; and *haym*, meaning "falling in love." The combination of the two words sounds like an abbreviated version of "Abraham." When Muḥammad ascended to the sky, in each of the seven heavens He met with one of the Prophets. He met Adam in the first heaven and Abraham in the seventh heaven (implying Abraham's special station among the Prophets). Each heaven is associated with specific characteristics and attributes. The seventh heaven is for generosity, a characteristic of Abraham (Murata 1992, 133–35). Abraham's "falling in love" is His heart's natural or inherent desire (*fiṭrat*, فطرت) for truth and His attraction to the beauty of God indicated in Qur'án 6:76–80. Refer to the introduction to poem 5 for a more detailed explanation of this. Ṭáhirih makes references to other attributes of Abraham: His obedience (*taslím*, تسليم) in verse 88 of this poem, and His acceptance of the duty of pilgrimage in line 27 of poem 5.

88
Like *alif*,[80] He arose[81] in fulfillment of Noah's command[82]
and He adorned Himself with the garment of submission[83] and praise.

89
Indeed, this very moment He has boldly seized the pen!
He pulls the reigns in whatever direction He chooses![84]

90
Lo, on this night He is filled with Noah's ecstasy;
He has severed Himself from all earthly attachments.

91
He meditates on the peak of the Summit of Grandeur.
He speaks of the presence and the return of Noah,

80. This is a common allusion to that which is upright because the letter *alif* (الف) is itself upright.

81. "Standing": *qá'im*.

82. Like Noah before Him, Abraham was endowed with the power and authority of command—acting on behalf of God. And as with all Manifestations, Abraham fulfills the prophecies and allusions that Noah bestowed on His followers.

83. "Submission to the will of God." This refers to Qur'án 3:66 and 2:131 where Abraham is associated with the attribute of submission to the will of God (the origin of the word *Islam*). Abraham was proclaiming the same truth as Noah and, in that sense, was completely submissive to God's will as revealed to Noah. In the next verse, Ṭáhirih describes another aspect of the Manifestations of God—that each reveals a new truth or a more ample vision of reality than that which was previously unveiled.

84. Once the Prophet reveals His station and assumes His rightful authority, He likewise assumes the station of "He doeth whatsoever He willeth"—He may abolish old laws and reveal new laws. Here Ṭáhirih refers to this same concept that the Manifestation possesses the divine power to ordain whatever is appropriate. It is also worth noting that as Ṭáhirih discusses these observations about the continuity of revelation, she is noting distinct characteristics that are emphasized by each Prophet, while observing that, in truth, all the Manifestations have the same powers and capacities. In these verses Ṭáhirih alludes to the station of unity of the Manifestations of God (Moses, Abraham, Noah, and the Báb). Although They appear in different or distinct human guises, They manifest alike the power and semblance of the Holy Spirit. In lines 88–92, Ṭáhirih likens the Báb to Abraham, explaining that in the same way Abraham was in fact the return of Noah, the Báb is also the return of Noah in that He demonstrates Noah's attributes. In poem 7, lines 55–58, we see how the Báb, like Noah, is asking God, "My Lord, leave not of the disbelievers any dwellers on the land" (Qur'án 71:26).

92
for He[85] regards Noah[86] as One of Those Who return again and again.
He regards Him as the living *Qá'im* on earth.[87]

Ṭáhirih's Praise of the Beloved (Bahá'u'lláh)

93
O Bird of *'Amá'*, begin singing![88]
Pour forth in sparks Your pages of praise!

94
Bring Adam[89] back to the Garden of Paradise!
Bring Him back to the station of the mystery of unity![90]

95
From the mysteries of the command of the Eternal Living One,
recount the story of the Point of the Mystery of Eternity.[91]

---

85. Most probably an allusion to Bahá'u'lláh.

86. Abraham regards Noah as One of Those Who return (He acknowledges the Prophethood of Noah).

87. Here Ṭáhirih describes how the speaker ("He") is discussing the unity of the Prophets, that each manifests the attributes of being the Qá'im (the intended one of the previous dispensation). In particular, the speaker alludes to Noah as having the power of command, the attributes of perfection and detachment, and as being part of the divine process whereby the "return" of each Prophet is manifest in the succeeding Prophets.

88. The Bird of *'Amá'* (عماء) is an allusion to the reality of the Báb, Bahá'u'lláh, and all the Manifestations of God, and also to the realm of command, the station of unity of the Manifestations. Here she is invoking the Manifestation to reveal Himself to humankind.

89. Making an allusion to "humankind," Adam wishes to return to the original spiritual source of being (reunion with the Beloved). Adam, having been expelled from paradise, wishes to return to that paradise from which He was expelled and to manifest heavenly attributes before it was timely (before humankind was ready). Ṭáhirih is asking the hidden reality of the Manifestation to reveal His mysteries in this auspicious age, the promised Day when all will be revealed: "Thus it is recorded: 'Every knowledge hath seventy meanings, of which one only is known amongst the people. And when the Qá'im shall arise, He shall reveal unto men all that which remaineth.' He also saith: 'We speak one word, and by it we intend one and seventy meanings; each one of these meanings we can explain'" (Bahá'u'lláh, Kitáb-i-Íqán, ¶283).

90. "Unity" as opposed to the station of "separation" (failing to appreciate that all creation is an expression of divine creation). Also a reference to Adam's original condition in paradise.

91. This is an intensely complex allusion to the concept of the origin of creation, which, in fact, has no beginning, even though each planet has a beginning and, likewise, human life has various points or milestones of evolutionary change. These changes are brought about by the wish or will of God as they are translated into language and action through the intermediary of the Manifestations.

96
Usher the mysteries out from behind the veil!
Make manifest those concealed secrets of the heart!

97
From the Hidden Mystery of placeless powers,
make manifest the source of all power![92]

98
Make manifest to all[93] the splendor concealed in the ornaments of light
through the dawning of the Manifestation!

Ṭáhirih Continues Her Discourse on Religious History and the Theological Implications of the Adamic Cycle

99
The blazing Letter[94] that had been hidden
was a fire derived from veils of Divinity.

100
Perhaps it was illumined by the light from *'amá'*;
All else but God was taken to Túr by its splendor.

101
The realm of light itself appeared through its Manifestation!
Bounty rained down from the thick full clouds of the Bayán.

102
Because of the refulgence of the reflection from His face,
the sun of Wisdom turned face-to-face with the Moon.[95]

92. The word *tamkín* (تمکین) means "obedience," but in this context power derives from obedience to the will of God.

93. Literally *him*, but here referring to Adam as humankind.

94. The blazing Letter (*ḥarf-i-náríyyih*, حرف ناریّه) is an allusion to the manifestation of the hidden divine reality. See the introduction to this poem for a further discussion of this concept.

95. "Veil" in Ṣúfí terminology is at times a symbol for the intensity of the glory and majesty of God that makes it impossible for human beings to relate to His transcendent reality. In the next verse Ṭáhirih refers to the story of Moses, Who, seeing the intense light of the glory of God

103
(Mere) reflections and shadows vanished or were abolished!
All approached the shore of the Most Great Ocean![96]

Ṭáhirih Pauses to Reflect on the Nature and Origin of "Separation"

104
O God, O God, what is this light of "avoidance" [separation][97]
that appeared amidst the command (*fi'ál*)[98] of He who is Independent,[99]

105
as if the mystery of unity had been disclosed
or else the world of creation had become the land of "*you shall never see me,*"[100]

106
as if the shimmering veil had been removed
and the Concealed Unapproachable One were unveiled,[101]

---

on Mount Sinai (*Ṭúr*), became unconscious. In verses 104–6 and 116 of this poem we find these same concepts: "the light of separation" (نور احتراز, *núr-i-iḥtiráz*), "shimmering veil" (*ḥijáb-i-munkhafiq*, حجاب منخفق), "veils of grandeur" (*astár-i-izzat*, استار عزّت), and the story of Moses on Sinai. At other times the allusion of "veil" employs the idea that knowledge can become a veil to understanding.

96. Here it seems the Sun represents God, the rays emanating from the Sun are the divine attributes of God, and the Moon, being face-to-face with the Sun, represents the capacity of the Manifestation to reflect that illumination with effulgence.

97. The "shore" in mystic philosophy is the division between spiritual and physical realities.

98. The "light of avoidance" (*núr-i-iḥtiráz*, نور احتراز) in this verse and "the shimmering veil" (*ḥijáb-i-munkhafiq*, حجاب منخفق) in verse 106 refer to the dual nature of spiritual reality, which is both "hidden" and "manifest." See Qur'án 57:3: "He is the First and the Last, the Manifest and the Hidden: and He is Knower of all things." The paradox here derives from the nature of brightness that simultaneously enlightens and blinds the beholder.

99. *Fi'ál* (فِعال): actions (of God). This word is also very similar to the word *fa'ál* (فعّال) meaning "very active," an attribute of God (Qur'án 11:109, 85:14–16).

100. God: "He who is the one with no needs." The sentence starts in this line of the poem, continues for six more lines, and should be read with care.

101. "You shall never see me" (*lan taráni*, لَن تَراني). This is what God told Moses in Sinai according to Qur'án 7:143. The first half of this verse is about the immanence of the divine, and the second half is about the transcendence of the divine.

107
or the indivisible Essence of the Absolute God
were made manifest through the splendor of its own Purity,

108
as if God Himself had appeared with glorious splendor
from the stations of praise that are beyond "what is possible,"

109
or *Ṣamad* (the Eternal) had become manifest in the realm of time
and the sea of Power had become tumultuous?

110
Is the Hidden Mystery or the Concealed name
manifest from behind the Three Veils?[102]

111
Has Aḥmad[103] descended from the heavens
with the effulgence of lights from *'Amá'*?

112
Or has 'Alí come forth with "ceaseless attacks,"[104]
roaming throughout other constellations (saying):

113
"This mystery of ecstasy is illumined by Benevolence!
The circular Throne of Honor is near completion!"

114
Or was the "*cleft asunder*"[105] sky created,
pouring forth from behind thick, dark clouds?

---

102. The unveiling of the "Concealed" and "Unapproachable One" (two names of God) among other things alludes to the revelation of all the knowledge that had heretofore been too remote for human capacity to comprehend.

103. This series of rhetorical questions likewise continues through line 115.

104. Muḥammad.

105. "'Alí": He was given the title *karrar* (کرّار) because he used to attack the enemy repeatedly without fear or concern for his own safety.

115
Is this the Promised Day? Has the Mystery of manifestation
unveiled its face, adorned with resplendent ornaments?

Ṭáhirih Answers Her Own Rhetorical Questions

116
Indeed, from behind the veils of grandeur
The Face of God has appeared with honor and nobility![106]

117
The earth and the sky have begun to "quake"[107]
as the seed of *that which is revealed*[108] has been manifest by this transformation!

118
From radiant beams of light, the form of God
has appeared with perfection[109] and glory!

106. See Qur'án 73:17–18: "Then how shall you, if you deny (Alláh), guard yourselves against a Day that will make children hoary-headed? Whereon the sky will be cleft asunder?" Also see Qur'án 82:1–2: "When the Sky is cleft asunder; When the Stars are scattered . . ." Two variations of the word *faṭara* (فَطَرَ) are seen in this line of the poem.

107. Ṭáhirih now begins the affirmation of what has occurred, thereby answering forcefully the rhetorical questions she posed in the previous three sentences. This style is very similar to Bahá'u'lláh's tablet entitled Muballigh, originally part of a tablet revealed in honor of Ḥájí Muḥammad-Ibráhím. See *Tablets of Bahá'u'lláh,* pp. 117–118, in which there is a series of rhetorical questions followed by thundering answers, all of which recite the fulfillment of proofs associated with the appearance of the Manifestation in the Day of Resurrection.

108. This reference is to Qur'án 99:1–5: "When the Earth is shaken to her (utmost) convulsion, And the Earth throws up her burdens (from within), And man cries (distressed): 'What is the matter with her?' On that Day she will declare her tidings: 'For that your Lord will have given her inspiration ("revealed to her": *awḥá lahá,* اوحي لها).'"

109. *Má awḥá* (ما اوحي): what she has been inspired with, or what has been revealed to her—a reference to Qur'án 99:5 mentioned in the previous footnote. This means that through the growth and transformation that is taking place in the universe, we can know about the seed that God has sown on earth.

119
Lo, He[110] described the ecstasy of the Most Beneficent One!
[His words] unlocked all the closed portals!

120
Indeed, His reviving call of "*hasten unto me*"[111]
has dissolved the rust of doubt, superstition, and wavering.

121
Truly, with the first appearance He made everyone totally unconscious;
then, with the second appearance,[112] He will make everyone conscious from head to toe.[113]

122
In truth, in this very age every veiled allusion
has become unveiled through Him!

123
The fire of Sinai is manifest in this age!
The light of Paran is shining on you!

---

110. *Istivá* (استوی) means "attaining the completion and perfection of one's making and one's intellect." See Qur'án 53:6–18 regarding the station of Muḥammad and His nearness to God, a reference to the perfections of the Manifestation of God.

111. "Hasten unto me" (*háta lak,* هات لك). A word-for-word translation of this would be "Come forward. It is yours" (apparently this word comes from the Hebrew word *Hitalikh*). In Qur'án 12:23 this phrase (*háta lak*) is mentioned. According to the story in the Qur'án, when Joseph was living at the house of Potiphar, an officer of Pharaoh (cf. Gen. 39:2), Potiphar's wife "seduced him and locked the doors and said: "Come hither" (*hayta lak,* هيت لك). He said, "Alláh forbid!" This story has inspired Persian poets, and the love story of Yúsuf (Joseph) and Zuleikhá appears frequently in Persian literature. By including this phrase (*háta lak,* هات لك) in this verse of the poem, and with the phrase "unlocked all the closed portals" in the previous verse, Ṭáhirih might be alluding to this story from the Qur'án in order to explain that the appearance of the true Beloved (the Point) at this time has unlocked all the doors, bestowing freedom to all people with the words "Hasten unto me!"

112. The appearance of Bahá'u'lláh.

113. Here again Ṭáhirih alludes to the concept of the twin revelations, the first trumpet call (the revelation of the Báb) that will render all bewildered, drunk and unconscious; and the second call (the revelation of Bahá'u'lláh) that will awaken and inform the masses of humankind about their true identity and purpose.

124
The Greatest Name has appeared along with the One who was named,
and it has made all the cherubim ecstatic with delight!

125
It has illumined every other name[114]
and has led the way to the banquet of the Nearness of God!

126
He has colored all colors with the "color of God!"[115]
He has caused the face of God to be witnessed by all![116]

Ṭáhirih Marvels at How This Process Occurs

127
O God, O God, what benevolence, what bounty this is
that has been so clearly manifested through Glorified Essences!

128
What preeminence, what esteem, what distinction this is
that has been made to appear through the letters *"Be! And it is!"*[117]

---

114. "Name" refers to the "names" of God, or the attributes of God made manifest through creation.

115. Qur'án 2:138. In this passage the word *ṣibghat* (صبغة) is used, meaning "coloring" or "immersing in water" because Arab Christians used dye in the baptismal water. Thus Ṭáhirih is alluding to the verse "Our religion is the Baptism (or Color) of God: And who can baptize (color) better than God? And it is He Whom we worship."

116. *Mashhúd* (مشهود): "witnessed"; this word alludes to the Day of God or the Day of Resurrection. See Qur'án 11:103 and 85:03.

117. *Kun fa kán* (كُن فكان): "Be and it was." This is a slightly modified version of *kun fa yakún* (كُن فيكون, "be and it is"). In relation to God's authority and power, this phrase alludes to the process by which God has but to wish or will creation for it to come into being. See Qur'án 2:117, 3:47, 3:59, and 6:73. More specifically, this passage alludes to the fact that creation comes into being through the Prophets, Whose power is demonstrated primarily through speech or utterance and through Their immaculate character. In this case, Ṭáhirih seems to be alluding to the Prophet Himself Who has come into being to manifest perfectly all the divine attributes of God. In the Persian Bayán, the Báb symbolizes the Primal Will by the first letter of *kun* (كُن, *be*). In Persian poetry *kun fa kán* (كُن فكان) has been used to represent the whole process of creation or the entire created universe (see Dehkhoda 40:265).

129
The Command of God you witness appeared from two Commands![118]
The shade of the shadow was shattered by the Light!

130
The Light has been ignited from the fire-filled Lamp!
His Holiness Himself, its very origin, is humbled by portraying it![119]

131
This is that same sun-filled[120] lamp that is the source
through which the human temple becomes filled with spirit!

132
Neither roots nor branches can be assigned to Him!
Neither can there be conceived a dawning or setting for Him!

133
Verily, He was a firm root from the Day of Eternity,
So sanctified was He from all causes and limitations!

134
His bounty is manifest in verses of the Eternal![121]
His name is thereby established through the One!

135
The limits of the limiting[122] of *other than Him*[123]
are all bound by the aid of His boundaries.[124]

---

118. This could mean "faith" instead of "command." This verse clearly alludes to the twin Manifestations of the Báb and Bahá'u'lláh and Their respective religions.

119. The Manifestation Himself attests to His humility in being adorned with such a station to function as the intermediary between God and humankind.

120. *Qitbání*; *qitb* is "the sun."

121. The word is "signs," but alludes to "verses."

122. The *ḥadd-i-taḥdíd* (حدّ تحدید).

123. *Másivá* (ماسوی): other than Him.

124. The verse introduces the concept of laws as guidance and divine assistance, rather than as restriction or punishment. It also refers to the fact that the laws to which the universe is subject are divinely ordained laws.

136
The call for *Qadar*[125] had as its condition for benevolence
the manifestation of the "Hidden Mystery"

137
so that the Mystical Point became manifest in the world of creation,
and the Hidden Ecstasy became repeated in this present age.

The Uniqueness of This Day

138
The Point of Ecstasy has now achieved a new height
because Its emanation is beyond limitation or calculation.[126]

139
Through His aid the renewal of all ages was established,
and the outer garment of the created world took shape.

140
The plan of the universe was designed according to His plan,
and the order and movement of the spheres was arranged accordingly.

141
The Glorious Sun assumed its proper orbit
so that all creation might discover the mystery of *Há'*.[127]

142
Thus did the Moon reflect the Sun's light into the world of existence
as it traversed the constellations of the heavens.

---

125. *Qadar* (قدر): "measure" or the act of apportioning capacity, whether to human beings or to creation as a whole.

126. Fundamentally, this is Ṭáhirih's description of progressive revelation, that each successive revelation is capable of revealing ever more about reality without ever becoming exhausted in this capacity.

127. *Há'* (هاء): "the Essence." Here the term alludes to the fact that when creation is properly understood through the new revelation, all things will be seen as manifesting attributes of God. This process is symbolized in this verse by the Sun assuming its proper orbit (authority or primacy) in the minds and hearts of humankind.

143
And as the Moon arrived at each constellation and then was released,[128]
it discovered a new reality and assumed a new station.[129]

144
Since its mystery was concealed in the dust,
it was able to traverse the orbits of the spheres

145
while all were ignorant of Its hidden mysteries
and their endless levels of meaning.[130]

146
In the station of revealing the meaning of the Bayán,
It became illumined by the letters *"be and it was"!*[131]

147
When the body,[132] composed of the four elements,[133] achieved perfection,[134]
it began speaking of the mysteries of Bahá.[135]

---

128. Moved on to the next constellation.

129. Perhaps this line alludes to the early earthly existence of the Manifestation (the perfect reflection of God's [the Sun's] radiance). Ṭáhirih may be describing how the reality of the Manifestation assumes different degrees of ascendancy and revelation as humankind passes through successive stages of development, even though the Prophet is possessed of divine perfection from inception, as asserted in the doctrine of the "Most Great Infallibility." Also, Ṭáhirih might be alluding to the process of gradualness that occurs with the unfolding of each new revelation and, in the case of the Báb, with the disclosure of the Báb's true station.

130. Ṭáhirih seems to be dealing with the idea that the Prophets are concealed until the appropriate time for Them to assume authority and present the new revelation. She also might be referring to the fact that the Manifestations of God reveal Their heavenly attributes through Their earthly appearance.

131. *Kun fa-kán* (كن فكان).

132. The "temple" or *"haykal"* (هيكل) that the Manifestation assumes when He is born into the material world, a process and significance that Bahá'u'lláh elucidates at great length in the Súriy-i-Haykal.

133. The word *'anáṣir* (عناصر) can allude to the constellations through which the "Moon" has traversed (and thus gained knowledge), or here it may simply allude to the fact that the Manifestation as an earthly persona has achieved the point of maturity and is ready to reveal the Word of God.

134. "Balance," "harmony," the perfect "orbit" in terms of its metaphorical nature as a moon.

135. In this instance *Bahá* symbolizes not only the knowledge that Bahá'u'lláh alludes to in His epistle to the s͟háh, but also to the more encompassing sense of a degree of completeness of knowledge,

148
Verily, Beams of Divine light flash from this revelation,
the same Flaming Ecstasy that was Paran's fire![136]

149
By means of His splendor, Adam has become Adam;[137]
In one instant Adam was successively drunk then conscious.[138]

150
The Sun concealed Its face and went into hiding,
veiled in the luminescence of the Realm of the Placeless.

The Aftermath of the Báb's Execution

151
Adam then became afflicted with pain and sorrow,
remaining alone and isolated within himself in the plain of limitation,

152
sighing with regret because of His separation from Him,
like a waterless fish convulsing in bewilderment.[139]

153
In the realm of dust he endured so many
lamentations and scars from his suffering and toil,

Bahá representing the number 9 and thereby the idea of totality or completion. This also alludes to the condition of the Manifestation as a human persona operating through a human temple, as discussed in the Súriy-i-Haykal.

136. The light that emanated from the burning bush.

137. Adam here and in verse 151 most likely represents humankind. One sense of this line is that by means of this twin revelation, humankind can perceive and manifest its latent capacity. Humankind, having achieved maturity, will become universally aware of the essential reality of existence as a spiritual endeavor or exercise.

138. As mentioned before, this concept can be interpreted as an allusion to the twin revelations of the Báb and Bahá'u'lláh that correspond to the two trumpet calls, the first of which stuns humankind (Adam) into obliviousness, and the second of which awakens humankind (Adam) to the truth of reality. See Qur'án 22:2 regarding the intensity of the shock experienced in the Last Day or at the Time of the End when people seem to be drunk even though they are not.

139. The ancient notion of the Ptolemaic universe, here symbolizing creation as a whole.

154
prostrate, supplicating, pleading:
"Where is the direction of Your Face, O Self-Sufficient One?[140]

155
"Such memories of those days of unity and reunion!
Alas! Alas! This sunset and this separation!

156
"From what direction will the Sun of Unity arise?
From what point will the Mystery of Unity shine forth?"

What Bahá'u'lláh Will Bring about in Response to Adam's Wish

157
Lo, the Lord of Creation, the Hearer of prayers
became manifest throughout towns and cities![141]

158
With thousands of heart-ravishing splendors,
the ceaseless plentitude of His benevolence poured forth without limit

159
announcing to Adam,[142] "I am the Merciful Lord,
reviving the dried ones with my illumination.[143]

140. In addition to referring to the fall of Adam, we can infer that here Ṭáhirih is alluding to the turmoil that surrounded the revelation of the Báb, especially as the lines following depict that period, particularly the present tense of the speaker, Ṭáhirih, observing the events after the execution of the Báb but before Bahá'u'lláh revealed Himself to the Bábís.

141. This may well allude to the spread of the Bahá'í Faith throughout the world after the ascension of Bahá'u'lláh so that the source of unity and reunion is the Faith itself as manifest among the peoples of the world.

142. Adam as humankind. From this point onward the speaker is Bahá'u'lláh.

143. Dead souls that dance about like flecks of dust toward the sun when they are recreated.

160
"My countenance is concealed in the heavens!
My splendor can be discerned in '*amá'!*[144]

161
"My mystery is hidden in *huvíyyat,*[145]
but discerned through the veil of *váḥidíyyat.*[146]

162
"My sanctified name does not change from *aḥad*[147] to *ḥadd:*[148]
My revelation is illumined from the realm of the *Ṣamad.*[149]

163
"My exalted condition cannot be understood!
My glorious station is extolled in the Bayán![150]

164
"With the power of Our own flame we set you aglow
and adorned you with the Light of Honor.

---

144. "Clouds," an allusion to the Manifestation of God because the clouds assume a form and body that, as described in the next verse, conceal the transcendent sun of divine reality. However, the illuminated cloud also makes it possible for human beings to comprehend divinity since looking directly at the sun would otherwise blind the one beholding this reality.

145. *Huwíyyat* (هويّت): "the Divine." The mystery of the nature of the Prophet is ever beyond understanding.

146. *Váḥidíyyat* (واحد يّت): "unity" and "oneness." As opposed to *Aḥadíyyat* (احديّت) which refers to the transcendent oneness of the divine where God is beyond names and attributes, *váḥidíyyat* refers to the manifestation of the transcendent oneness in names and attributes. This is the station of distinction of the Manifestations of God and Their appearance as unique individuals at a certain age and time. However, as this verse points out, even the station of the Manifestation is a veil. It is not possible for humankind to fully understand the Manifestation of God. The Manifestations can only be "discerned through the veil of *váḥidíyyat.*" As the following verses point out, although the nature of the Prophet is concealed, the evidence of His presence can be found in peoples' actions wherever unity and oneness are apparent.

147. *Aḥad* (احد): the "One," the "Single."

148. *Ḥadd* (حدّ): the "reality of limitations."

149. *Ṣamad* (صمد): the "Eternal."

150. Ṭáhirih is referring to all the allusions made to Bahá'u'lláh in the writings of the Báb as the source of fulfillment for the long-awaited unification of humankind (Adam) and the maturation (enlightenment) of the peoples of the world (i.e., the reunion of Adam with God after eons of separation).

165
"There is not a particle of imperfection in creation!
The perfection of creation is one Animate Essence.

166
"From the most sublime heights of that which seems to be separate,[151]
recount our *jaláliyyat*![152]

167
"Make manifest the Hidden Ecstasy![153]
Ignite the firebrand with that same Fire!

168
"Dismiss (from your mind) the quarrel you had with Us[154]
and come now before Us in a condition of peace and reconciliation!

169
"These hints (and signs)[155] in your mysterious hearts
were formed between *B* and *E!*[156]

---

151. "That which appears to be distinct from Divine Essence." God is commanding Adam (humankind) to manifest God's attributes in the world of creation to the highest degree possible. The perfect manifestation of God's attributes is possible through the Prophets. "Adam" here could also refer to the reality of the Manifestation of God, Who, in this age, appears with utmost effulgence (i.e., because humankind has achieved the stage of maturity).

152. *Jaláliyyát* (جلاليّات) represents God's attributes of grandeur and majesty—the transcendence of God—as opposed to *Jamáliyyát* (جما ليّات), God's attributes that relate to His immanence such as beauty, kindness, and mercy. The Manifestation of God represents the transcendent divine in the world of creation.

153. *Ja<u>dh</u>bih* (جذ به): "ecstasy" or "attraction."

154. The separation of humankind from the Creator. This also refers to Adam's (i.e., humankind's) disobedience that caused Him to be expelled from paradise.

155. Perhaps indicative of spiritual instincts or inclinations.

156. *Káf* and *nún* (كاف و نون): the concept of the will or wish of God that brings creation into being by means of the Intermediaries or Manifestations who "join" and "knit together" these dual aspects of the process of creation. That is, the concept of the will of God is followed by the creative process manifest in planned action. Thus, however ignominious human history might seem at a given point in time, the human heart is constantly nourished by the guidance implanted by the appearances of the Prophets. The "mysterious" human heart is an emanation from the Creator, and the heart's longing or affection will ultimately be satisfied with nothing less than reunion with the Beloved.

170
"Ignore[157] the counselors and the consulting ones[158]
and relinquish the station of free will![159]

171
"There is no cessation in the outpourings of God! No cessation!
For there can be no delay in responding to God's command! No delay!

172
"How long will you remain veiled by your (own) veils,
shutting out yourself with a hundred gates by closing one Gate?[160]

173
"It was you yourself who contrived the idea of 'otherness'[161]
and you who made yourself concealed from Us!

174
"How long do you wish to remain imprisoned,
dwelling in the region of limitations?

175
"Behold, My resistless Faith has become manifest!
Behold the binding commandment, the subduing verses!

176
"Cast off the garments of old laws and outworn traditions!
Immerse yourself in the Sea of my Bounteousness!

---

157. There seems to be a transcription error in this verse. The phrase in the manuscript appears as *darguzar dar* (درگذر در), but it should be *dar guzar az* (درگذر از), which means "ignore."

158. The knowledge, guidance, advice, or learning "current among men."

159. The intended irony here, of course, is that the believer must employ free will in order to set aside free will and thus achieve alignment with what the will of God requires.

160. The implication seems to be that by closing oneself to the recognition of the Báb (the Gate), one shuts out all other knowledge and progress, including true recognition of all the other Manifestations of God.

161. You chose to perceive physical reality and yourself as somehow distinct from spiritual reality and God. Likewise, you chose to accede to the insistent self and vain imaginations instead of adhering to the straight path to God.

177
"In that same moment, behold all the beauteous mysteries!
Behold how all that was hidden has been made manifest!

178
"How long in this world—rabid with passion and corruption—
will you remain so far from your purpose, so pitifully far?

179
"Establish yourself on the seat of Our throne of Authority
and manifest that effective[162] power latent within you.

180
"From but two letters, *B* and *E,* Our command has appeared!
Say: *'from God'* and *'To Him shall we return.'*[163]

181
"Indeed, I am manifest solely for the sake of My Beauty!
Indeed, I have appeared with the mystery of i'tidál"![164]

---

162. The word *fa"álah* (فعّاله), as in line 165, refers to various qualities of being "active" and "efficacious."

163. Qur'án: 2:46.

164. *I'tidál* (اعتدال): "justice," "moderation," or "equilibrium." This verse is Adam's response to the call of the Manifestation of God or the way God wants Him to respond. "Moderation" refers to God creating man in the most perfect way. It is a reference to Qur'án 82:7. Refer to line 130 of poem 7 and its explanation in the introduction to that poem (section 1, part 3: "Free Will and the Process of Creation").

Poem 2: In Praise of the Advent of God

A recurring image in Ṭáhirih's poems is an allusion to people in a state of drunken stupor. Traditionally, this condition is a religious / poetic image implying that people have completely lost their composure and identity by becoming wholly absorbed in their adoration of and affection for the Beloved. In this sense they are portrayed as being unconscious, as having fallen to the earth, or even as dead.

This total loss of self (*maḥv,* محو) in one's encounter with the beauty of the Beloved is the station of *faná'* (فنا) or "nothingness." The sobriety (*ṣaḥv,* صحو) that succeeds this condition represents the station of enduring in God, a sobriety that occurs because of magnetic attraction to the Beloved. Even as the sun seems to attract particles of dust in its beams, or as the sound of the trumpet revives and resurrects the dead bodies, or as a flame attracts moths, so the Manifestation of God, standing erect (*qá'im,* قائم) among the fallen bodies, revives them and calls them back to life through His sublime melodies.

The images of *maḥv* (total self-absorption, drunkenness, or loss of reason) and *ṣaḥv* (sobriety and recognition of the truth), in addition to having mystical implications of *faná'* (nothingness) and *bqá'* (بقاء, "lasting in God"), terms related to the wayfarer's journey toward God, can also refer to the first and second trumpet blasts.

For Ṭáhirih (and according to the writings of the Báb), the first trumpet call represents the Manifestation of the Báb, which is so startling and severe that it causes all creation to be stunned and rendered unconscious. The second blast from the trumpet represents the manifestation of Bahá'u'lláh, which causes all of creation to become resurrected, conscious, and capable of comprehending the drastic changes that are taking place.

We can also observe in these poems how Ṭáhirih applies the image of *maḥv* and *ṣaḥv* to the Manifestation Himself, the One Who has been resurrected and is standing (*qá'im,* قائم) among the dead bodies as He calls them to Himself. As we will see in poem 5, Ṭáhirih applies the Qur'ánic story of Abraham to this image. Abraham's attraction to the heavens with the stars, the moon, and the sun leads to His loss of consciousness, and the *fiṭrí* (فطري) call of the Beloved recreates Abraham. Also, in line 2 of poem 1 the spiritual creation and resurrection of Adam are alluded to by the terms *maḥv* and *ṣaḥv*.

As is clear in verses 26 to 36 of poem 1, Ṭáhirih in her direct and indirect references to *ṣaḥv* and *maḥv* in various poems is providing her mystical and theological interpretation of the famous ḥadí<u>th</u> "What is the Truth?" (*má al-ḥaqiqat,* ما الحقيقة), which is very important to Ṣúfís and Islamic philosophers. The Báb Himself penned a short interpretation of this ḥadí<u>th</u> in Arabic (Rádmihr, pp. 123–151). Also, in *Risáliy-i-Dalá'il-i-Sab'ah,* the Báb identifies five stages for His revelation, stages derived from this same ḥadí<u>th</u> (Afnán, 35).

In poem 2 we are presented with the image of people falling unconscious because of the sudden revelation of the unveiled beauty of the Friend (the Point) and because of the severity and power of a revelation that erases all signs of superstition and vain imagining. We also witness the image of the "Upright One" (the *Qá'im*), the only one remaining conscious and the one who attracts the dead particles by his melodies and bestows on them new life.

Poem 2: In Praise of the Advent of God

Alláh, Alláh, by Your truth, by Your truth, through Your Divine Plan, render us whole and gather us together at the seat of Your Glory that we all may be established on the throne of Your exaltation. Praised be God Who has fulfilled His covenant with us!

1
Praise be to God that He has cast off the veil from His face!
Unveiled, He is manifest with splendor from the place of His dawning!

2
He cleanses away the rust of imaginations and doubt
with the sanctified call of "Hasten unto Me!"

3
Observe how all in His presence have fallen to the ground,
have fallen down drunk, intoxicated, and disheveled!

4
How joyous that the One Who is inebriated from the undefiled goblet
has appeared, so beguiling with brilliant illumination.[1]

5
He attracts all the fallen specks of dust
with melodies pouring forth from His words.

6
They are all unconscious, but He is conscious
because of the inherent[2] luminescence of the cloud.

7
O God, O God, He has appeared!
The Hidden Mystery! *Indeed, it is an astonishing mystery!*

---

1. Here we have used Mohammadhoseini's version.
2. *Fiṭrí* (فطري)

8
From the pages (of the history) of manifestation,
an entrancing Temple has arisen,

9
enticing and sanctifying every speck of dust
with His warbling voice.

10
O God, I see His beauteous face,
illuminated by ornaments and veils!

11
O God, except for Him there is no one in existence
able to assume the station of "*that which is the answer*"![3]

12
Praise be to that life-giving Power
Who appeared without disguise or veil!

13
I will fearlessly proclaim that *bihjat*[4] has descended
with attractions from the supreme and exalted Height![5]

---

3. "The station of that which is the answer" is most probably a reference to the Promised One, for Whose appearance people have supplicated God for ages.

4. "Happiness" or "felicity." The fact that Ṭáhirih is addressing Bihjat throughout this work allows her to make a number of double entendres relating to the fact that his name, *Bihjat,* means "happiness."

5. In Mohammadhoseini's version this verse would be translated as "it descended for my Bihjat." In the manuscript we have used for our translation, the verse is translated as "*bihjat* has descended."

14
He is captivating all those who possess intelligence
with His melodies intoned from the paradisiacal Essence.[6]

15
Indeed it is an astonishing mystery!—the account of *bihjat*—
how everything descends from a single source of genesis!

6. Ṭáhirih will employ the term *essence* a number of times in this poetic discourse to allude to the ultimate source of reality and creation—the Essence of God, as distinct from the attributes that emanate from God through His Manifestations. Likewise, she will distinguish between the essential reality of the Manifestations and that of ordinary human beings. Here she seems to be alluding to the spiritual realm that is the essential reality, as opposed to the physical world that is but a shadowy reflection of that realm.

Poem 3: The Joy of Bihjat

Introduction

As mentioned in the main introduction to this book, "Bihjat" is the title of Karím Khán-i-Máfí, a follower of the Báb from Qazvín, the hometown of Ṭáhirih. Ṭáhirih corresponded with Bihjat while she was imprisoned in the house of the governor of Tehran, Maḥmúd Khán-i-Kalántar, where she was confined in a small second-story room for more than two years.

The chamber where she dwelled was so small that Ṭáhirih had hardly enough room to stretch her legs. What is more, since there were no stairs to the room, she had to climb a ladder to get in and out. But in spite of these severe restrictions, the Bábí women used any means possible to reach her. At times they would change their clothes to look like beggars. It was in this context that the secret communication took place between Ṭáhirih and Bihjat.

By order of the prime minister, the governor had commanded that Ṭáhirih's actions be carefully monitored. He especially forbade her having access to pen and pencil so that she would not be able to correspond with her friends; however, this mandate did not stop Ṭáhirih. Using vegetable juice as ink and broom straws as pens, she would write on the torn pieces of paper used for wrapping cheese and other food (Mohammadhoseini, 294).

It is no wonder, then, that errors appear in the transcriptions of her poems and in the transcribed versions of her work, or that there are differences among some of the copies of her poems. Doubtless it was difficult for the recipients of these poems and letters to read some of the words. Furthermore, had her poems and other written works been simple, readers might easily have made accurate guesses about words that could not be readily recognized, but such is not the case.

For one thing, these works are often composed in what may be coded poetic allusions and symbolic terms, for had they not been, the life of the recipient would have been endangered. Therefore, as we see in this poem, the word *Bihjat* may have various meanings: the personage of Bihjat, the Primal Point, or the Manifestation of God in this day. We are convinced, however, that there is another more important reason for the cryptic and abstruse nature of Ṭáhirih's poems.

Ṭáhirih was a remarkably talented artist, and she thus writes in images and symbols that reach beyond any obvious meaning intended solely for her immediate audience. She possessed an incredibly deep understanding and appreciation of the significance of the age in which she lived. Consequently, her analysis of theology, religious history, and Islamic philosophy is so immense that it is often difficult to penetrate the outer shell of language to comprehend the layered meanings veiled in her works. Certainly her work was as difficult for the Bábí recipients of her communication as it is for the modern reader.

Ṭáhirih was extremely well educated in spiritual philosophy and frequently alluded to the political intrigue surrounding the persecution of the Bábís and the manipulation of governmental affairs by clergy and corrupt officials. Most important, she was keenly aware of and attuned to what she regarded as a momentous point of transition in religious history and the particular part that she had to play in this unfolding drama.

It is obvious from a number of dramatic episodes in her life, as well as from her writing, that she was imbued with a spiritual capacity and station beyond that of the other Bábí believers. Hints about the loftiness of her spiritual station abound in virtually every reference to her throughout the authoritative texts of the Bahá'í Faith.

In this poem, as in the previous piece, the Manifestation of God is the only one in the universe Who is not unconscious and Who is aware of the mysteries of the hidden or concealed reality. The Arabic letter *ṭá'* (طاء)[1] pronounced as *ṭá* in the first verse of the poem is perhaps a reference to the city of Tehran, or to Bahá'u'lláh since this letter has the numerical value 9, equal to the numerical value of the word Bahá. In either case, we can conclude from this poem and from

1. In another version of this poem translated in *The Poetry of Ṭáhirih,* the first couplet includes the Arabic letter *fá'* (فاء), which can be a reference to the province of Fars, the home province of the Báb. In the Persian Bayán by "the land of fá'" (*arḍ-i-fá',* ارض فاء) is intended the province of Fars, and "the city of *fá'*" (*madíniy-i-fá',* مدینه فاء) implies the city of Shíráz. The letter *fá'* is also repeated in the seventh couplet.

the next poem that both Ṭáhirih and Bihjat were aware of the role Tehran would play in the future course of the Bábí Faith and that they were also aware of the station of Bahá'u'lláh.

The Concept of "Mirrors"

The word *mirrors* in the context of the verse of Ṭáhirih could have various symbolic meanings. In the Báb's writings, the hierarchy of the spiritual world is symbolized by a sequence of mirrors, each reflecting in itself the image of a higher mirror. The Primal Will is at the top of this sequence or chain of reality. Then, in descending order, are the mirrors that represent Manifestations Who reflect perfectly the attributes of God, the mirrors that are the first believers in each revelation (e.g., the disciples of Christ or the eighteen "Letters of the Living" in the case of the Báb), and the mirrors that are the other believers who reflect the light of these first believers (see *Persian Bayán,* 5, 203, and 208).

Thus the "Drop of a new creation" in verse 2 of the poem would be the Primal Will as manifested through the Báb and reflected in the mirrors—the early believers. The Báb explains in His writings that in the mirror of the station of "The Gate," the sun of the station of the Imám is reflected; and in the mirror of the station of the Imám, the sun of Prophethood is reflected; and in the mirror of Prophethood, the sun of Lordship is reflected. These various aspects of the Manifestation of God could also be what Ṭáhirih is alluding to in this couplet.

The term *mirror* may also be an allusion to the prominent early believers on whom the Báb bestowed the title "mirror." For example, in the following passage He addresses His followers as "Mirrors," warning them that, though they have recognized Himself, they may still fail to recognize the Manifestation of the Latter Resurrection (Bahá'u'lláh):

> Beware, O concourse of Mirrors, lest on that Day titles make you vainglorious. Know ye of a certainty that ye, together with all those who stand above you or below you, have been created for that Day. Fear ye God and commit not that which would grieve His heart, nor be of them that have gone astray. Perchance He will appear invested with the power of Truth while ye are fast asleep on your couches, or His messengers will bring glorious and resplendent Tablets from Him while ye turn away disdainfully from Him, pronounce sentence against Him—such sentence as ye would never pass on yourselves—and say, "This is not from God, the All-Subduing, the Self-Existent" (*Selections from the Writings of the Báb,* 6:14:5).

In the third couplet, the transformation of *Há'*[2] (هاء) to *Abhá* (ابهاء) most likely refers to the transformation of the Primal Will, as it is manifested in the Báb's revelation, to the reflection of the Primal Will manifested in the revelation of Bahá'u'lláh. Because of the immaturity of the people and as an act of kindness to them, the Báb revealed His station to the public gradually and in stages. First He was known as the gate to the Hidden Imám, then as the Imám himself, next as an independent Prophet, and finally as the Lord, the Manifestation of God's names and attributes.

Though some believers could perceive His true station in His earliest writings, to the average believer the magnitude and severity of the new revelation was not originally known. Bahá'u'lláh explains that if the Báb had revealed His station at the beginning of His mission, people would have done to Him immediately what they eventually did do (execute Him). Even a gradual disclosure of the mission of the Báb caused severe tests for some believers.

To reduce the magnitude of the shock associated with the new revelation, the Báb hid His true station from the majority of the people. Additionally, Manifestations of God appear on earth as human beings. On the one hand, their human qualities make it possible for the people to relate to Them. On the other hand, this becomes a veil that hides Their true exalted station. In one epistle to Muḥammad Sháh He says: "In brief, I hold within My grasp whatsoever any man might wish of the good of this world and of the next. Were I to remove the veil, all would recognize Me as their Best-Beloved, and no one would deny Me" (*Selections from the Writings of the Báb,* 1:4:15). This is an obvious reference to the appearance of the Manifestation of God from behind the veil as alluded to in Ṭáhirih's poems. In the seventh couplet of this poem, for example, Ṭáhirih alludes to the removing of the veil so that people may behold the full glory of the Manifestation of God.

2. In this manuscript, the word *há'* (هاء) has been written as *já* (جا). This is clearly a mistake, considering other manuscripts of this poem.

Poem 3: The Joy of Bihjat[3]

1
Praised be Thee, O our[4] Joy, All Praise!
Praised be Thee, O *bihjat* of *Tá'*![5] All Praise!

2
Greetings! O Ye Drop of a new creation,[6]
illuminated in these mirrors. All Praise!

3
Hail, O thou imbibing from the Pure Goblet,
the first cause of revival, all hail!

4
When Your exaltation was commanded[7] by *'Amá'*,
You were transformed from *Há'* to *Abhá!* All Praise![8]

---

3. *Bihjat* (بهجت) means "joy," but here it does not seem to be referring to Ṭáhirih's delight in and appreciation of Karím Khán-i-Máfí, who became an intermediary between her and her followers. Rather, the term alludes to the appearance of Bahá'u'lláh.

4. In Mohammadhoseini's version, the word *our* (ما) is "*fá*'" (فا). *Fá'* can be a reference to the region of Fárs in Iran, where Shíráz is located.

5. *Tá'* (طاء) is a reference to Tehran and to Bahá'u'lláh (Who lived in Tehran). The word *bihjat* ("joy") may also be a reference to Bihjat (Karím Khán-i-Máfí).

6. "Creation" is a translation for the word *fiṭr* (فطر), a short version of *fiṭrat* (فطرة).

7. We have used the past tense *bíyámad* (بیامد) instead of *bíyáyad* (بیاید) because this is the way it appears in Mohammadhoseini's version of the text, and it makes more sense.

8. *'Amá'* (عماء) meaning "cloud" is explained previously as the stage of the essence of God (*aḥadiyyat,* احدیّت) in contrast to the stage of Manifestation or *váḥidíyyat* (واحدیّت). It should be noted that some mystics have defined *'Amá'* as the stage of *váḥidíyyat,* explaining that as the cloud is located between the heaven and the earth, *'Amá'* is the intermediary between the unity of God and the multiplicity of the world of creation. (Refer to Ra'fatí's article on *Rashḥ-i-'Amá'*, a poem by Bahá'u'lláh, p. 51 of *Safíniy-i 'Irfán, Book Two*). *Há'* (هاء) is the Arabic letter equivalent to number 5 (the word *Báb* equals 5 according to the *abjad* system). *Abhá* (ابهاء) is the superlative form of *Bahá* (بهاء) and means "most glorious." This line could thus allude to the ascent from the stage of being "glorious" to becoming perfected or "most glorious." It is likely that this phrase alludes back to the first couplet and the transition from the Manifestation of the Báb (represented here by *Há'*) to the Manifestation of Bahá'u'lláh (represented here by *Abhá*). In other words, the Faith of the Báb that appeared in the region of Fars (*Fá'*)—assuming that the first couplet of the poem should be as it is

5
All (ye) particles, unconscious and swooning,
  praised be thee who have discovered this Hidden Treasure![9]

6
Descended (as You are) from God Almighty,
  without any doubt an unequaled Essence.[10] All Praise!

7
Indeed, behold this face from the glorious province of *Fá'*[11]
  but hidden from the world. All Praise!

8
O friend, come sing with us in joyful praise
  that you too may discover the secret of certitude. All Praise![12]

---

in Mohammadhoseini's version—will be followed by the Faith of Bahá'u'lláh in the city of Tehran (*Tá'*). *Tá'* at times is a reference to Ṭáhirih herself.

If we take the letter *Há* to symbolize the Absolute, the phrase might refer to the process by which the Unknown Absolute (the "Hidden Treasure") desired to make itself known by manifesting itself gradually until it becomes understood in its greatest glory (*Abhá*).

9. Probably the followers of the Báb who have begun to recognize Bahá'u'lláh.

10. Literally the verse is "an unequal Essence, a command, All Praise!" In the version we used in *The Poetry of Ṭáhirih*, the word *essence* is followed by the phrase *lá mit͟hl-u-mir'á* (لامثلُ و مِرا). We assume this is a poetic way of using the Arabic expression *lámit͟hl-va-lá mir'á* (لامثلُ ولامرا) meaning, "It (the Essence) has no equal without any doubt." This phrase most probably alludes to the same concept found in a passage in the Kitáb-i-Íqán in which Bahá'u'lláh states the following regarding the Báb: "He also saith that the Qá'im will reveal all the remaining twenty and five letters. Behold from this utterance how great and lofty is His station! His rank excelleth that of all the Prophets, and His Revelation transcendeth the comprehension and understanding of all their chosen ones" (¶272).

11. A literal translation would be: "Indeed, behold this face from the glorious *Fá'*." *Fá'* (فاء) must be another reference to the province of Fars. In this verse, we have replaced the word *bá-istinár* (با استنار), meaning "with illumination," with the word *bá-istitár* (با استتار) meaning "hidden," as it is written in the version of this poem in *The Poetry of Ṭahirih* and in Mohammadhoseini's volume.

12. What we translated as "the secret of certitude" is literally "the secret of *'ífá'* (ایفاء)," which we believe should have been *Ibqá'* (ابقاء), meaning "to sustain," "to protect," "to keep alive," "to establish," "to strengthen," "to protect someone's life," "to leave intact and in place," or "to be kind and benevolent."

9
It will become clear to you *quicker than the twinkling of an eye,*
the Hidden Treasure made manifest. All Praise!

10
O my Bihjat, from your *bihjat* it is *bahíj,*[13]
Bihjat's face among those mirrors![14] All praise!

13. *Bahíj* (بهيج): "delightful" or "cheerful."

14. As we have noted, the symbol of "mirrors" is used frequently throughout Ṭáhirih's work and, though sometimes alluding to the Manifestations, most probably here alludes to the pure-hearted first followers of the Manifestation. In this case she is exhorting Bihjat to be among these exemplary followers.

Poem 4: Sing Praises to God!

Since the last verse in many Persian poems includes a reference to the poet—normally a title the poet gives himself—to signify that this is his poem, it may be that this poem was penned by Bihjat. The title "Bihjat" in the last verse of the poem might support this idea. Also, compared to poems in the manuscript that precede and follow it, this poem has less energy, is less ecstatic, and has a slower metrical pace, even though in some sense it is more musical. The verses of Ṭáhirih's ma<u>th</u>naví's are normally shorter but more abrupt and filled with greater power and energy than are those that scholar Baydá'í seems to have attributed to Bihjat.[1]

However, the last verse of the poem could be taken as an exhortation by Ṭáhirih to Bihjat to behold and to appreciate the appearance of the Manifestation of God, as indicated by the references to the region of *Ṭá'* and the words *Bahá'u'lláh* and *Abhá* in line 10. Consequently, the poem may be taken as an indication that Bihjat was, like Ṭáhirih (or perhaps because of Ṭáhirih), already aware of Bahá'u'lláh's unique station.

1. He indicates this in a handwritten note on his copy of the facsimile text.

Poem 4: Sing Praises to God!

1
That same God Who fashions whatsoever He desires,
has in His benevolence opened the gate to the exalted Garden of Riḍván.[2]

2
Goblets filled with pure wine have descended,
setting ablaze the verdant trees of the Garden of Riḍván.

3
O God, Praiseworthy indeed be Thy doings! It is Aḥmad,
the reflection of whose beauty has illumined the plain of Párán[3]

4
O Lord, such beauteous faces have come into being,
each so ineffable that no metaphors are worthy of similitude.

5
O God, through Thy bounty Thou hast made the Hidden Treasure manifest![4]
By God, Thou hast revealed the truth, O *Subhán!*[5]

---

2. *Riḍván* means "Paradise," but here the reference is not to the specific gardens associated with the life of Bahá'u'lláh (the Garden of Najíbíyyih in Ba<u>gh</u>dád and the Garden of Na'mayn near 'Akká).

3. A mountain range north of Sinai and south of Seir. The verse means that the reflection of Aḥmad's beauty is so intense that it even illumines Sinai, where Moses witnessed the burning bush. The allusion to Párán in Bahá'í scripture symbolizes the eternal Covenant of God with humankind: "As for the reference in The Hidden Words regarding the Covenant entered into on Mount Párán, this signifieth that in the sight of God the past, the present and the future are all one and the same—whereas, relative to man, the past is gone and forgotten, the present is fleeting, and the future is within the realm of hope" ('Abdu'l-Bahá, *Selections from the Writings of 'Abdu'l-Bahá,* no. 181.2).

4. The tradition or ḥadí<u>th</u> of the "Hidden Treasure" is discussed by both Bahá'u'lláh and 'Abdu'l-Bahá. The tradition states, "I was a Hidden Treasure. I wished to be made known, and thus I called creation into being in order that I might be known" (quoted in Bahá'u'lláh, *Kitáb-i-Aqdas,* "Notes," 175).

5. *Subḥán* (سبحان): "far above" and "transcendent." It is an attribute of God also meaning "Great" and "Glorious."

6
I can view clearly, O God, that Thy Mighty Throne hast become manifest
in the plain of *Ṭá'*, O Beloved, O *Dayyán.*[6]

7
O *Subhán*, all thy people from the lofty summit of the Throne on High
are descending and circumambulating the sacred sanctuary.

8
O God, pour those scented drops into my goblet
that through acknowledgment from the beauteous face of *Ḥumrán,*[7]

9
with divine honor I may arise from my place
and extract whomsoever You desire from the heart of *Ḥumrán.*[8]

10
Supreme is God the Most High from Whom *jalálíyyát*[9] has descended!
Glorious is God, the Most Glorious, from whom the illumination of *jamálíyyát*[10]
has emanated!

11
O Bihjat of *Fá'*, behold the sign dawning from the West!
With a pure heart, read all the verses of proof!

---

6. *Dayyán* (دیّان): a "judge," a "requiter of good and evil"; as an attribute of God it means "the Rewarder."

7. *Ḥumrán* (حُمران) is the plural of *aḥmar* (احمر), meaning "red."

8. Literally, this reads, "*from the belly of the land of Ḥumrán.*"

9. *Jalálíyyát* (جلالیّات): see footnote to the second half of verse 166 of poem 1.

10. *Jamálíyyát* (جمالیّات): see footnote to the second half of verse 166 of poem 1.

Poem 5: Be Thou Prepared, O Bihjat!

This poem is another correspondence with Bihjat. In it Ṭáhirih is urging Bihjat to understand the station and greatness of the Manifestation of God in this age. She offers a mystical interpretation of the verses in the Qur'án about Abraham and His progressive spiritual journey and transformation. The whole poem is dedicated to this concept and to the conclusion that Ṭáhirih derives from her interpretation of this allusion.

The story of Abraham in the Súra of Cattle in the Qur'án can hardly be taken literally, but its value as a parable is significant. Abraham, not being satisfied with the lowly idols His father was worshipping, takes the stars as His God. But in the morning the stars disappear. Abraham is puzzled and comes to the conclusion that anything that disappears so quickly can hardly be worthy of being His God. He then selects the moon as His God, but the moon also disappears. Therefore, He thinks the sun should be His God. When the sun disappears, Abraham comes to the conclusion that: "Being upright, surely I have turned myself wholly to Him who created the heavens and the earth, for I am not one of those among the polytheists" (6:80).

Ṭáhirih's interpretation of verses 75–83 of the Súra of Cattle is focused on the concept of progress and the process of change. The progress of Abraham's thought might symbolize the wayfarer's progression in his journey toward the truth and his transition from the state of being unconscious and ignorant (*maḥv*, محو) to the state of sobriety and certitude (*ṣaḥv*, صحو). In this regard, Abraham can represent not only the personage of Bihjat but also each and every wayfarer.

The progression of Abraham's enlightenment can also be understood as God's progressive revelation at the various ages of the spiritual and social development of humankind (e.g., Adam, Noah, and Abraham in lines 15–19), concluding with the crucial turning point in this process at this unique and magnificent stage of human development—the maturation of humankind. The poem also points to the simultaneous reappearance of the perfections and attributes of all the Manifestations of God of past ages at this glorious age and time.

Another way to understand this poem is to read it as Ṭáhirih's advice to Bihjat to appreciate and understand fully and perfectly the true station of the Manifestation of God. In this sense, the various stations associated with the Báb and the gradual and progressive unfolding of His exalted condition can be seen as parallel to the progressive enlightenment of Abraham in the mythic story of His successive adoration of the stars, the moon, the sun, and finally God, the Creator of all these.

In line 12, Ṭáhirih points out that the reality of Muḥammad and of the Lord Himself has appeared. Then, at the conclusion of the poem, Ṭáhirih hints at the expectations of the revelation of God that is about to occur—the revelation of Bahá'u'lláh—an event so close in time that it will occur in less than the twinkling of an eye.

Many images in this poem are taken from the verses in the Qur'án about Abraham. In 6:76 God says: "And thus we show Abraham the kingdom of heavens and earth that he might be of those having certainty." In lines 2–5 of the poem, the phrases "the prize descended," "the scenery," "the glorious (*bahá'íyyih*, بهائيّه) constellations (skies)," "the glorious lands," and "the inhabitants of the clouds" are images of the kingdom of heaven and earth which made Abraham totally absorbed and intoxicated (*maḥv* in line 5). Like the stars, the moon, and the sun observed by Abraham, these are all expressions of God's glorious creation.

However, the most perfect and final revelation of God that brings Abraham back to sobriety is the melody or call of the Creator Himself, "He who originated (created) the heavens and earth" (6:80). The word used in this verse of the Qur'án for the act of creation is *faṭara* (فَطَرَ), meaning "originated it" and "brought it into being." This word also has the meaning of splitting—it is said that since the act of creation is like cleaving the darkness of nothingness and manifesting existence, this word means "to create" (Javádí Ámulí, 23).

This term is thus a crucial key to understanding Ṭáhirih's poetry. Ṭáhirih uses many variations of this word, and the reader needs to watch for these variant uses since they often relate to Ṭáhirih's own interpretation of the story of Abraham. Ṭáhirih seems to offer a certain philosophical point of view based on this word in the Qur'án and in ḥadíth.

A word close to *faṭara* is *fiṭrat* (فطرت), meaning "a certain way of originating" and "the nature of a thing." This word is used only once in the Qur'án, but variations of it occur elsewhere in the Qur'án (Javádí Ámulí, 24). In contemporary Arabic this same word means "nature," "form," "(natural) disposition," "(innate) character," "moral constitution," "temper," "instinct," "primitiveness" and "origination" (Al-Mawrid, 829). In literature the word has also been used to mean "religion," "wisdom," "sagacity," and "idiosyncrasy" (Steingass, 933). In this poem, variations of the word *faṭara* are seen in lines 3, 12, 23, and 24 in the following forms: the "*faṭṭárí* ear" (*sam'-i-faṭṭárí*, سمع فطّاری) meaning "original, pure, and natural ear"; *fiṭrah* (فِطره) "nature"; "*fiṭríyyih* splendor" (جلوه فِطريّه) meaning "original and natural splendor"; "*faṭṭárí* ecstasy" (جذبه فطّاري) meaning "original ecstasy."

The mystical point of view that Ṭáhirih seems to be presenting in this poem is that the transformation of Abraham—and in another sense, the transformation of every human being and of humanity in general—is the result of a natural interaction between the human soul and God. The word *natural* (qualified in various ways that we will explain) is at the heart of this mystical perspective. For example, in this poem, we observe how God attracts Abraham through natural splendor (line 23) and His natural attraction (line 24). In line 26 God appears to Abraham in the name of the creator (of one's nature). In line 3 Ṭáhirih advises Bihjat to hear with a "natural ear," a capacity endowed within Bihjat as a human being. In line 12 she refers to the Manifestation of God's (Muḥammad's) natural benevolence (*fiṭriy-i-mann*, فطره منّ) that enlightens Bihjat's heart.

This illumination that originates from God takes place within the heart of each human being. In lines 10–14 the notion of "heart" is alluded to with various images: "in the bosom of paradise," "the robe of God covered your chest," or, as we have translated it, "the robe of God became flesh," and finally, "the light from the mirror of your heart."

The notion of love and attraction are likewise significant in this poem. God's splendor and beauty resonate with man's natural affinity for and inherent attraction to the Beloved. For example, we find the word *attraction* (*ja<u>dh</u>bih*, جذبه) repeated in line 1 twice, and in lines 20, 24, and 27. In line 29 God is "the Attractor" (*ja<u>dh</u>dh</u>áb*, جذّاب) and in line 30 God is the "Beloved with embraces and kisses waiting for Bihjat to take her veil off her face."

Natural attraction and love is the basis for Abraham's transformation (Qur'án 6:77): "So when the night overshadowed him, he saw a star. He said: Is this my Lord? So when it set, he said: I love not the setting ones." The phrase "I love" (*uḥibbu*, أُحبُّ) in this verse has led some Islamic scholars, such as Allámih Ṭabáṭabá'í, to argue that the human being naturally seeks the divine eternal reality (Javádí Ámulí, 232–33). The ḥadí<u>th</u> "Religion is love and love is religion" (*Tafsír-i-Nuru'<u>th</u>-<u>Th</u>aqalayn*, 5:84) and another ḥadí<u>th</u> "And is religion anything except love?" (Majlisí, *Biḥaru'l-Anvár*, 27:84) from Imám Báqir have been used by Muslim scholars to support this idea (Javádí Ámulí, 230).

However, the concept of something being "natural" does not imply "effortless"—that free will is not involved, that such an action or response is automatic or deterministic. Ṭáhirih's poem asserts that the transformation that takes place in Abraham, Bihjat, and humanity, although a "natural" transformation, can only be realized when each person employs free will, a point emphasized in line 18: "Your determination must be unrelenting, O Bihjat." Of course, she also notes that God's aid and assistance make such a transformation thoroughly possible, something she notes in the last line of the poem.

The English word *nature* has been adopted in our translation for the Arabic word *fiṭrat* (فطرت) because we have not found a word in English precisely equivalent to *fiṭrat*. It is obvious in Ṭáhirih's poems that the term *nature* does not denote man's lower nature, but instead alludes to the concept of nature as defined by Bahá'u'lláh when He observes, "Nature is God's Will and is its expression in and through the contingent world" (*Tablets of Bahá'u'lláh,* 142). Considering the notions of "heart" and "attraction" explained earlier, Shoghi Effendi's adoption of "The voice of the true Faith" for the word *fiṭrat* is most enlightening and appropriate.[1] According to Javádí Ámulí, *fiṭrat,* although encompassing nature as a whole (*ṭabí'at,* طبيعت), is in one sense the opposite of nature. In the sense that everything was created by God, the Qur'án employs a derivative of the word *fiṭrat* to refer to God as the Creator of all that is in the heavens and the earth (Súra *Fáṭir,* verse 1). But in the context of this discussion, *fiṭrat* takes on a special meaning. In his analysis of the word nature (*fiṭrat,* فطرة) in the Qur'án, Javádí Ámulí indicates four characteristics of the word (pp. 2–3): (1) This natural consciousness is not imposed on human beings; rather it is endowed in man's nature. It is not like acquired knowledge, which is an external addition. (2) One cannot eradicate this natural tendency by force. In other words, it is always there, although it can be

1. Bahá'u'lláh calls Himself *fiṭrat* (فطرت): "The voice of the true Faith calleth aloud, at this moment, and saith: O people! Verily, the Day is come, and My Lord hath made Me to shine forth with a light whose splendor hath eclipsed the suns of utterance. Fear ye the Merciful, and be not of them that have gone astray" (*Epistle to the Son of the Wolf,* 29). "The voice of the True Faith" is Shoghi Effendi's translation of the word *fiṭrat*. In the Báb's writings, the prophetic nature and genius for revealing verses is a sign of the Manifestation of God. Some Bábís opposed Bahá'u'lláh, claiming that His writings are not the result of natural genius but are learned, thoughtful, and artificial (*Asráru'l Áthár,* 451, under *fiṭrat*). Bahá'u'lláh responds to this on various occasions by calling Himself the true source of revelation and explaining that *fiṭrat* was created by His own command.

weakened. (3) It is universal since every human being is created with this reality. (4) Since the human being's natural tendency and awareness is directed toward Absolute Existence and pure perfection (God), it has real worth associated with it and is the cause of humanity's progress. This inherent capacity is how human beings are differentiated from other living things.

This specific definition of *fiṭrat* is what the Qur'án (30:30) refers to when addressing Abraham as follows: "So set thy face for the religion, being upright (*ḥanífan*, حنيفاً), the nature (*fiṭrat*, فطرة) made by Alláh in which he has created (*fuṭirat*, فُطِرَت) men. There is no altering of Alláh's creation. That is the right religion—but most people know not." Ṭáhirih is most probably referring to this Qur'ánic verse in line 21 of the poem: "O my beloved soul, do not observe any change in the Divine tradition. One who would seek God must relinquish allegiance to the moon and sun."

"Relinquish allegiance to the moon and sun" is a reference to Abraham, Who, at the final stage of His spiritual journey, declared Himself to be upright (Qur'án 6:80): "surely I have turned myself, being upright (*ḥanífan*, حنيفاً), wholly to Him who originated (*faṭara*, فَطَرَ) the heavens and the earth, and I am not among those who are polytheists."

The word *qá'im* (standing upright) in line 26 of the poem can refer to Abraham after He reaches His final station of enlightenment and has arisen conscious and sober. The word *qavvam* (قوّام) in line 20, meaning "correct" and "rectified," is related to the attribute of *ḥaníf* (حنيف) mentioned in Qur'án 6:80 for Abraham. *Ḥaníf* means "the one who has abandoned false religions and has aligned himself with the true religion of God." When used in conjunction with the word *muslim*, *Ḥaníf* means "the pilgrim of Mecca." Abraham was the One Who left His native land and at an old age reached Arabia. There He built the house of God (*Ka'bih*) in Mecca. This house was renewed and reconstructed during Muḥammad's youth, and Muḥammad placed the Black Stone in its present position in the wall of that house (Haykal, p. 340).

In line 27 of the poem, "M" turns into "Abraham," which is possibly a reference to the Báb's interpretation of the three letters of *A*, *L*, and *M* (*alif*, *lám*, and *mím*, الم) at the beginning of the Súra of the Cow: "A, L, M, This Book, there is no doubt in it, is a guide to those who are faithful to their duty." The Báb, in His commentary on this súra, *Tafsír-i-Súriy-i-Baqarih,* (13–14) interprets the letter *A* as a reference to God, the letter *L* as a reference to Muḥammad, and the letter *M* as a reference to the Imáms. He explains that the manifestation of these three letters cannot become complete without the manifestation of the Book. The Book, He interprets to be the Fourth Foundation (*rukn-i-rábi'*, رکن رابع). The

"Fourth Foundation" is a Shaykhí term referring to the special representative of the Hidden Imám whose recognition is a duty (Dehkhoda, 26:602). In Shaykhí terminology this phrase refers to "the Commander of the world of humanity and the Existence of the Age."[2] Therefore, the Fourth Foundation, also referred to as the Perfect Shí'ih (*Shí'iy-i-Kámil*, شیعه کامل) seems to be the Shaykhí parallel to the Ṣúfí concept of the Perfect Man, a man who has lost his human identity (become selfless) by manifesting perfectly the names and attributes of God. Among these Shí'ih, the Báb explains, are the Shí'ih of 'Alí, one of whom was Abraham since He entered the city of "vicegerents" (*viláyat*, ولایة).

Abraham thus symbolizes one who has abandoned his human condition by means of dedicating himself completely to God. Abraham left His homeland at a very old age and migrated to a strange land. He sacrificed all He had and was even willing to sacrifice His own son in order to be obedient to the command of God.

According to this background information, the letter "M" turned into "Abraham" in the sense that the fruition or objective of the first three stages of manifestation (*A*, God; *L*, Muḥammad or the station of the Manifestation of God; and *M*, the Imáms or "vicegerents") was completed by the manifestation of the fourth stage—again, the Shí'ihs who have lost their own identity by aligning their wills totally with God's Will, even as Abraham did.

The special station assigned to Abraham in Islamic literature can be observed in various legends and stories attributed to Him. Abraham migrated to Arabia where, with the help of His son, He constructed the Ka'bih, the first house built for public worship in Mecca (Haykal, 29). After His arrival in the new land, there came a time when Abraham's wife and son suffered from lack of food and water. Seven times His wife Hágar ran to the valley of Makka and back, between Safaa and Marwah, to find water, but without success. Finally, when she returned to her son, she discovered that by scratching the surface of the earth with his foot, he had uncovered a water fountain (Haykal, 27). This water fountain, called Zamzam, is in the vicinity of the Ka'bih. Also, "Abraham's standing place" (*maqám-i-Ibráhím*, مقام ابراهیم) is a rock very close to the Ka'bih. It is believed that Abraham stood on this rock when building the Ka'bih (Dehkhoda, 39:599, under Ka'bih) and that his footprints are on it.

2. See Fáḍil Mázandarání (*Asráru'l Áthár*, 36, under *rukn*).

The famous Black Rock (*Ḥajaru'l-Asvad,* حجرالأسوَد) was placed by Muḥammad in one of the four foundation walls of the Ka'bih, the most important of the four foundations of the Ka'bih (Riaz-ul-Lughat, 4:714), at the side that is closest to the spring of Zamzam and "Abraham's standing place." It is believed that Muḥammad's ascent to the heavens (*mi'ráj,* معراج) started from a location in between the spring and "Abraham's standing place."

These legends indicate the very special station of Abraham, the Prophet or Manifestation Whose title among Muslims is "the Friend of God" (*Khalílu'lláh,* خليل الّله). The second half of verse 27 in poem 5 seems to be a reference to this station and to the fact that the transformation of Abraham, together with the appearance of a people with a spiritual station similar to that of Abraham, has occurred in this new age: "Indeed, by the Lord's attraction *mím* became "Abraham"/ so that He instantly circumambulated the Ka'bih which was beside him."[3]

Line 28 of the poem refers to Abraham's completion of His spiritual journey and His pilgrimage to the house of God. This mystical perspective of Ṭáhirih is prophetic in the sense that Abraham, representing humanity as a whole, is destined to complete His spiritual journey. In other words, Adam's wish, in one way or another, is destined by God to be realized. The individual's free will and God's unchangeable plan for humanity, which will be fulfilled regardless of specific individual choices, are simultaneously in effect.

Bahá'u'lláh states that if an individual fails to fulfill his duties, God will raise up the least pebble of the desert to perform that duty. This observation likewise recognizes the simultaneous operation of the Greater Plan of God as the plan incorporates the particular choices and efforts put forth by each individual human being.

Ṭáhirih's choice of various derivatives of the word *nature* (*fiṭrat,* فطرة) is an indication of this theological perspective. A ḥadíth by Muḥammad states, "Each new creature is born in accordance with *fiṭrat*" (from Majlisí's *Biḥáru'l-Anvár,*

3. Figuratively, "to circumambulate . . ." most often alludes to "circumambulating the City of God," which as a metaphor signals adherence to the word of God as it is revealed with each new Dispensation. As already noted, Abraham signifies one who inherently (by nature) discerns the reality of God. *Mím* (the letter *m*) may be a reference to the station of the Báb as an Imám or Guardian of the Faith of Islam—i.e., a "Gate." The idea of *Mím* becoming Abraham seems to be a reference to Abraham's gradual recognition of God and the Báb's gradual declaration of His station. God's mission for Abraham was to leave His homeland and go to Arabia so that He could eventually build the House of God (the Ka'bih). By fulfilling this mission, Abraham achieved God's purpose for Him. See Qur'án 2:122–27 and 3:96 regarding the construction of the Ka'bih by Abraham and His son.

3:279 and 281, quoted by Javádí Ámulí, 74). This ḥadí<u>th</u> suggests a positive perspective on human nature (as opposed to the view that humankind is born in sin), and it also seems to refer to the spiritual potential of humanity as a whole. Ṭáhirih, in line 20 of this poem reminds Bihjat that he was born into this world to become rectified and upright (*qavvam*, قوَّم): "You must hasten forth with attraction to the Beloved / so that you may become erect and your seed scattered throughout the regions."

Ṭáhirih's selection of the word *seed* here seems to allude to the seed of Abraham. Therefore we have translated this passage as "In order that your seed might be scattered throughout regions." As such, this verse indicates that the seed of Abraham, which is the source of future civilizations, was created for the purpose of achieving this final rectification—this destiny to fulfill the plan of God on earth.

Another metaphorical representation of this point of view that the world is moving toward an exalted spiritual destiny is the concept of the covenant. In the Qur'án (7:172–73) we find the following verse: "And when thy Lord brought forth from the children of Adam, from their loins, their descendents, and made them bear witness about themselves: Am I not your Lord? They said: yes; we bear witness. Lest you should say on the day of Resurrection: we were unaware of this, or (lest) you should say: Only our fathers ascribed partners (to Alláh) before (us) and we were (their) descendents after them. Wilt Thou destroy us for what liars did?"

This covenant between God and human beings at the beginning of creation has been interpreted by some to mean that humanity as a whole has an inherent attraction to grow ever closer to God, both in knowledge and in character. Otherwise, such a covenant would have not been taken from them (Javádí Ámulí, 119). To avoid misinterpreting this process to imply a deterministic view of the covenant, Siyyid Káẓim-i-Ra<u>sh</u>tí in his analysis of this concept divides people into five groups according to their individual responses to God's call: "Am I not you Lord?" (*alastu birabbikum,* اَلَسْتُ بِرَبِّكُم).

First are those who without any hesitation respond with a resounding "Yes!" Second are those who respond rhetorically or sarcastically "Yes," even though they have no true faith or conviction. They are, as it were, merely mocking the enthusiasm of the believers who responded in recognition of the truth (*Risáliy-i-Uṣúli-'Aqáyid*, 77).[4]

4. Refer to *Raḥíq-i-Ma<u>kh</u>túm* under *<u>dh</u>arr* (1:507–506) for the Bahá'í writings on this subject.

Shoghi Effendi's translation of the closing to the prayer commonly referred to as the Long Healing Prayer seems to refer to this covenant of God with man: "and by Thy grace whereby Thou didst respond, in Thine own Self with Thy word 'Yea!' on behalf of all in heaven and earth, at the hour when Thy sovereignty and Thy grandeur stood revealed, at the dawn-time when the might of Thy dominion was made manifest" (*Bahá'í Prayers,* 109). Shoghi Effendi's translation of this sentence is novel and differs from the common reading of the sentence in the original language. Commonly it is assumed that "on behalf of" (*min qibali,* مِن قِبَلِ) "all in heaven and earth" should be read "before" (*min qabli,* مِن قَبْلِ) "[the creation of] all in heaven and earth" (*Tasbíḥ-va-Taḥlíl,* 212). According to Shoghi Effendi's interpretation of this prayer, God through His grace and bounty, at the outset of creation and on behalf of humankind, responds positively to His own call to humanity. This means that humanity is not doomed to fail but destined to achieve the noble station God desires for it. Therefore, Adam's wish is destined to be realized, but in due time and through tests and difficulties associated with physical existence.

The Báb's statement that all revelations of the past will be aided by the latest revelation of God seems to support the existence of a positive dynamic force in the universe that moves humanity toward its destiny. In the Persian Bayán, the Báb writes, "If thousands of thousands of Manifestations appear in the future, . . . the aid (*madad,* مدد: "influence" or "victory") of all these Manifestations will result from the assistance of the very last Manifestation, who is the same First Adam who has no beginning in the world of existence. This is the mystery of Truth, and if one swims about in this ocean, one will witness that *there is no might and power except through God,* and one will come to understand that neither free will nor destiny can alter the plan of God" (provisional translation, 123).

This passage could be interpreted to mean that the purpose and objective of all the Manifestations of God has ever been and will ever be to manifest the wish of the first Manifestation of God—what we have termed "Adam's wish." Adam's wish was not attainable in His own time, at the outset of creation, but will become realized through successive ages and appearances of the Manifestations of God. In this connection the Báb says on another occasion, "The Point of Bayán is the same wondrous [new] creation (*fiṭrat,* فطرة) of the beginning" (provisional translation, *Bayán-i-Fársí,* 95). In other words, the potential of revelation endowed at the outset of creation has been realized with this latest revelation.

According to the Báb, in this new revelation every created thing can realize the potential for which it was created: "and He has created all things in a manner that in the Day of Resurrection, all would according to the existence of their nature (*fiṭrat,* فطرة) confess at His presence that for Him there can be no equal, no match, no companion, nor similitude" (*Bayán-i-Fársí,* 1).

Bahá'u'lláh in the *Kitáb-i-Badí'* (276) makes reference to God's address to Abraham in Qur'án 30:30: "So set thy face for religion, being upright, the nature (*fiṭrat,* فطرة) made by Alláh in which He has created (*faṭara,* فَطَرَ) men," and to the aforementioned ḥadíth that "Every child is born according to the nature (*fiṭrat,* فطرة)." He explains that this is true only so long as one has faith.

In other words, these Islamic verses do not mean that every child will fulfill the potential with which he or she has been invested by God. He explains that the ḥadíth goes on to say that the parents of the child can exert a negative influence that may cause the child to adopt erroneous beliefs. The child, therefore, though born with the natural capacity to recognize and worship God, can be influenced by external impulses to deviate from this inherently pure nature. Most important of all, the individual's will determines the extent to which he or she will reject the negative influences that may derive from acquired knowledge.

The difference between this Islamic view of the nature of man and the Christian view of original sin is that, according to the Islamic view, one is born in a condition of goodness and will remain in that condition so long as one does not deviate from the natural or inherent tendency of the soul to be pure and undefiled. Siyyid Káẓim-i-Rashtí cites the Islamic ḥadíth that states, "Every child is born according to its original nature (fiṭrat,فطرة), but the parents make the child a Jew or a Christian." He explains that as long as we do not alter that original purity (*fiṭrat*) or alter the child's nature (*ṭabí'at,* طبيعت) from the way God has created it, all human beings will inherently or instinctively be able to recognize God and understand His attributes and names (*Risáliy-i-uṣúl-i-'Aqáyid,* 29 and 33).

The Báb explains that "All existing things, in their primordial nature (*fiṭrat*) have been created in the most beauteous of forms, and if they do not become deterred from manifesting that inherent beauty, they will appear in their original created form" (provisional translation, *Bayán-i-Fársí,* 286). Therefore the Báb ordains that believers gaze into the mirror, behold their own creation, and give thanks to God for the splendor of their own beauty (286). The passage from Bahá'u'lláh's Hidden Words that states, "I created thee rich" (Arabic no. 11) reaffirms this positive view of human nature as created inherently noble and beautiful.

Of course, the concept of original sin assumes that one is born with a sinful nature and can become reformed only through personal salvation, an act achieved by means of the sufficient grace wrought by God's sacrifice of His son—an act of atonement prefigured by Abraham's willingness to sacrifice Isaac. But both perspectives urge humankind to accept responsibility for spiritual development by means of persistent effort in the struggle for growth; however, the psychological and cultural impact of these two distinctly different and somewhat antithetical perspectives is well worth noting.

For example, for those who have assimilated the concept of original sin, it would be difficult to feel comfortable with the notion that Adam's sin was not really a sin, that this is a mythological portrayal of desire for human progress, the very concept that Ṭáhirih deals with in poem 7. The image of man that Ṭáhirih portrays in this poem is not only optimistic and positive in terms of individual human beings, but also in terms of human society and the vision of the ultimate outcome of human civilization. So it is that while urging Bihjat to live up to his true destiny, she joyfully announces the advent of the realization of humanity's glorious destiny. The tone of the poem is thus upbeat and ecstatic, even as is the philosophical perspective of the poem.

Finally, it is also worth noting that the concept of progressive change and the philosophical debate over free will versus determination are introduced in this poem by Ṭáhirih in an implicit way and with metaphorical language, once again utilizing the story of Abraham. In poem 7 Ṭáhirih will deal with these particular issues in a more detailed and explicit manner by employing the stories of Adam and Noah.

Poem 5: Be Thou Prepared, O Bihjat!

1
O Bihjat, *bahj*[5] itself is flourishing because of your *bihjat,*
that magnetic ecstasy exploding into sparks of ecstasy!

2
From the Source of all honor and glory a bounty descended for you!
Behold now the panorama,[6] how He arrived with honor and dignity.

3
O Bihjat, hearken with an attentive[7] ear
that you may clearly observe how Moses came to this same region:

4
From His sacred cycle the *Bahá'íyyih*[8] stars[9]
revolved in the circle of existence by God's command![10]

5
With but one glimpse of them,[11] the inhabitants of *'má*, the *Bahá'íyyih* angels,
became absorbed, then intoxicated!

6
Oh Bihjat, I have read all your signs,[12] and your station is assured
in the presence of the Lord of the Throne on High!

---

5. "To be happy" or "to make someone happy."

6. What God showed Abraham. As already noted, Abraham ultimately realized the ascendancy of God, first by beholding the majesty of the stars, then the moon, then the sun, and then the Creator of all things.

7. *Faṭṭárí* (فطّاري): "original," "natural," or "inherently capable or good." The idea here is that, like Abraham, Bihjat should respond to his natural goodness or inherent capacity to perceive reality and truth. See Qur'án 6:79.

8. "Glorious."

9. The constellations or the heavens.

10. This concept of a "refreshed" or "renewed" cycle can have many allusions: to the advent of a new Manifestation or to the eternal cyclical process by which creation itself is ever renewed.

11. The constellations.

12. Astrological signs.

7
Blessed are you, a hundred times blessed, for *that which appeared from constellations!*[13]
Verily, your destiny[14] was discerned from the realm of light![15]

8
With certitude, behold how your soul (is) the great prize,
for your movement,[16] unmatched and splendid, aligned itself with (His) orbit.

9
O beloved one, receive this wondrous bounty from God—
your beautiful countenance ever in God's presence.[17]

10
The young trees in the bosom of Eden
exploded into sparks from the dome of Ṭúr.[18]

11
O Bihjat, that tree in Eden was inflamed by you,
and the sparks from that tree set the universe aflame.

12
Praised be (God), that Aḥmad, the *Ḥabíb*[19] of God, is the *Qá'im*,[20]
that from the nature[21] of His favor, your own light has become ignited.

---

13. Because of what happened as a result of what he has done.

14. As foretold in the stars or caused by fate. Destiny is a translation for *ḥukm* (حکم), which is the effects each star has, according to the astrological rules (Dehkhoda, 19:754).

15. "Enlightenment" or "illumination."

16. Bihjat's actions, portrayed here as a celestial body orbiting the sun or the moon.

17. Qur'án 75:22–23, 83:22–24.

18. An allusion to Moses and the burning bush. In verses 10 and 11, Ṭáhirih interprets some Qur'ánic verses (e.g., see 28:20–30, 24:35, and 23:20). She makes a connection between the forbidden tree in paradise (Eden) and the tree that was inflamed at *Ṭúr*. She implies that the same tree in paradise (the reality of the Manifestations of God) manifested itself to Moses and is manifesting itself again in this age.

19. *Ḥabíb* (حبیب): "Beloved." The "Beloved of God" is one of the titles of Muḥammad.

20. *Qá'im* (قائم) here means the "upright" one, the one who has "arisen," the Promised One, or the twelfth or hidden Imám. Ṭáhirih's association of the forbidden tree of paradise with Muḥammad can also be found in 'Abdu'l-Bahá's interpretation: "The tree [represents] a station specialized for the Master of Existence. . . . The Ḥabíb [friend] of the kind God, Muḥammad, salutation and praise be upon Him" (*Min Makátíb 'Abdu'l-Bahá*, 76, provisional translation by Hatcher and Hemmat).

21. *Fiṭra* (فطره): used throughout as signifying "inherent" or "original nature."

13
By God, He is the Beloved and from the Supreme Robe
and through His great *Zikr*,[22] the robe of God assumed a human form.[23]

14
Bihjat, O Bihjat, behold the divine signs
illumined by the light from the mirror of your own heart.[24]

15
O beloved, O my beloved, O Bihjat full of joy,
from the unfolding of the Bayán, Adam has come into these regions.[25]

16
From the panorama before you, gaze upon God!
The ark has paused that you might board it,

17
that you might arrive at my presence in the twinkling of an eye
the *Bahá'íyyih* mirror orbits in the universe.

18
Your determination must be relentless, O Bihjat,
if you ask your Lord for the One Who has appeared among men!

19
Your destiny surpassed the illumination of the Sun,
the influence of either stars or the moon.

22. "Utterance," one of the titles of the Báb.

23. Literally, "came (or was placed) on the chest," though the idea is that our knowledge of God derives from the earthly appearance of the Manifestations in a human temple.

24. Your sincerity and spiritual capacity make the panorama of the constellations and signs of God reflected in your heart comprehensible to you. "Signs" (*áyát,* آيات) also refers to holy verses.

25. "Adam" here seems to be alluding to humankind, which, because of the fidelity of the "mirrors," like Bihjat, will become illumined by the light of the new revelation.

20
You must hasten forth with attraction to the Beloved
so that you may become erect and your seed scattered throughout the regions.

Ṭáhirih Explains the Signs of the Advent of Bahá'u'lláh

21
O beloved one, no change is there in this divine tradition:[26]
One who would seek God must relinquish allegiance to the moon and sun.[27]

22
A star appeared to Him in the heavens!
It then faded, turned pitch black.[28]

---

26. A reference to God's tradition (*sunnat,* سنّة) of gradual revelation of truth as was the case for Abraham.

27. This verse and the following ones refer to Qur'án 6:77–80 on the gradual enlightenment of Abraham. First He saw a star, and He said, this is my Lord, but when the star faded, He took the moon and subsequently the sun as His Lord. Eventually He took the invisible God as His Lord. According to Qur'án 2:122–127 and 3:96, Abraham and His son renovated the Ka'bih in Mecca and purified it from idol worship. "The place of Abraham" (*Maqám-i-Ibráhím,* مقام ابراهیم) mentioned in the Qur'án is a name used for a small building situated in the Ka'bih, but it is also used as a title for Ka'bih where the Muslims go for pilgrimage. "One who would seek God" (literally: "The one who came to visit") in this verse of the poem should be a reference to Abraham as the first pilgrim of the Ka'bih after He built it. In addition to a reference to the story of Abraham, in these verses Ṭáhirih here might be alluding to the appearance in the heavens of a celestial sign that heralds the new dispensation, even as the "mirrors" (sanctified souls) also appear to awaken the hearts. See the Kitáb-i-Íqán:

> By "heaven" is meant the visible heaven, inasmuch as when the hour draweth nigh on which the Daystar of the heaven of justice shall be made manifest, and the Ark of divine guidance shall sail upon the sea of glory, a star will appear in the heaven, heralding unto its people the advent of that most great light. In like manner, in the invisible heaven a star shall be made manifest who, unto the peoples of the earth, shall act as a harbinger of the break of that true and exalted Morn. These twofold signs, in the visible and the invisible heaven, have announced the Revelation of each of the Prophets of God, as is commonly believed (Bahá'u'lláh, ¶66).

28. The sense of this repeated allusion is that, while impassioned by the spiritual revival unleashed by the appearance of the Báb, few were conscious of His true station or purpose in terms of this turning point in the religious history of humankind on the planet.

23
Then, without peer or likeness, the *fiṭríyyih*[29] splendor
descended beside Him from the cloud of *'Amá'*[30]

24
[and] lifted His head from the dust by means of *faṭṭárí* attraction [saying]:
"O obliterated one God descended from the heavens[31] [for you] to discern,

25
"behold with your own eyes how flawless is His handiwork!
Since God has appeared in your own garments,[32] your duty is refinement.[33]

---

29. *Fiṭríyyih* (فطريّه): "primordial," "natural," or "inherent." As an adjective, this word derives from the root word we have already glossed in several forms, especially as it has related to Abraham; it implies an inherent or essential splendor, as opposed to an acquired attribute.

30. *'Amá'* (عماء): "a thin cloud that is not easy to discern." In mystical terminology it is a reference to the station of Hidden Treasure, the fact that God, like a hidden treasure, is unknown (*Riaz-ul-Lughat,* 6:1189). Here Ṭáhirih seems to allude to Bahá'u'lláh, Who, though manifest to humankind after the Báb, was a contemporary of the Báb (indeed, He was two years older than the Báb) and a follower and prominent teacher of the Bábí religion prior to the revelation of His own station to the Bábís.

31. Considering verse 14 ("Bihjat, O Bihjat, behold the divine signs / illumined by the light from the mirror of your own heart"), we might infer that the illumination of the heavens in which stars, the sun, or God can be observed is dependent on the heart of the observer.

32. The Manifestation appears as a man among men—i.e., in the guise of an ordinary human being.

33. Qur'án 95:4: "We have indeed created man / In the best of moulds." The meaning of this might be that God not only created human beings in His image spiritually, but also fashioned us in the most beauteous physical form as a sign of that relationship. Here humankind (Bihjat) is being told that because we have been created nobly, we must act accordingly.

26
"O Qá'im, surrounding *mím,*[34] you have now become like *Hím.*[35]
Your Lord came from the deserts of *Rayy* in the name of *faṭár.*"[36]

27
Indeed, by the Lord's attraction *mím* became "Abraham"
so that He instantly circumambulated the *Ka'bih* which was beside him.

28
O Bihjat, thou who art my *bihjat,*[37] now must you comprehend
the meaning of that dark night[38] that came from the deserts.

29
Behold that He is attracting you from the Celestial Concourse!
Embrace Him, for His patience has now become established.

30
Remove the veil from the *Bahá'íyyih* face![39]
Your Lord has come with embraces and kisses, with majesty and grandeur![40]

---

34. *Mím* (م, the letter *m*) in the Báb's writings alludes to Moses, to the station of Vicegerent (or Guardianship), and to the Eleventh Imám of Shí'ih Islam (observations from the glossary of the *Bayán-i-Farsí,* The Persian Bayán). As mentioned already, Ṭáhirih might be referring to the Báb's gradual proclamation of His mission. Although He was known to be the Qá'im, an Imám, and a Vicegerent, He gradually made it known that He was also a Prophet of God of the same station as Abraham. In addition, though God told Moses, "You shall never see Me," He called Abraham His intimate and close Friend; therefore, *Khalíl'u'lláh* is Abraham's title in the Qur'án.

35. *Hím* means "sand." In this verse the Qá'im (the Báb) may have become like "sand" in that, like Abraham, the Báb had forsaken His own identity to become absorbed by God's revelation. Also like Abraham, the Báb became unconscious on the desert sand (see Pines, 17–25). Bahá'u'lláh, from Tehran (the deserts of Rayy), is believed to have heeded the Creator's call to Abraham.

36. The Creator.

37. "Delight."

38. *Laylá* (ليلا): "dark night." This could be an allusion to the intervening period of turmoil between the appearance of the Báb (1844) and the occurrence of the "Latter Resurrection" with the appearance of Bahá'u'lláh (1863). The essence of *laylá* can also be a reference to Muḥammad in Qur'án 73:1–2 or Abraham in Qur'án 6:77.

39. Possibly this passage is commanding Bihjat to help others to perceive the reality of Bahá'u'lláh as fulfillment of the promises of the Báb regarding "Him Whom God shall make manifest."

40. There is a delightful contrast of qualities here—both personal and intimate affection, together with lofty and macrocosmic powers.

31
By God, He will appear sooner than the twinkling of an eye![41]
In that Day, will you dare suggest that His authority derives from these regions?[42]

32
At your feast with God, aid and assistance will arrive
with a paradisiacal melody from the Iraqi quarter.[43]

---

41. Again, though Ṭáhirih is keenly aware of Bahá'u'lláh's station, she was executed in 1852 before Bahá'u'lláh revealed Himself or revealed His station to aught but those who had discovered it for themselves.

42. Refer to various verses in the Qur'án on the authority (*idhn*, اذن) and power of the Prophets and the chosen ones (4:64, 13:38, 40:78, and 97:4 in relation to the return of Christ). The line reads, literally, "from the region of cities," but the implication is clear—that Ṭáhirih is cautioning Bihjat (and those to whom he will deliver her writings) to examine whether or not the unleashed power of Bahá'u'lláh has a celestial or an earthly source. Naturally, she is being ironic, stating that all earthly powers will attempt to confound and prevent this force.

43. This is an allusion to the fact that the transformative power of Bahá'u'lláh will first become manifest to the world at large after He is exiled to Baghdád.

Poem 6: The Appearance of "Him Whom God Shall Make Manifest"

While some consider this poem to be a response from Bihjat to the previous poem (poem 5) by Ṭáhirih, it seems that these exalted verses extolling the advent of Bahá'u'lláh could not have been penned by a poet with less capacity than Ṭáhirih herself. What is more, underlying the ostensibly simple expression of rejoicing is a very powerful conjoining of symbols alluding to this period in the history of humankind when all will at last be made plain that was understood previously only piecemeal.

Of particular power is the emphasis Ṭáhirih places on the emergence of this long-awaited time in which humankind can understand the truth directly, rather than through the "crystalline couplets" alluded to in line 11—the various poetic traditions that, while steeped in symbol and metaphor, had so often been misconstrued to befit the perverse and sometimes corrupted interpretations through the ages by Islamic clerics.

In this sense, the poem is much more than the announcement of both the Day of Resurrection alluded to in the Qur'án and the Day of the Latter Resurrection alluded to in the Bayán. Ṭáhirih is proclaiming that, to those with discerning eyes who are able to escape from the constraints of superstition and clerical literalism, the evidence of the unity of creation and the fulfillment of the Divine plan is everywhere to be seen.

Though the poem is not as imagistic or as complex as the previous poem, Ṭáhirih's purpose here is totally distinct, and she bends her remarkable skills to befit the task at hand. Even as the poem itself notes that the time for allusions, symbols, and "names" (indirection) has passed, so she in this verse articulates with astounding clarity, power, and concision that what in past ages has been veiled in allusions and images is now revealed bright as the sun to all who dare study the world around them with discerning vision.

In this context Ṭáhirih urges the reader to set aside the troublesome allusions, abstruse images, and misinterpretations of scripture from past traditions and follow instead the inherent or natural (*fiṭáríyyih*, فطاريّه) capacity that lies dormant within every soul. Like Abraham, Who in His spiritual journey surpassed the images of star, moon, and sun; each one in this day can, by transcending images and similitudes, observe the effulgent Sun of Truth and perceive that the Beloved has occupied the throne of Bayán with utmost glory and majesty (line 9).

In line 10, Ṭáhirih reminds the reader of the advice she has already bestowed in line 30 of poem 5: "Remove the veil from the *Bahá'íyyih* face!" In effect, she is exhorting the believers to discern in Bahá'u'lláh the fulfillment of the promises foretold by the Báb in the Bayán. In this same context in lines 12 and 13, Ṭáhirih declares poetically that Muḥammad Himself has descended from the heavens in the figure of Bahá'u'lláh.

We can find a similar reference to Muḥammad's return (descending from the heavens) in line 199 of poem 7. In both instances, Ṭáhirih is most probably alluding to verse 2:210 of the Qur'án, which says, "They wait for naught but that Alláh should come to them in the shadows of the clouds with angels." This verse has been interpreted by Siyyid Káẓim-i-Rashtí to mean that the Apostle of God, Muḥammad, will descend from the sky in a cloud with a weapon in His hand fashioned from light (*Uṣúl-i-'Aqáyid*, 209). Since Ṭáhirih begins poem 7 with the allusion to this same verse, she discerns in this passage the basis for the structure of this entire work.

Poem 6: The Appearance of "Him Whom God Shall Make Manifest"

1
It is another world, and another command is being unfolded!
Another Revelation is descending from the Sun of Destiny!

2
Amid the dawning light, It has appeared in the constellation of Praise!
Drops of praise spring forth from It!

3
(The Sun) says, "It is I! No one is alive except Me!
All people prostrate themselves in My presence.

4
"It is My wish to withdraw the cord of my crimson tongue from the depth of my heart
and unfold the mysteries of all that has been concealed beneath the covers!"

5
The One Who came but Who did not come has now arrived![1]
He has cast off the veils of distinction to reveal the same Personage.

6
O thou hearer, hearken, and, if you examine with care the world around you,
you will recognize clearly revealed the One Who has been concealed.[2]

1. This may be a reference to the fact that though the Báb came, He was unable to fulfill the entirety of His purpose because He was imprisoned and executed, whereas Bahá'u'lláh, in fulfilling His mission, is also completing some of what the Báb would have accomplished. An even more helpful explanation might be that Bahá'u'lláh, though already at hand and a follower of the Báb, could not reveal His station until the time was ripe. Ṭáhirih is cautioning Bihjat (and by implication all Bábís) that the time of that unveiling is close at hand.

2. This statement alludes to the fact that Bahá'u'lláh, though as yet veiled from public knowledge, was already known by Ṭáhirih and other close followers to be the One Whose advent the Báb had come to announce.

7
The next instant you may discover another world made manifest,
made to shine with light through the mystery of Truth.

8
But first you must cleanse yourself from the (dust of) names in the kingdom of names[3]
and bring yourself into the station of *fiṭáríyyih*[4] which He Himself occupies.

9
God, the Venerated, the Beloved, the Matchless One,
assumed the throne of the Bayán with effulgence and song!

10
Since He has at last arrived, remove the veil!
Since truth is now apparent, the days of names have passed!

11
In the past, all the mysteries were revealed in crystalline couplets![5]
Verily, this is the revelation of that exact same truth![6]

12
Far from Celestial Heights the Friend of God[7] has descended
Whose name in the Bayán is now manifest in the exaltation of light![8]

---

3. *Mit͟hál* (مثال) could mean "example," but we have used "names" because in the Bahá'í texts physical reality is alluded to as the "kingdom of names" since each virtue (or name of God) can be understood only as it becomes manifested in some physical object or analogue. Here Ṭáhirih is saying that since the truth is now clear, this indirect understanding is not necessary. It is also a reference to Abraham's story in the Qur'án in which Abraham first took the stars, moon, and the sun to be His Lord before He recognized the unseen God.

4. *Fiṭáríyyih* (فطاريّه): "creation" or the "act of creating"; here the term alludes to the spiritual realm as the source of the kingdom of names.

5. The prophecies and allusions of the scriptures.

6. Here, too, the poet is distinguishing between the veiled imagery of past scripture and the "unsealing" of those books through the unambiguous verses of the Prophet.

7. *Ḥabíbu'lláh* (حبيب الله): "the Beloved of God," one of the appellations of Muḥammad.

8. Throughout the Bayán, the Báb alludes to the advent of "Him Whom God shall make manifest" in the year nine (1853). Ṭáhirih states here that this One (Bahá'u'lláh) is present, though as yet concealed to the world at large.

13
Now He is speaking of the face of the Appointed One[9]
proclaiming: "I am He! I am Aḥmad! He is the manifest name!"

14
By God, Alláh, it was manifest in the world, that mystery
which is a secret concealed in the heart of Holy Texts.

15
By means of the flawless Mirror, the past is now made plain![10]
By Alláh, He is (the One) exalted in the Bayán.[11]

16
Verily, in this Day the Truth has become revealed!
Verily, the light[12] has been ignited by sparks flashing from the Bayán.[13]

---

9. Literally, "the One Who was named."

10. Bahá'u'lláh will make all the mysteries of past prophecy and veiled images understandable. This statement is exemplified throughout the writings of Bahá'u'lláh, beginning most obviously with the Kitáb-i-Íqán, wherein Bahá'u'lláh renders a lengthy explication of a passage from the New Testament and, in doing so, also explains parallel passages in the Qur'án and in the prophecies of the Báb.

11. Throughout the Bayán and other works of the Báb, Bahá'u'lláh is alluded to as the fulfillment of the Bábí Faith and all the previous revelations of the Adamic Cycle.

12. *Zahrá'* (زهراء): "luminous" or "light." This was a title for Muḥammad's daughter Fáṭimih, who was the wife of Imám Alí and who is referred to by some Muslims as "Our Lady of the Light."

13. Here the important point is made that the Bayán, though of secondary importance once Bahá'u'lláh appears, is still the essential source of preparation for the advent of "Him Whom God shall make manifest"—poetically, the shower of sparks from the Bayán started the fire that now will illuminate the whole of human existence.

Poem 7: Adam's Wish

Introduction

This seventh and climactic poem is a weighty discourse that serves as the heart of Ṭáhirih's insights into how humankind has been fashioned to experience spiritual development through trial and struggle. As throughout this entire work, the figure of Adam is important—more as an allusion to the awakening of human intellect and self-awareness than as a reference to the historical figure Who was a Manifestation of God.

As does Muḥammad in the Súra of Houd and Bahá'u'lláh in the beginning discourse in the Kitáb-i-Íqán (Book of Certitude), Ṭáhirih here employs the story of Noah as the starting point of human guidance. It can be seen as a point in religious history that tests the fidelity and capacity of humankind to renounce vain imaginings by going aboard the Ark—the ancient symbol of the Covenant of God through which humanity can be protected from the stormy seas of strife and struggle that are often experienced in the physical world.

Part I: Progressive Revelation and the Advent of a New Manifestation (lines 1–15)

The poem begins with the glad tidings of the coming of the One with authority (Him Whom God shall make manifest). Ṭáhirih advises Bihjat to purify himself from conditions of customary logic and discourse and elevate himself so that he can hearken with his heart and spirit to the message that "Him Whom God shall make manifest" will utter to the world.

The words that the next Manifestation of God will utter begin with: "I am the One Who made Adam appear and thereafter Noah." Ṭáhirih then teaches the principle of progressive revelation. Even as with the advent of Noah when the believers had to detach themselves from the previous Manifestation, Adam, so will it be a test for the Bábís when Bahá'u'lláh reveals Himself. This she teaches through the words of Noah commanding Adam's absolute obedience to Him (lines 13–15).

Part II: Noah and His Return (lines 16–113)

In this rather long part of the poem, which by itself can be divided into five distinct sections, Ṭáhirih retells the story of Noah and the Ark and applies that allegorical narrative to the relationship between God's Manifestation and humanity in this age. She ends this part by describing a particularly trying test involved in the process of progressive revelation—that God can send to the world of being a Manifestation with any physical attributes He desires. Then she focuses on the station of the Báb and the coming of "Him Whom God shall make manifest." In the following paragraphs each of the five sections of Part II will be explained with references to specific lines of the poem indicated in parentheses.

SECTION 1: THE INHABITANTS OF THE ARK (LINES 16–35)

In this section Ṭáhirih explains what transpired after the appearance of Noah and how a chosen number of people were brought forth. These special individuals possessed highly developed souls and unique stations, as do the first followers of every Manifestation. They received God's command from Noah, even though the command of God had been previously conveyed through Adam. They were aware that when a new revelation arrives, there is no benefit in holding on to past traditions. They were further aware that in the world of limitations there is no more than one representative of God for each age (at least in a particular part of the world), and that no one else has an equivalent station—no two Manifestations of God vie for the allegiance of the same people (16–35).

SECTION 2: INHABITANTS OF THE ARK IN THIS NEW AGE (LINES 36–50)

Ṭáhirih explains how the story of Noah has been repeated in this age. God's command has again arrived (36), and those special souls now aboard Noah's ark can be seen (38). They utter words that appear as sparks. They express their obedience to God and call out to others to come aboard the Ark of salvation by recognizing the covenant of the new Manifestation (39–50).

SECTION 3: NOAH'S ANGER (LINES 51–69)

Ṭáhirih explains that Noah again is uttering the same angry words He uttered at His first coming when, after finding so few faithful souls, He asked God not to leave any of the faithless ones alive on earth. The present anger of the Lord of the Bayán (Bahá'u'lláh) is caused by the martyrdom of the Báb, the Primal Point, Who is the source of all creation (51–69).

According to the story, Noah, after showing patience with His people, finally gave up on them and saw no alternative but the destruction of the faithless ones and the construction of a new society using only the few who followed Him. The anger of the Manifestation of God at this age is also due to the fact that the corrupt society the Báb had been sent to save had, by and large, failed to respond appropriately. After His martyrdom, those who persecuted Him seemed spiritually dead and without hope for resurrection or revival.

SECTION 4: ADMONITIONS TO BIHJAT (LINES 70–79)

Next, Ṭáhirih advises Bihjat to learn his lessons from this story, not to forget for a moment the bounties of God, and to praise God's loved ones so that he might deserve to be one of those who ride the Ark (70–75). She also warns Bihjat not to share the mysteries about "Him Whom God shall make manifest" until the new Manifestation of God reveals Himself and in an instant enlightens him and enables him to become detached from his past (76–79).

SECTION 5: NOAH IN THE NEW DISPENSATION (LINES 80–113)

In this section (verses 80–113) Ṭáhirih resumes retelling the story of Noah and unfolding corresponding events in the dispensation of the Báb. She describes how the stories of the past have been repeated in this very age (80) and that Noah (that is, Noah as He has returned in this age) has raised again His angry cry: "O God do not leave anyone alive in these regions" (Qur'án, 71:26) (82).

In spite of persecutions and the apparent failure of the religion of the Báb, the courageous believers who came aboard the Ark became inspired and spiritually prosperous, even in the physical world. The rest of the people were tested and purified through Noah's anger.

In this age, the reality and authority that was manifest in Noah (the Point) is the same authority that has made various Manifestations of God appear at different ages of the past (verses 95–101). God is the One Who brought Adam into existence out of dust. He made the Truth appear from the water (perhaps an allusion to Noah), then He made it manifest from the fire—possibly a reference to Abraham when fire turned into a flower garden for Him, or a reference to the burning bush on Sinai that appeared to Moses. God will manifest Himself to whomsoever He wishes, in whatever form He chooses, until He brings about the Great Spirit, the countenance of Bahá.

Verses 102–106 describe the period of time between the dispensation of the Báb and the dispensation of Bahá'u'lláh. Finally, verses 107–113 allude to the station of the Báb, Who manifested the same reality of Muḥammad in this new dispensation.

Part III: Adam's Myth and the Concept of Free Will (lines 114–57)

In literary traditions and in religious texts, Adam represents not only the first Prophet of God in the Prophetic or Adamic Cycle, but also all of the Prophets Who have appeared on earth with different human personalities in different ages. In an allusion to this same concept, Bahá'u'lláh in the Kitáb-i-Íqán says, "Why should Muḥammad, that immortal Beauty, Who hath said: 'I am the first Adam' be incapable of saying also: 'I am the last Adam'?" (¶172).

In Christianity, Jesus Christ is called "the last Adam" inasmuch as Paul refers to Jesus Christ saying, "And so it is written, The first man Adam was made a living soul; the last Adam was made a quickening spirit" (Cor. 15:45). Christ is also called "the Second Adam" since the apostle Paul speaks of Adam as "the figure of him who was to come" (Rom. 5:14–19).

The same concept is seen in Islamic culture and texts. In Kháqání's poetry, the term "Second Adam" (*Ádam-i-thání*, آدم ثانی) has been employed to signify "God's Vicegerent," one who possesses the nature of Adam (Farhang-i-Luqat va T'bírát-i-Kháqání, 1995, 1:22). In lines 114–57, Ṭáhirih deals with the story of Adam by providing three interpretations of the Adamic myth: philosophical, theological, and eschatological.

The first interpretation (lines 115–36) is about the creation of Adam, which signifies the Will of God made manifest through the emanation of the reality of the Manifestations of God. This is a purely philosophical discussion on the Manifestation of God's Will on earth and what that creative process means in terms of providing human beings with free will. The Báb refers to this as the creation of the First Adam (*Ádamu'l-Avval*, آدم الأول) since this creation is a primordial reality that manifests itself repeatedly in different ages (*Risáli-i-Nubuvvat-i-Khassih,* 29).

Lines 137–48 contain an allusion to the historical figure of Adam as a distinct and unique Manifestation of God. This interpretation explains the explicit claims of the individual Manifestations of God and elucidates the individuality of Their specific purposes and missions (to which Bahá'u'lláh alludes as the "station of distinction" in the Kitáb-i-Íqán, ¶191).

The third interpretation concerns the return of Adam in this age, the dispensation of the Báb (lines 149–75). This section explains how the Báb, as a Manifestation of God, has incarnated the same attributes, character, and actions as did the historical Adam, Who was the first Manifestation in the religious cycle that the Bahá'í writings categorize as the Adamic or Prophetic Cycle.

In each case, Adam has been created with free will and wishes "to eat from the tree of knowledge" so that He can bring about the immediate transformation of the human spiritual condition. As a result of Adam's "selfishness" or "presumption" in this sense, the divine reality descends to earth and is manifested within the confines and limitations of physical reality.

In this third part of the poem, Ṭáhirih utilizes two related and similar words to make a connection between the mythological recounting of Adam's sin and the philosophical and theological allusion to creation as the extant relationship between God and the universe. The two terms Ṭáhirih uses are *ananíyyat* (اَنانيّت), meaning "selfishness," and *inníyyat* (اِنّيّت), meaning "selfhood" and "existence." The two words are very similar in meaning, and at times each is used to imply the meaning of the other one. The second word literally means "indeed me" (*inní*, اِنّي). Therefore, although denoting "existence," the word has some connotation of "selfishness."

Similarly, the first term ("selfishness") has been interpreted by some mystics and philosophers as implying the concept of "existence" or "selfhood." "Selfishness" (*ananíyyat*, اَنانيّت) in mystical and Ṣúfí terminology is "Manifestation of the Absolute existence in logically and sensibly perceptible stages" (Gowharin, *Sharḥ-i-Iṣṭiláḥát-i-Taṣavvuf*, 2:76). Because each existing thing reflects some of God's attributes, it also expresses its own "selfishness," but not in a negative or exclusive sense.

Mullá Ṣadrá, the Shí'ih philosopher of the seventeenth century, also discusses a relationship between these two terms. He uses the term *ananíyyat* or selfishness to mean the identification of self as a separate entity (*tashakhkhuṣ*, تشخّص), or the rational soul (*nafs-i-náṭiqih*, نفس ناطقه) that is always aware of self (Sajjadí, *Philosophical Glossary of Mullá Ṣadrá*, 106). Accordingly, "to exist" necessarily implies "to express one's self as an entity distinct from one's origin." Based on this existential point of view, realization of all things depends on the intense light emanating from "Absolute Existence" (*vujúd*, وجود), a reality that is independent of all things and yet bestows existence on all. In this context, the "selfness" (*inníyyat*, اِنّيّت) or "selfhood" of that source of all being is, according to Mullá Ṣadrá, the most manifest and obvious reality for those with discerning eyes (Amin, 44).

Therefore *selfishness* in this context does not have a moral meaning but rather an ontological meaning. The selfishness of Adam that causes His dismissal from paradise is, in one sense, His appearance in the physical world and His ability to demonstrate God's perfection in the physical realm.

In the Báb's writings we also encounter a discourse on the concept of "self-hood" as a virtue. In the Risálihy-i-Qaná' (رساله غناء) the Báb explains that music is not forbidden as long as it does not cause one to turn away from "the tree of existence (selfhood)" (Radmehr, *Andalíb Magazine,* 22:88:38). The "tree of selfhood" (*sh̲ajariy-i-inníyyat,* شجره اِنّیّت) in this case is a positive and spiritual essence, the Manifestation of God Himself, or the spiritual nature of man which, in itself, is the spiritual reality or essence (that is, the rational soul) that emanates from God.

Another entirely distinct but related meaning for "the tree of selfishness" is the possible allusion once again to the burning bush, the tree on Sinai through which God talked to Moses, a metaphor for the reality of the Manifestations of God. Though this tree is different than the forbidden tree of the primordial paradise, Ṭáhirih employs this allusion in her shorter poems, and much mystical and poetic literature at times implies a possible link or connection between the two, as in verse 11 of poem 5. The "forbidden tree" can thus assume a positive connotation; instead of being associated with disobedience and sin, it can become a source for the reflection of the attributes and perfections of God. Part III of the poem can also be divided into various sections in terms of its content.

SECTION 1: FREE WILL AND THE PROCESS OF CREATION (LINES 115–36)

This section addresses two complex issues—the transcendence of the Absolute and the operation of free will in the world of existence, two critical questions regarding philosophical and ontological perspectives that underlie Ṭáhirih's longer and more discursive poems. For example, Ṭáhirih considers how existence could be created by an absolutely transcendent God, Who, by definition, is completely self-sufficient and totally independent of His creation. She also discusses how human beings could be created through a binding command of the Creator and simultaneously possess (or be granted) free will.

Ṭáhirih's discourse is based on the Qur'án, on some ḥadíth̲, and on interpretations of these by Siyyid Káẓim and the Báb. These texts define the process of creation taking place in various stages (causally, not chronologically, since the metaphysical realm is timeless), dealing with the subtle question of the relationship between a transcendent reality of God and the contingent world of creation. This relationship occurs through the intermediary element of Will, explained in a rather complex system of terms describing various aspects of Will in an Islamic ḥadíth̲ and in the references to it in Siyyid Káẓim's and the Báb's writings. This ḥadíth̲, attributed to the seventh Sh̲í'ih Imám (Imám Ja'far Ṣádiq), defines seven stages for the process of creation, the first three being Will, (*mashíyyat*, مشيّة), Determination (*irádih*, اراده), and Measure (*qadar*, قَدَر). In the commentary on the Súra of Baqarah, the Báb designates Adam as the first stage or "Will," and Eve, the second stage or "Determination," an entity being receptive to the "Will" (*Asráru'l-Áthár*, 1:11).

In this section of poem 7, Ṭáhirih provides the same interpretation of Adam and Eve symbols. According to Ṭáhirih, God's own Essence is first manifested as "the one with a free will" (line 122) in accordance with the Báb's designation of the First Adam as the "Will" (*mashíyyat*, مشيّة). Following this all things were created according to their own will and their acceptance of their own creation (lines 124–25). The first stage of creation, the "Will," is the first being created with free will and is likened unto a husband, or to a beautiful, admirable, worthy, and beloved Lord. The wife in this analogy thus represents the recipient of that Will, or the one who accepts, admires, and serves her husband with complete obedience in the second stage of creation, referred to as determination (*irádah*, اراده). In this condition, she becomes the source or mother of all particles of existence (lines 126–29).

In line 130 Ṭáhirih talks about the third stage of creation, (*qadar*, قدر) "measure," also making a reference to the condition of "the right good state" mentioned in Qur'án 82:6–8: "O man, what beguiles thee from thy Lord, the Gracious? Who created thee, then made thee complete, then made thee in a right good state. Into whatever form He pleases he moulds thee." The four-stage process described in the above passage with four phrases—"created thee" (خَلَقَكَ), "made thee complete" (فسواك), made thee in "the right good state" (فَعَدَلَكَ), and then "moulds thee" (رَكَّبَكَ")—has been interpreted by Siyyid Káẓim as the four stages of creation that take place before a thing can become manifest in its fifth or final stage (*ẓuhúr*, ظهور) (Siyyid Káẓim-i-Rashtí, 109). He equates the third stage of this Qur'ánic verse with the third stage in the hadíth mentioned before: "measure" (*qadar*, قَدَر), describing it as putting things in the appropriate state or condition (*t'díl*, تعديل) (Siyyid Káẓim-i-Rashtí, 111). A reference to this last stage is made in line 130 of the poem as "conditions of moderation" (*sh'n-i-i'tadal*, شأن اعتدل). Thus in this line, the first Adam is the Primal Point from which all created things emanated or issued forth.

In the rest of the verses of this section (lines 130–36), Ṭáhirih describes the mystery of selfishness (*anáníyyat*) of the Point (or of Adam, Who represents the Point), a condition that causes His separation from the Divine, His descent from paradise, followed by His redemption through God's grace.

The terms "selfishness" (*anníyyat,* انيّت) and "face-to-face" (*rúb-i-rú,* روبرو) are key to understanding Ṭáhirih's discourse in this context. The term "face-to-face" in line 131 seems to have a negative connotation in that by seeing Himself face-to-face and in conversation with God, Adam's selfishness (*anníyyat,* انيت) is manifested. But the very opposite effect occurs earlier in the poem. In lines 126–39, Ṭáhirih describes how Eve, the Mother of all existence, found herself face-to-face with her Lord, and as a result of that transformative encounter, manifested the exalted stations of servitude and obedience. Similarly, in line 137, Ṭáhirih implores the reader likewise to come "face-to-face"—"face-to-face" here being likewise a noble and praiseworthy condition.

By using the term "face-to-face," Ṭáhirih seems to be making a delicate philosophical point on the subject of free will versus determinism. One's free will assumes meaning only when one is faced with another source of authority and command. Only in facing that authority does one become free to decide whether to obey or to oppose that authority.

In such a moment of choice one truly exercises one's distinct identity and freedom. Where Eve, as the "mother of existence," exercises complete obedience to her Lord, Adam's expression of "self" as an independent entity results in separation, thereby distinguishing Him from God. That is, He was originally more or less identical with His Lord—the condition of "He is I" as noted in verse 133 of the poem. However, after He identifies Himself as a distinct entity and comes "face-to-face" in conversation with God, His selfishness is manifested, and He descends to the station of "He is He and I am I" (a reference to the ḥadí<u>th</u> in which Muḥammad says: "*I am He, Himself, and He is I, Myself, except that I am that I am, and He is that He is,*" quoted in *Gems of Divine Mysteries,* 30). Adam's selfishness is thus demonstrated by His desire to make manifest God's perfections by His (Adam's) own actions (*fi'ál'iyyát,* فعاليات).

Adam's descent, however, is followed by the redemption that takes place through the aid and intervention of God. Adam's personal doings, His self-attained perfections, and all expressions of His identity will be burned away, and His return to paradise will be made possible by the aid of the Beloved (lines 134–36).

SECTION 2: THE ROOT-TREE AND THE MANIFESTATION OF ADAMIC QUALITIES (137–48)

In this section Ṭáhirih repeats the story of Adam and talks about His desire for the root-tree. This time, however, Ṭáhirih is referring to Adam as the first

Manifestation of God in the Adamic Cycle, though her discussion is equally appropriate as an allusion to any Manifestation of God in the Adamic Cycle.

The root-tree, the mystery of God's free Will, proclaims its authority saying that it is the executor of God's Will, actions, and commands. Adam, upon hearing God's voice from the root-tree, desires to partake of the fruit of the tree—the fruit symbolizing the Creator's wisdom and power—and thereby manifest God's attributes and perfections. However, like Moses, Adam finds the intensity and brilliance of the fire emblazoned in the tree unbearable to behold. He then finds Himself thrown into remoteness and far from that exalted station.

Adam's desire and His subsequent expulsion and descent are therefore repeated in the sense that prior to the Day of God—the time of the maturity of humankind—it is premature and presumptuous for one to desire the full manifestation of God's glory.

SECTION 3: ADAM'S DESIRE, ONCE AGAIN (149–57)

In this section Ṭáhirih describes how the same qualities and conditions of the First Adam have appeared in this new dispensation. One can observe Adam's face in the "mirrors." As we noted earlier, "mirrors" refers primarily to the early heroic believers of the Bábí Faith, but generically it can refer to the whole of existence, which is a mirror or reflection of spiritual reality. 'Abdu'l-Bahá notes: ". . . the Kingdom is the real world, and this nether place is only its shadow stretching out. A shadow hath no life of its own; its existence is only a fantasy, and nothing more; it is but images reflected in water, and seeming as pictures to the eye" (*Selections from the Writings of 'Abdu'l-Bahá,* no. 150.2).

Seeing Adam's face in the mirrors implies that the Báb's revelation reflects the First Adam or the Will of God—that is, the reality of the First Adam, Who appears from time to time to educate humanity, has appeared again. This time, however, Adam does not desire to partake of the root-tree. Rather, His whole existence is branched from the root-tree. In this sense, He has effectively become the tree that proclaims I am God (that is, a Manifestation of God).

Adam's act of selfishness that took place at the outset of creation can be seen today in the Mirror of the Báb Himself, Who is manifesting Adam's selfishness *(anáníyyat,* انانيّت). Ṭáhirih then describes what this selfishness is. She addresses the problem of the identity and the station of the Manifestations of God. The question she is addressing is a long-standing one: Is Jesus the same as God or different—is Jesus the same "essence" as God, as the literalist interpretation of the Christian Trinitarian doctrine asserts? Naturally this question is extremely relevant to the ontology of all Manifestations of God.

Ṭáhirih's answer is that in one sense the Manifestations are God, but at the same time They are not God. She responds to the matter in the poetic language of line 153: "The concept of *anáníyyat*[1] was manifest through Him / however, for an instant He ignored God." This passage implies that although the Manifestation of God appears as an individual, it is difficult to consider Him separate from the divine reality from which He appears, inasmuch as He is preexistent and a perfect manifestation of that reality in His spiritual attributes. And if we consider Him existing as a separate entity, this essential reality of the Manifestation of God encompasses the whole of existence since existence is sustained by and is living through His grace (line 154): "True, He [the Mirror] exists, but in the realm of existence / there exists only One; All else is mere nothingness." The uniqueness of the station of the Manifestation of God in this age is explained in the rest of the verses of this section (lines 155–57).

SECTION 4: THE MYSTERY OF ADAM'S FAILURE (LINES 158–79)

After explaining the uniqueness of the station of the most recent return of Adam, Ṭáhirih describes why Adam failed to achieve this station at the outset. Whereas the Báb manifests the attributes of the tree itself, Adam had the desire to partake of the tree through the exercise of His own will and action. That is, the concept of His desire to partake of the tree signified His wish to manifest God's attributes immediately. By His own actions He wanted to demonstrate the reality of His nature. This exercise of free will caused Him to be deprived of the stages of growth and the final maturity of mankind because a gradual and progressive revelation of God's attributes (God at work in human history) was required in order for the stage of maturity to be achieved.

In line 159 of this poem, we see the expression of the stages of *váv* and the ornaments of *nún—váv* (و) and *nún* (ن) being the letters of Arabic and Persian alphabets that create the sounds "v" and "n," respectively. The verse thus reads as follows: "Being a human[2] caused Adam to be rejected / from the stages of *váv,* from the ornaments of *nun.*"

In the writings of the Báb we encounter this same concept—"the stages[3] of váv" (*ḥudúd-i-váv,* حدود واو) (*Risáli-i-Nubuvvat-i-Khassih,* 29–30). Here the Báb

1. "Self" or "selfishness"; more appropriate here would be "self consciousness."

2. Here *Adam* signifies "human being."

3. "Stage," "limit," "boundary," "separation," and "a restrictive ordinance of the divine law" are some of the meanings of the word *ḥadd* (حدّ); its plural is *ḥudúd* (حدود).

discusses the concept of progressive revelation using the symbolism of the letter *váv,* which possesses the numeric value six according to the *abjad* system, the ancient Arabic system of allocating a numerical value to each letter in the alphabet.

By referring to Qur'án 23:12–14 (and a similar concept in 22:5), the Báb speaks of the six stages of creation of man. According to the Qur'ánic verse, the stages of formation and growth of the human body after its creation from clay (*ṭín,* طين) are: the "life-germ" or sperm (*nuṭfah,* نطفه), the clot (*'alaqah,* عَلَقه), the embryo (*muḍghah,* مُضغه), the bones (*'iẓám,* عِظام), the flesh (*laḥm,* لَحم), and the final and highest form of creation (*khalq-i-ákhar,* خلق آخر), which is the beginning of the stage of the complete human being.

According to the Báb, these six stages allude to the major religions of the Adamic Cycle, after which "the First Adam" (*Adamu'l-Avval,* آدم الأول) will appear at the beginning of the "moderation" and "equilibrium" (*i'tidál,* اعتدال) of the station of man.[4] The Báb thus explains that by means of this progressive path, each religion has been changed and perfected by the religion that followed it.

In this context Ṭáhirih's verse can be interpreted to mean that Adam's wish to partake of the tree at the beginning of creation deprived Him of the tree at its final stage of maturity. That is, Adam did not want to wait patiently for the progressive growth of the Faith of God. He assumed that because He possessed a free will and an understanding of what needed to happen, He could bring about the foreordained destiny of humankind immediately. He wanted to determine on His own the extent to which revelation could be measured out, instead of abiding by the guidance and wisdom of God. In this sense, He was ignorant or heedless of the fact that instead of partaking of the tree at the outset of creation, He needed to wait to partake of the tree when it became timely or appropriate to do so—at the time of the tree's maturity.

According to this symbolic interpretation, the tree at the stage of its maturity represents the Faith of the Báb, which appeared after the completion of the process of progressive revelation that occurred during the Adamic or Prophetic Cycle. Because of His desire to partake of the tree at the beginning of this process, Adam

4. Ṭáhirih alludes to the station of equilibrium in line 130 of poem 7, referring to the phrase "[He] proportioned thee, or made you in the right state and symmetrical" (*fa-'adalaka,* فَعَدَلَكَ, Qur'án 82:7).

(humankind) deprived Himself of the stages of progressive revelation that took place prior to the Manifestation of the Báb. In other words, humankind was collectively oblivious to the dynamic process by which human history proceeds to fruition and then to further progress.

Such an interpretation offers a useful and, in terms of contemporary religious tensions, timely observation about the failure of humankind to recognize the essential unity of the foundation of all successive religions. Humankind thus deprived itself of the six stages of progress as symbolized by the stages of *váv* or "six."

The ornaments of *nún* of which Adam similarly deprived Himself can be interpreted as the completion of the process of creation. The process of creation alludes to God's command "BE!"— a translation of the word *kun* (كُن) in Arabic. This is a process rather than a simple command because it consists of two reciprocal stages: the stage of *káf* (represented in English by the letter *b*) and the stage of *nún* (represented in English by the letter *e*), the completion of the process of becoming or bringing creation into existence. Stated another way, the process of coming into being is completed when the wish or will is carried out in action. This process is thus symbolized in English by the simple conjoining of the letter *b* with the letter *e* to complete the word of command *Be!*

While this process of creation can be seen as one act, it can also be understood to consist of two parts: the Creator's wish, desire, or will that something occur, and the actual process whereby the concept is carried out in terms of physical actions. In other words, the will exerts a transformative power by which the Holy Spirit proceeds through the intermediary of the Manifestation of God to creation itself, so that physical reality in all its infinite forms comes into being and by degrees begins to manifest divine attributes.

The completion of the process of creation—symbolized by *nún* or *e*—can thus be interpreted to be the "ornament of *nún*," of which Adam deprived Himself by wishing that the maturity of creation be realized instantly at the outset of creation, thereby circumventing this divine plan or process.

In lines 160–70, Ṭáhirih deals with the problem of free will as part of this process. Adam's awareness of Himself as a being of independent thought and action led to His desire to make His nature known through His actions (*'af 'ál-i-máhíya,* افعال ماهی). This desire to bring about change on His own caused Him to be deprived of God's assistance (*madad,* مدد). He thus ignored the fact that for His own will to be effective, it needed to be aligned with God's Will as manifested through the root-tree. Adam (humankind) needed to partake of the tree gradually and repeatedly, clearly an allusion to the successive and progressive appearances of the Manifestations of God. In lines 166–70, Ṭáhirih emphasizes the station of the tree as symbolizing perfection in and of itself, as well as perfection achieved by degrees through willful action.

In line 170, Ṭahirih refers to verses of the Qur'án (51:7–9). She seems to be offering an interpretation of these verses similar to what is known as Ibnu'l-'Arabí's interpretation of the Qur'án (Ghalib, 2:54). In this súra of the Qur'án, God swears that His promised Day of Judgment will be realized. God says, "By the heavens with its myriad paths, truly you people are in discord in what you say, but those who speak not the truth turn away from God and speak in discord." Here "the heaven full of paths" is interpreted to be the various paths of the soul. The interpreter asserts that based on their own free will, people choose different paths. These alternative paths might allude to the path of lying and corruption or might allude to the path of salvation.

In line 170, Ṭáhirih implies that to make the path of truth revered and distinguished from all other revered paths, God has created many inferior alternative paths so that the followers of truth might be distinguished from those who are deceivers: "He is unique, and any hint of similitude to Him is false! / That is why the heavens contain a multitude of paths [to His Presence]."

In lines 171–75 Ṭáhirih provides a summary of her philosophical interpretation of the creation myth—Adam's expulsion from the paradise of divine unity and His entrance into the physical realm. Adam's intention to demonstrate His wisdom caused His limitations to become manifest. He was expelled from His original divine condition and was forced to descend to earth. Therefore, He repented and shed tears. From His tears, the waters that reflect God's attributes were formed, and the limitations of the physical reality were generated. In sum, the cause of the creation of physical reality was Adam's wish to manifest God's names and attributes, and Adam's repentance and weeping are allusions to His desire for a return to the sanctity of the spiritual realm and the paradise of perfection.

So it is that the objective of all the Manifestations of God has been to educate humanity so that progressively humankind can become capable of demonstrating the attributes and perfections of God. All the Manifestations desired the redemption of humankind from the darkness of the material world and their return to that original paradisiacal and spiritual state of their souls. Therefore, according to the Qur'án, because all the Manifestations of God possessed this same desire, They all have repented and all have desired to return to the original paradisiacal purity of the spiritual world.

Adam's descent to physical reality can also be interpreted as a symbolic portrayal of the appearance of the Manifestations of God on earth, since it is through the appearance of each successive Manifestation of God that a new or rejuvenated creation is brought into being.

In lines 176–79 Ṭáhirih beseeches Bihjat to bear witness that through the revelation of the Bayán, the mystery of oneness will be manifest on earth. The purpose of the Báb's revelation is that the true nature and destiny of all things may thereby become realized. By this means, God's power will be manifest, and His acceptance of His creation, His forgiveness, and His redemption of Adam (humankind) will be complete.

SECTION 5: THE TWIN DUTIES (LINES 180–88)

In this section of the poem, Ṭáhirih urges Bihjat to manifest Adam's mysteries at "this time"—during the dispensation of the Báb. There are thus two mysteries or reciprocal responses involved in this process. The first part of this process is God's revelation of His beauty to humankind so that humankind has the opportunity to discern that beauty. The second part of this process is the subsequent response of humankind to manifest their true nature—their inherently divine, godly, or spiritual nature—in fulfillment of their purpose as emanations from God. This freely chosen process is signaled by pure deeds and sustained by determination and purpose.

Adam's "wish"—that the kingdom of heaven be rendered on earth—is thus fulfilled incrementally with the successive revelations whereby the articulation of spiritual truth is renewed, the laws of human society are updated, and humankind is refined and educated by degrees. However, while this change is ultimately carried out by human response, the change itself is not man-made. This progress results from the divine plan as it is revealed, manifested, and implemented through the successive unfolding of the laws of God with the advent of each Manifestation.

Because the new revelation signals a milestone in the completion of this process, it is indeed magnificent. Its flame is so intense that it burns away all "stations of wish" and sin. Indeed, God Himself, the Creator of the universe, is made manifest unto the whole of humankind.

The "stations of wish" (*sha'nháy-i-'umníyih,* شانهای اُمنیه) in line 187 of the poem is a reference to the Qur'ánic verse 22:52 in which God addresses Muḥammad saying: "And never did we send a messenger or a prophet before thee who, when he desired some course of action, was not tempted by Satan regarding how this desire might be fulfilled. But Alláh annuls that which Satan suggests to Them, and thus does Alláh establish His Messengers. For Alláh is Knowing and Wise."

Ṭáhirih provides an interpretation of the "desire" (*'umníyyah,* أمنيه) in this line of the poem. As we noted earlier, in Ṭáhirih's poems "Satan" and "Satanic thoughts" always symbolize the temptation to accede to the promptings of the insistent self—the temptation to utilize knowledge and power for personal gain, the classical and tragic Faustian flaw. Thus the sinful desire of the Prophets, she implies, is the same as Adam's wish for the maturation of humankind, a wish that is replaced by God's Will for each age in which a Manifestation of God appears. In this glorious age, however, the fire of revelation is so intense that all sinful (personal and individual wishes) are burnt away and seen as naught when viewed in the light of the unity of God's plan. Likewise, the wisdom of timeliness becomes clear—now the time has at long last arrived for humankind to attain the stage of maturity wherein the true nature and purpose of human creation can be made evident to all.

SECTION 6: PRAYER AND PRAISE (LINES 189–203)

In this last section (verses 189–203), Ṭáhirih first prays that Bihjat will be able to understand her discourse. She concludes the poem with an ecstatic announcement of the new dispensation, the appearance of the eternal and timeless reality of Adam, the first Manifestation of God, at this Day of the End, the Day of Resurrection, the promised day of God alluded to throughout the Qur'án and virtually all sacred scriptures of past religions.

Poem 7: Adam's Wish

1
With delight will I dip from the pure ocean[5]
  and pour a portion into Bihjat's goblet

2
So that boundless healing may come to him
  from the pure station of God the Eternal.[6]

The Signs of "Him Who Will Be Made Manifest"

3
The ages will pass by and He will appear
  with splendors that have never appeared before.

4
Unprecedented, [He will descend] from the clouds of *'Amá'*[7]
  so lucid in His reasoning as to be distinguished from [any] ordinary clamor.

5
Indeed, His very essence[8] will disclose the secrets of the Bayán,
  unveiling the secrets of the Lord of *"be and it is."*[9]

6
He will gaze on nothing else but His own essence,
  beside which all else will become as ashes, from the first to the last.

---

5. Errors in the transcription have been corrected. The word *'arf* (عرف) has been changed to *qurfi'h-'í* (غرفه ای), meaning "a handful of water."

6. In this line we have corrected an obvious error in the transcription by adding the letter *alif* to *du* (دو). Thus "two" is changed to *davá* (دوا), meaning "medicine" and "healing."

7. "Clouds pregnant with potentiality"; also "plentitude" or "portentous."

8. According to the Bahá'í texts, the two most evident proofs of the Manifestation are His person and His revealed utterance. As we have mentioned, each Manifestation perfectly manifests all the attributes of God.

9. See note 134.

7
He will reveal no word save the mention of God:
"Indeed, I am the Pure One[10] *acting in all affairs."*[11]

8
O my Bihjat, if you approach this knowledge of Him,
sanctified from the station of listening and conversing,[12]

9
you might be seated in the place of prominence,
and adornments from the Supreme Authority may descend on you.

10
Verily, listen to the ecstatic warbling
of His melodies, so plenteous and ascendant:

The Station of the "Point"

11
"I am the Creator of Adam in the world of Being;[13]
I made him appear from the dawning place of the Bayán.[14]

10. The word *Quddús* (قدّوس) or "Pure One" is a name of God in the Qur'án (59:23 and 62:1). Therefore this may be a reference to God. Or, as further allusions to early Bábí history in this poem will demonstrate, this could be an allusion to Quddús, the last "Letter of the Living," who, like Ṭáhirih, had a special station even among the other Letters of the Living.

11. "Affairs" is a translation of the word *sh͟a'n* (شأن), which could also be translated as "station" or "occasion." We have put this line in italics and quotes because (1) it is in Arabic, and (2) it seems to represent the first-person statement of the holy personage being described by Ṭáhirih. It may be an allusion to Qur'án 11:107 regarding the Day of the End in which God will be acting as He deems appropriate, separating those deserving paradise from those deserving hellfire. This same idea could also refer to the Qur'án 55:29 describing God as acting differently in each age according to the needs and capacities of the people at a given stage of human spiritual evolution (see also *Persian Bayán,* 44).

12. Common discourse or the petty concerns of the clerics and the learned, what Bahá'u'lláh alludes to as "learning current amongst men" (*Epistle to the Son of the Wolf,* 11).

13. Here the Point itself is speaking.

14. "Utterance" here is not necessarily alluding to the work of the Báb. As discussed at length by Bahá'u'lláh in the Kitáb-i-Íqán, the "utterance" of the Prophet is one of the primary proofs of His station. Likewise, in John 1:1, there is the well-known doctrinal passage "In the beginning was the Word, and the Word was with God, and the Word was God."

12
"After Him I manifested Noah
that He might make plain the burden of faith.[15]

13
"There is no Creator of existence except Me!
I will manifest whomsoever I wish!

14
"It is not for Adam to breathe a word save by Me,
since naught but Me exists in the sight of the One!

15
"Moment by moment Adam should become
more and more humble, as if He were utter nothingness![16]"

The Meaning of the Past

16
O Bihjat, hear from us the secrets of God
that you may bear witness to our utterance.[17]

17
It is at the command of God[18] that I have come
to sing for you about the past and what it means:

18
After manifesting the perfections of God,
Noah, Who was raised up by the command of Power,

15. Noah prophesied something that did not come to pass and thus tested His followers to remain faithful in spite of His ostensible fallibility.

16. This concept of "selflessness" is not to be confused with abasement or self-effacement; it is the same objective elucidated by Bahá'u'lláh in the Seven Valleys—the "True Poverty and Absolute Nothingness" that is the goal of every mystic, the concept of *faná'* (فناء).

17. By employing the editorial "we" in this shift in speakers from the voice of God to Ṭáhirih, the poetess implies the exalted station she occupies, speaking as one among the heavenly concourse and speaking with the voice of wisdom and authority. In short, she demonstrates her awareness of her own station without any tone of superiority, conveying this as a simple matter of fact.

18. *Ḥaqq* (حقّ) is "God" and also "Truth."

19
declaimed the mystery of divine Unity
and delivered the people of Unity to the shore.[19]

20
He lifted the veils of vain imaginings
and He opened the gate of the lights of learning.

21
Verily, that is the manifest Truth—
Cannot be Questioned was the nature of His station.[20]

22
Indeed, since naught is manifest save *Cannot be Questioned,*[21]
no soul can question Him Who is made manifest.[22]

23
New creations poured forth from Perfection Itself,
whereby the exalted signs of God came into being,

---

19. The "shore" here clearly alludes to the myth of Noah and the Ark, a story that Shoghi Effendi states is symbolic: "The Ark and the Flood we believe are symbolical" (from a letter dated October 28, 1949, written on behalf of the Guardian to an individual believer, *Bahá'í News,* no. 228, February 1950, 4, qtd. in *Lights of Guidance,* no. 1716). The symbolism of this story is amply explicated in what follows. The shore represents safety, and the "people of unity" are those who were faithful to Noah and did not cavil at His teachings, even when what He seemed to predict did not appear to come to pass.

20. A reference to the divine authority of the Manifestations of God, Who can abrogate the laws of the religion that precedes Them. In this poem, the passage refers specifically to Noah's authority to replace the commandments of Adam with His own commandments (see lines 12–15 of this poem).

21. An allusion to the Manifestation of God. See Qur'án 21:23: "He cannot be questioned about His acts, but they will be questioned (about theirs)."

22. While this may seem like circular logic, the statement is consistent with Bahá'í theology in its assertion that all human knowledge and progress is dependent on the revelation of truth unto human beings through the Manifestations of God. Consequently, by asserting that Noah was a Manifestation and therefore bore the emblem of *Cannot Be Questioned* or *He Doeth whatsoever He willeth,* the people should have followed whatever Noah said by virtue of His station alone, whether or not they immediately understood the rationale for His observations, exhortations, and commands.

24
each one with a strong and capable body,
[each] able to manifest[23] divine attributes.[24]

25
Each creation became worthy of withstanding calamities,
and a chosen few became perfected and complete.[25]

26
Their eyes turned towards nothing else in the entire universe
save God Himself.

The Nature of Progressive Revelation

27
That same Book[26] descended from Adam.[27]
[The Prophets] obtained it, that mighty command, from God (alone).

28
From Him Who is the Creator of *be and it is,*
there has appeared each Day something new from Their souls.[28]

29
There is no one [who can] question Him regarding *what He did*[29]
since He is exalted beyond peer or likeness.

---

23. *Iẓtihár* (اظتهار), a word derived from *ẓahara* (ظَهَر), which means "manifested." Ṭáhirih seems to have coined this term to mean "capable of being exhibited or displayed."

24. In the fullest sense of this verse, Ṭáhirih is actually responding to the Darwinian notion of natural selection published in 1859 approximately nine years after she is writing this. Instead of accepting the Darwinian concept of the deterministic forces of "natural selection," she asserts that every created thing has a distinct and prescribed destiny.

25. "Complete" in Their ability to manifest the attributes of God—that is, human beings, the only being in creation that is capable of manifesting all the attributes of God.

26. The term "Book" is used throughout the Qur'án and the Bahá'í scriptures to allude to the Word of God revealed by each Manifestation of God, whether or not it was actually recorded in written form.

27. Adam here is alluded to as the previous Manifestation Who brought a "Book" or revelation.

28. This seems to be an allusion to the concept of progressive revelation, and each "day" represents a new "day of God"—that is, a new revelation.

29. *"What He did"* (*máfa 'al,* مافَعَل) refers to Qur'án 21:23.

30
He brought Adam into existence through *fa'ál*[30]
that He might mirror forth the Beauty of (God's) countenance.

31
God (then) took Adam unto Himself that God
might bring forth (another) unique One like Adam.[31]

32
The command that [then] became manifest through (Noah)
was invested with the same majesty and utterance.[32]

33
Whensoever the command for a new creation descends,
all must needs be faithful to that which has been created![33]

34
No longer is it beneficial to follow the previous revelation:
what has passed has become the past, the command of destiny.

35
In the plain of limitation, there is no God except the One God!
Neither does He have any peer or likeness.[34]

36
O thou who heareth the songs of Truth,
verily, the Faith of God has come to you! [hearken to] what He said!

---

30. *Fá 'ál* (فَعال): "generosity," "acting," or "doing" that refers to God's creative action.

31. The Prophet Noah. Here again the ontology of the station of the Manifestation is explicated as Ṭáhirih states that when God fashions the Prophet, the Prophet is a perfect manifestation in human terms of the qualities and attributes of God. Likewise, the Manifestations of God uniformly assert that what They proclaim is naught but the Word of God conveyed through Them.

32. The perfect character and the Divine guidance.

33. This is the "judgment" or test that befalls the followers of the previous Prophet whenever a new revelation appears.

34. When the new Manifestation appears, the old laws are nullified and the Manifestation is, effectively, the only access to God for those who dwell on the plain of limitations (the world of existence or material reality). It is in this context that Christ asserts, "I am the way, the truth, and the life: no man cometh unto the Father, but by me" (John 13:6).

37
Behold those aboard[35] the Ark,[36] the chosen ones,
those Letters that are so illumined![37]

38
Except for that which descended in the form of a new revelation,
there is nothing else remarkable about them.[38]

39
Fiery sparks pour from them emblazoning:

The Chosen Ones (Mirrors) Speak

"We are Him! Naught endureth save us![39]

40
"Since He is aware of the secret of all mysteries,
there is nothing new in creation save us.

---

35. The word *rákibín* (راکبین, "those who are aboard") we take to be the word intended rather than *ráki'ín* (راکعین, "those who are prostrating"), which appears in the manuscript, though either works well poetically and semantically.

36. The ship is used both in the myth of Noah and in Bahá'u'lláh's Tablet of the Holy Mariner to symbolize the Covenant of God and those who are sheltered within it through their fidelity, reverence, and obedience.

37. Most probably this is an allusion to the Letters of the Living as well as to those who in every age are the few who initially perceive the station of the Prophet.

38. This alone distinguishes them.

39. The first to believe in every dispensation have a special recognition or status, a station sometimes alluded to with terms like "disciples," "apostles," "letters," or "mirrors." Because they are the first to believe, it is through their transformation that the power of the Manifestation of God is first unleashed and observed. In the Kitáb-i-Íqán Bahá'u'lláh cites this capacity as one of the proofs of the Prophet: "Amongst the proofs demonstrating the truth of this Revelation is this, that in every age and Dispensation, whenever the invisible Essence was revealed in the person of His Manifestation, certain souls, obscure and detached from all worldly entanglements, would seek illumination from the Sun of Prophethood and Moon of divine guidance, and would attain unto the divine Presence. For this reason, the divines of the age and those possessed of wealth, would scorn and scoff at these people" (¶246).

41
"He would not replace our station with any other
except for that which was established through the revealed verses.

42
"To them who have goaded us with antagonism,
their very actions have become their own worst punishment.

43
"For them there is no escape from what has been decreed
from the heaven of Command by the Lord of destiny.

44
"Because the Faith of God descended with illumination,
it replenished the four elements with fire![40]

45
"But we heard and have obeyed and thus
have severed ourselves from aught *except what hath descended.*

46
"Because we are aglow with the light of the Truth we have accepted,
the Ark itself has been provided for our assistance![41]

---

40. The sense here is that all creation is reinvigorated or energized, even as Bahá'u'lláh notes in a prayer on this same theme, "This is the hour when Thou hast unlocked the doors of Thy bounty before the faces of Thy creatures, and opened wide the portals of Thy tender mercy unto all the dwellers of Thine earth. I beseech Thee, by all them whose blood was shed in Thy path, who, in their yearning over Thee, rid themselves from all attachment to any of Thy creatures, and who were so carried away by the sweet savors of Thine inspiration that every single member of their bodies intoned Thy praise and vibrated to Thy remembrance, not to withhold from us the things Thou hast irrevocably ordained in this Revelation—a Revelation the potency of which hath caused every tree to cry out what the Burning Bush had aforetime proclaimed unto Moses, Who conversed with Thee, a Revelation that hath enabled every least pebble to resound again with Thy praise, as the stones glorified Thee in the days of Muḥammad, Thy Friend" (*Prayers and Meditations,* 144).

41. The "ship," "boat," or "ark" symbolizes the covenant of the Manifestation, the guidance and laws that provide a safe abode for the believers as they encounter the tumultuous waves of rejection and discord caused by those who persecute them—most frequently the followers of the previous revelation.

47
"Verily, O assemblage of liars, clearly our condition
has descended from heaven

48
"that we may gather together, may become stalwart and faithful,
so that each of us may become established in the Center.[42]

49
"O people of pride, perversity, and aversion,
verily, our Center is the Ark of the Revelation.

50
"Quickly come aboard and take your seats!
You can no longer brook any delay!"

Reflections on the Process of Revelation[43]

51
O attentive one,[44] behold all that surrounds you,
how that Great Hidden mysterious Source has come!

52
The fiery Point became aflame so that
the semblance of God surrounded it like a halo.[45]

53
By the power of that fire it reached its full stature!
No longer was there respite for patience or tranquillity!

---

42. The Manifestation is compared to a "center" that holds the rest of a system together (e.g., the Sun of the solar system, the nucleus of an atom, etc.).

43. Here Ṭáhirih discusses the process of revelation as exemplified by accounts of the past. However, she presents them from an objective point of view, as if she and Bihjat are able to perceive a panorama of history as it is occurring—the narration is thus presented in the present tense.

44. Presumably Bihjat, though obviously the listener, is also the reader.

45. We assume that there is a transcription error in the manuscript, that the word intended by *ḥálih* (حاله) is *háli* (هاله). A more literal translation of this is "The reflection of Him [the light emanating from His face] formed a halo around Him."

54
Sparks began to fly from that fiery Point!
Instantly the waters transformed into flame!

The Story of Noah

55
Behold that [same] flame burning in Noah's breast
as Noah mounts the Ark with a troop of true believers.[46]

56
Hearken to His wrathful tone!
Behold His wrathful countenance!

57
Lo, how clearly He says in the Bayán:[47]
"My Lord, leave not a single one dwelling on the earth!"[48]

The Dwellers of the Ark[49]

58
[He casts] a glance at the assemblage of liars.
Behold the shower of flames flowing from the heaven of His eyes![50]

---

46. This line and what follows is a remarkable shift in perspective whereby Ṭáhirih has Bihjat (and by implication the readers) imagine that they are viewing the scriptural story of Noah as it occurs, almost like a liturgical drama.

47. The Bayán here does not allude to the Báb's work by that same name, but rather to the revelation of the Báb or the Báb's dispensation.

48. See Qur'án 71:26.

49. Here Ṭáhirih is describing the point of view of those who occupy the Ark (i.e., who are faithful to the Covenant of the new Manifestation), which, in the case of the Báb, includes Ṭáhirih herself as she considers her condition and that of her coreligionists.

50. The word *samá'* (سماء) means "sky" (heaven), "cloud," and "rain." This should be a reference to the rain that caused Noah's flood. The word "sky" here can also refer to God's or Noah's eyes looking down at the assemblage of those who persecute the first believers; through that look, a showering fire of punishment descends on them.

59
O my God! What could it be—this fiery ecstasy
that has descended from the realm of the abode of *Qadar?*[51]

60
O Sublime Creator, all have become ablaze!
Nothing exists but the face of the Beauteous One!

61
O God, as I, too, enter the presence of cold and shivering death,
I am perplexed by those who have descended to the depths![52]

The Báb as Inheritor of the Mantle of Prophethood

62
O God of the Bayán, the reason for Your wrath
is naught but the burning Point of the Manifestation.[53]

63
Since this Point is the mystery of the renewal of creation,
nothing in creation exists except what was created by Him!

64
From Him new laws have come into existence!
From Him all the verses of light have issued forth!

65
O God, He is verily the cause of all created things!
O God, He is verily the cause of guidance for all creation!

---

51. Meaning "portion" or "measure," the word *qadar* (قَدَر) here implies the realm of Command where the First Will doles out capacity, power, and understanding to whomsoever it wishes.

52. Here Ṭáhirih is comparing those who drown in the story of Noah with those souls who inevitably reject the new Manifestation of God. In effect, she seems unable to fathom how anyone could take an action that would be so detrimental to the destiny of their own soul.

53. This verse can also be translated as: "O God of the Bayán, the reason for Your victory / is naught but the burning Point of Manifestation"—an allusion to the burning bush, as well as to the concept of the "Point" as the source from which the Prophet receives His power and station.

66
O my God, from Him emanates all assistance for the whole of creation
beyond limit and beyond measure![54]

67
Indeed, whosoever absconded with Him
stole Him but was not ignorant of You![55]

68
O God, after that Point, a respite
is no longer needed, not by virtue of any wisdom.[56]

Ṭáhirih Celebrates the Advent of "Him Whom God shall make manifest"

69
Since He is the source of conveying (Divine) assistance,
all who are separated from Him shall become destroyed!

54. This portion of the discourse parallels 'Abdu'l-Bahá's statement in *Some Answered Questions* that "the enlightenment of the world of thought comes from these centers of light and sources of mysteries. Without the bounty of the splendor and the instructions of these Holy Beings the world of souls and thoughts would be opaque darkness. Without the irrefutable teachings of those sources of mysteries the human world would become the pasture of animal appetites and qualities, the existence of everything would be unreal, and there would be no true life" (162–63).

55. There is an error in transcription that makes the verse incomprehensible. We have compared this manuscript with another version and made our best guess at its meaning. Everything Ṭáhirih has observed thus far in this section seems intended to apply to what occurs with the advent of each new revelation; she now shifts to the specific events surrounding the advent of the Báb and the imminent advent of Bahá'u'lláh. Here she seems to allude to the body of the Báb. After His execution in 1850, officials left the body of the Báb beside a moat so that it might be desecrated and devoured by scavengers, but at night the Bábís secretly absconded with the remains and kept them in hiding (they were eventually entombed on Mt. Carmel in 1906). Ṭáhirih may be alluding to this event even as in the next couplet she seems to allude to the imminent appearance of Bahá'u'lláh.

56. The Báb foretold that the next Manifestation ("Him Whom God shall make manifest") would appear in the year nine (i.e., 1844 + 9 = 1853). Ṭáhirih was executed in 1852.

70
O my Bihjat, let your (voice) roar forth
that the ocean of manifestation may engulf you like a thrashing sea![57]

71
Dare not ignore it, even for a moment,
so that all your deeds may become manifest to us![58]

72
Join with us in chanting the verses of God, O friend,
so that you neglect not your share of this bounty!

73
Sing about the attributes of the beloved of God
who truly attained *There is no God save God!*[59]

74
Pour out into the world that pure drink[60]
from the melodious verses of manifest light

75
so that you may establish yourself in your proper place,
and the Ark of God may become your eternal abode.

57. This is a charming line in which Ṭáhirih admonishes Bihjat to accept Bahá'u'lláh with enthusiasm and joy, even as he might jump into the water at the seaside. The water in this case is not a negative image of tumult, trials, and affliction; instead it is the abundant "ocean" of Bahá'u'lláh's revelation, an image Bahá'u'lláh employs with the command: "Immerse yourselves in the ocean of My words, that ye may unravel its secrets, and discover all the pearls of wisdom that lie hid in its depths" (Kitáb-i-Aqdas, ¶182).

58. While not the first allusion to Ṭáhirih as having a special station, this pronoun seems to make it clear that Ṭáhirih recognizes her own authority in what she says and does.

59. A state of ecstasy and annihilation (*faná*) in which the believers exist solely in their love of God.

60. See Qur'án 76:21.

76
Verily, heed your duty with esteem and splendor!
Yet, be silent, even before the pebbles and mud.[61]

77
Thus concealed, you will be the concealer of the Concealed
until that time when He casts aside the veil from His face.[62]

78
The glorious tidings will descend to you from the West,[63]
and in an instant He will scatter all the clouds of darkness.

79
Thereafter He will draw you into the Presence of God,
without any of the limitations of the stations of the past.[64]

---

61. An idiomatic expression meaning "to hold one's tongue even when no one else is around." It seems to be advice to Bihjat that he should not disclose the advent of "Him Whom God shall make manifest" until Bahá'u'lláh reveals it Himself.

62. Throughout these passages Ṭáhirih is alluding to the fact that soon Bahá'u'lláh will reveal Himself, that the interval between the appearance of the Báb and Bahá'u'lláh is drawing nigh, but that those (like Ṭáhirih) who already know Bahá'u'lláh's station must keep that knowledge concealed until it is timely to reveal what they know.

63. The "West side" can be a reference to Qur'án 28:44, where God talks to Moses from the West side of Mt. Paran. Ṣúfís have interpreted "west" as the physical aspect of the human reality, as the body within which the divine reality is concealed (Nourabsh, 2:288.) Mystics have also interpreted the self of Moses as the West side where the tree appeared to Him. By "West side" Ṭáhirih might mean the appearance of the divine reality through the Manifestation of God to humanity. Also, Bahá'u'lláh finally revealed Himself openly to the Bábís after His exile west of Persia in Ba<u>gh</u>dád in 1863, then to the rest of the world even further west from the city of Adrianople beginning in 1864.

64. Bahá'u'lláh discusses in the Kitáb-i-Íqán that "entering the presence of God" means entering the presence of the Manifestation by following His guidance. Likewise, while all the Manifestations are capable of revealing the attributes of God perfectly, the revelation of Bahá'u'lláh represents the maturation of humankind when the entire planet will become aware of this divine process.

Ṭáhirih Returns to Her Theme

80
Again I return with you to discuss the Bayán.[65]
In this very time in which there appear allusions to what transpired in the past.[66]

81
Like Noah! He appeared upright through His command!
[The Báb] has now appeared in the selfsame station of perfection.[67]

82
The same Lordly power has appeared again,
as has His command: *My Lord, leave not any unbeliever!*[68]

83
The chosen people of the Ark have descended from Him,
detached from names and idle speculation.[69]

84
The faithful beheld Him manifest and peerless
in spite of what the liars tried to steal from them.

85
Praised be God that continuously they became ever more inspired!
Even on earth have they become beneficent and perfect guides.[70]

---

65. The Báb's dispensation.

66. The Bayán is replete with allusions to this process of history repeating itself.

67. See Qur'án 11:112: "Therefore stand firm (in the straight Path) as thou art commanded . . ."

68. See Qur'án 71:26, where Noah prays that God destroy all who dwell on earth. This also may allude to Bahá'u'lláh's prophecies revealed after the kings and rulers rejected His admonitions to disarm and bring about universal peace. Baháu'lláh revealed that this peace would still come, but only after dire upheavals such as the world has never known, though one might question that Ṭáhirih could foreknow such a process would occur after her execution.

69. "Names" represents the "kingdom of names" or the physical world of distinction, as opposed to the spiritual world of Oneness. The "idle chatter" most likely alludes to the vain imaginings of the learned and the clerics.

70. *Muṭrib* (مطرب): "singer" or "musician." This translates as "a perfect guide" in Ṣúfí terminology (Dehkhoda), and as "the one who enlightens" (Nurbakhsh, 1–131).

86
From them, their (spiritual) descendants appeared among men,
progressed, and achieved the degree of perfection.

87
These riders charged out from the house of annihilation[71]
and approached God with the glory of the light of Bahá![72]

88
For the purification of those descendants, God's command,[73]
the same subduing verses,[74] descended into His hand.

89
With dignity,[75] but without fear or dread,
and without pity did He cast dreadful conditions (throughout the world)

90
so that after His manifestation of the *fiṭríyyih*[76] countenance,
He manifested the mystery of Noah's (will).

---

71. "Nothingness"—the material world. These are the martyrs who sacrificed their lives.

72. All this narration now begins to allude to the purity, power, and courage of the early believers, particularly to those at the battle of Fort Shaykh Ṭabarsí from October 1848 until May 1849.

73. *Sunnat* (سنت): "God's command"; also "a traditional and unchanging rule."

74. A reference to Qur'án 71:26: "My Lord, leave not any dwellers on earth."

75. In the tradition of Noah, the Báb was fearless in His appearance before those arrayed against Him. At His examination in Tabríz He proclaimed unabashed, "I am, I am, I am the Promised One" (quoted in Shoghi Effendi, *God Passes By*, 21).

76. *Fiṭríyyih* (فطريّه): "original nature." This refers to the manifestation of God's creative power, as was accomplished with Abraham, Who turned His face toward the Creator (Qur'án 6:79).

91
The spark that emanated from the point in Noah's breast[77]
opened its lips proclaiming, *"Indeed it is He!"*[78]

92
God made manifest Him Who descended
in the strong *Ka'bih*[79] among the fortified nations.

93
With steadfastness He stood up (to proclaim):
"Indeed I am the barr-i-hám,[80] *the desert of deserts!"*[81]

94
From the stations of the Bayán He manifested
the secret of the Ancient, the Beloved, the Placeless,

---

77. "Breast" is our translation of the word *ṣudúr* (صدور), the plural for *ṣadr* (صدر) meaning "breast." Since Noah is a single person, use of a plural word by Ṭáhirih seems erroneous. However, Ṭáhirih might be alluding to the unity of the Manifestations of God and to the Qur'ánic verses that she has referred to previously (29:48–49). In these verses, the Qur'án teaches that what is revealed by the Manifestations of God is not acquired knowledge: "Nay, it is a clear message in the hearts (*ṣudúr*) of those who are granted knowledge."

78. In this verse and in verses 54–55 we see that the Point sparks and glows in the heart (*ṣadr*) of Noah. Mystics interpret the burning bush through which God spoke to Moses to be God's voice raised in the heart of Moses.

79. The word *Ka'bih* is what we have chosen for the word *davar* (دَوار), meaning "turning around," since pilgrims circumambulate the *Ka'bih* (see Dehkhoda 23:300, *davvár*). The *Ka'bih* was renovated and built by Abraham, so verses 91–93 refer to the appearance of Abraham after Noah. *Ka'bih* can also be an allusion to the body of the Manifestation of God.

80. *Barr-i-hám* (بَرّهام) means "exciting," "sad," "important," and "desert." It is also a name for God. *Barr* pronounced differently as *birr* means "pilgrimage," "obedience," and "generosity." All these words have been in some way associated with Abraham. *Barr-i-hám* could be a play on words, alluding to *Ibráhím* (Abraham), indicating the high station of the Manifestation of God—that is, Abraham was titled the intimate "Friend" of God (*Khalílu'lláh*, خليل الله). See the following footnote. Also refer to poem 5, verse 26.

81. The desert in Rúmí's poems refers to the Word of Command, the spiritual realm beyond our understanding that is the cause and foundation of the material world (see Gowharín 2:186 and 6:143 under *bíyábán* 'بيا بان' and *ṣaḥrá* 'صحرا').

95
saying that the Point exists because of Its Absolute Existence
and It will make manifest whomsoever He wishes.[82]

96
At times He will make Himself manifest in mere specks of dust,
at other times through the ocean and its waves.[83]

97
When the waters become tranquil,
He may arise with a robe of fire.[84]

98
At that time, when you gaze upon Him,
your destiny and capacity are bestowed on you from Sinai.[85]

99
He manifests whomsoever He wants to manifest,
not One whom you might desire from the past.[86]

100
Thus does He cause the Most Great Spirit to appear in human form:
Indeed, I am the harbinger of the mystery of all created things.[87]

---

82. This is one of the most profound and illuminating statements Ṭáhirih makes about the ontology of the Manifestations and the process by which the Primal Will becomes known and actuated through the Prophets. Here, the "Point" seems to be neither the essence of God *per se* (though it represents the will of God) nor the Manifestation, but the "point" or "source" of intersection between the Primal Will or Wish of God, and the transmittal of that wish into knowable concepts in the soul and then into the words of the Prophet.

83. Manifesting His power through dust and water may refer to the revelations of Adam and Noah. The ocean and its tumult often symbolize, both in Ṭáhirih's verse and in Bahá'í scripture, the turmoil, strife, heedlessness, and oppression of the faithless. She also may be alluding to the successive appearances of God through Noah, Moses, and the subsequent Manifestations of God.

84. This may be an allusion to Abraham since the fire transformed into a flowering garden for Him.

85. "Sinai" is a reference to Moses.

86. The Manifestations will not appear according to your expectations.

87. In the original, "all creative acts" or "acts of creating." This line could allude to a new Manifestation and a new religion, or to the fact that God brings about creation through the intermediary of the Manifestation.

101
He will appear in [the vault] of the sky
so that the countenance with Bahá beauty might become visible:

The Báb Speaks about the Advent of Bahá'u'lláh

102
"Now the aid of the Helper no longer need assist Me.
For Me the time of being assisted has passed.[88]

103
"I came forth that He might become unconcealed!
I pour forth like luminous drops from the clouds!

104
"Indeed, I will disclose all the Hidden Treasures:
Indeed, You are the Truth! Only You endure!

105
"Even as I observe the sun cycling in the heavens proclaiming,
'Verily, am I the Truth shining through the clouds.'"[89]

Ṭáhirih Praises the Advent of Bahá'u'lláh

106
The Splendor of the One True God shone to its limit:
to the limit of all that is limited! He Himself is not limited!

107
Let us sweep aside all the trivialities of this world!
One with the station of Muḥammad has become manifest!

88. When the Manifestation assumes His full power, He is the channel through which the power of God is conferred. In this sense, He is now the source of power.

89. The term "clouds" is explicated at length in the Kitáb-i-Íqán by Bahá'u'lláh. In general, He ascribes to this term an allusion to the obfuscation of the holy texts that has been perpetrated by the clerics and divines.

108
No one is intended by "the One" except Him,
and verily, His assistance has come to the aid of all.

109
Anyone else who came with the desire to assume that station
doubtless soon fell from favor with God.[90]

110
Since He appears in the station of Creator,[91]
No one else among humankind appears like Him.

111
His temple is the handicraft of the Ancient Lord!
His nature is the creation of the Great Living God![92]

112
His action is unaffected by ought but God:
He does what he wishes, to what He wishes, as He wishes.

113
The one who wanted to become manifest like Him
doubtlessly fell pitifully from the throne of the Bayán.[93]

---

90. As with the story of Adam, Who wished to attain the station of Muḥammad.

91. According to Bahá'í theology, God as Creator employs the Manifestation as intermediary in the process of effecting material progress.

92. While ontologically distinct from ordinary human beings, the Manifestations of God, like all of creation, are emanations from God.

93. This would seem clearly to be an allusion to Mírzá Yaḥyá, who was the "nominee" of the Báb but who, at the instigation of Siyyid Muḥammad-i-Iṣfahání, pronounced himself to be the Manifestation, "Him Whom God shall make manifest."

Ṭáhirih on the Origin and Nature of Free Will[94]

114
Lo, my Bihjat, look around you! Ponder [everything]
that you may discover manifest the face of the Sign [of God on earth].[95]

115
Ask us about the secrets of the divine mysteries
that you might attain the hidden stations of the spirit.

116
O my dear Bihjat, O light of Ṭáhirih's heart,
you who come to us with splendor and veneration,

117
Say: What was the wish of His Holiness Adam?
Let us make His hidden mysteries manifest in the world of existence.

118
Indeed, hearken to the ecstasy of my chanting
that you may discover the mystery regarding the beginning and the end.[96]

119
Know that the Venerable, Omnipotent God has endowed all with free will
and capacity according to a preordained measure.[97]

---

94. Ṭáhirih in lines 115 to 157 provides three interpretations of Adam's story. The first (lines 115–36) is the creation of the First Adam (آدم اول), which is the Will of God or the reality of the Manifestations of God. The second (lines 137–48) is the second Adam (آدم ثانی), or Adam as a distinct Manifestation of God. The third is the return of Adam in this age in the dispensation of the Bayán (lines 149–75). In each case, Adam wishes to eat from the tree of knowledge and by this "selfishness," the divine reality descends to the earth and is manifested in the locus of the limitations of physical reality. "Selfishness" in the mystical and Ṣúfí terminology is "the observance [manifestation] of the Absolute existence in the stages of sensory and logic, and since each existing thing reflects some of God's attributes, it thus demonstrates its own 'selfishness'" (Gowharin, Sharḥi Iṣṭiláhát-i-Taṣavvuf, Vol. 1–2, 78–79).

95. *Áyat* (آیت): "sign," as in *Áyatu'lláh* (آیت الله), "the Sign of God," a title used for high clergy. Here it refers to the Manifestation of God.

96. The "beginning" is a reference to the story of Adam, and the "end" is a reference to the Manifestation of God in this age.

97. This line juxtaposes *qaḍá'* (قَدَر), meaning "free will," with *qadar,* meaning "measure of things, destiny" as in (*qaḍá' va qadar,* قضاء و قدر). This is an important ontological and theo-

120
In order that He might fashion free will in this world of existence,
He made manifest in these regions One who suffers ceaseless torment.[98]

121
From the dawn of eternity, the Beloved, the Friend, the Eternal,
has endowed everyone with the power of free will.[99]

122
Since there is nothing in existence except God Himself,
God established His own essence as the first of the first free-willed ones:[100]

---

logical point. Bahá'u'lláh states, "Unto each one hath been prescribed a preordained measure, as decreed in God's mighty and guarded Tablets. All that which ye potentially possess can, however, be manifested only as a result of your own volition. Your own acts testify to this truth" (*Gleanings,* no. 77). This is a reiteration of a point made by Muḥammad in the Qur'án (54:49; 5:21; and 42:27). See also this same point discussed by 'Abdu'l-Bahá in *Some Answered Questions,* chapter 35, where *qaḍá'* and *qadar* (قضاء و قدر) are translated as "predestination."

98. This is in the precise context that Bahá'u'lláh discusses free will when He states that without the capacity to recognize the attributes of God through the Prophet and without the capacity of free will to choose whether or not to respond to that recognition, humankind could not be held accountable: "It follows, therefore, that every man hath been, and will continue to be, able of himself to appreciate the Beauty of God, the Glorified. Had he not been endowed with such a capacity, how could he be called to account for his failure?" (*Gleanings,* no. 75.1). A part of this process of search and discovery is the capacity of human beings to recognize the Prophet even though He may appear among us as an ordinary human being.

99. This concept of free will being a property possessed by all human beings is explained by the Báb in *Ṣaḥífiy-i-'Adlíyyih,* page 21. In this text, the Báb, in His explanation of the concept of free will, refers to the term *dharr* (ذرّ). "The world of *dharr* (عالم ذرّ) in Siyyid Káẓim-i-Rashti's *Uṣúl-i-'Aqayid* (pp. 56–60), refers to the beginning of creation when God asked all who will be created, prior to their creation, "Am I not your Lord?" (based on Qur'án 7:172–73). Some immediately said "yes," some said "yes" but with hesitation, and some said "no." According to Siyyid Káẓim, after their creation, people act in this world according to the decision they personally made in the world of *dharr.* In verses 121–25 of this poem, Ṭahirih makes a reference to this myth.

100. See the chapter on fire in *The Vision of Islam,* pp. 104–117, in the section titled "The Measuring Out" for a discussion on free will and predestination. Also refer to the Súra of Jinn (72) of the Qur'án. This súra was revealed when opposition to Muḥammad had reached its climax. In spite of the severe opposition to the Prophet, the djinn followed the Prophet. Here we see that man disobeys God but djinns obey Him. Man's free choice to accept or reject the message is explained in this súra (verses 11 and 14).

123
"I am the One with free will at the beginning of the beginning
for Me there is neither beginning nor end!"[101]

124
After that, each one of the specks of existence[102]
parted its lips to reveal the nature of its reality.[103]

125
Each existent thing through its own will became clothed
and appeared from the station of *"be and it is!"*[104]

101. This is the Point speaking. Also see the Persian Bayán, pages 112–14, on the meaning of "beginning," *bidá'* (بداء) as referring to God's (or the Manifestation of God's) free Will and His unquestioned authority to judge people and to accept or reject their actions.

102. "Specks" is our translation for the word *dharrát* (ذرّات), which is the plural for *dharrih* (ذرّه), meaning "a small particle." In mystical Ṣúfí terminology *dharrih* is an allusion to "the First Essence," "Tablet," "the Mother Book," "Earth," "Eve," "the womb," and "that which is the source of the universe and existed prior to Adam" (Gowharin, *Sharḥ-i-Iṣṭiláḥát-i-Taṣavvuf,* 1–19). By *dharrát* or "particles," Ṭáhirih means the source of existence of all things prior to their creation in the universe.

103. "The nature of its reality" is our translation for *má híyah* (ماهِي), meaning "what she (or it) is" (Haím, 2:792). This is an important term that is repeated in lines 164, 177, and 182 of this poem. The term is very similar to the word *máhíyyat* (ماهيت), meaning "the essence or nature of the thing itself, its value, worth, or condition." Refer to note 372 of *The Poetry of Ṭáhirih* (Hatcher and Hemmat, 2002, 197) for grammatical details of the term *má híyah.*

104. "Be and it was" (كن فكان) is a variation of "be and it is" (كن فيكون) seen in many verses of the Qur'an such as 36:82, 3:59, and 6:73. In this verse Ṭáhirih interprets these Qur'ánic verses by making a contrast between God's command of "Be and it was" and the "free will" of each and every thing regarding its own existence. Regarding the free will of each thing in its becoming created, the Báb explains in *Ṣaḥífiy-i-'Adlíyyih* (p. 21) that God is aware of the will of each thing and creates everything according to its own will. If God created anything with a station different from that which that thing has accepted, then God would not be just to that thing.

Creation Recognizes Its Own Station and Condition

126

The first form that took shape was his *umm*[105]
which came face-to-face with her Free One[106]

127

and which manifested stations of excellence, proclaiming:
"It is I, the abject one, the lowly servant!

128

"There (surely) must exist for me One Who is adored, beloved, and beauteous,
One for whom I can become a humble and submissive servant.

129

"For me, being possessed [by him] is the foundation of my existence!
Without this possession there would be no standard for comparison!"[107]

---

105. The "mother," "root," or "source." The mother symbolizes the second station in the process of creation. In these verses Ṭáhirih provides an interpretation of the Qur'án (82:6–8) "O man, what beguiles thee from thy Lord, the Gracious? Who created thee, then made thee complete, then made thee in a right good state. Into whatever form He pleases he casts thee." The process of "created thee" (*khalaqaka,* خَلَقَک), then "made thee complete" (فسَوّاکَ), then "made thee in the right good state" (*fa-'adalaka,* فعَدَلَكَ), and finally "molds thee" (*rakkabaka,* ركبك) has been interpreted by Siyyid Káẓim as the four stages of creation before a thing is manifested (*ẓuhúr,* ظهور) (Siyyid Káẓim-i-Rashtí, 109). In a similar description of the process of creation Siyyid Káẓim defines five stages: "will" (*mashyy'at,* مشّيه), "determination" (*irádih,* اراده), "measure" (*qadar,* قدر), "destiny" (*qaḍá',* قضاء) and "completion" (*imḍá',* امضاء) (Siyyid Káẓim-i-Rashtí, 111). These two processes of creation offered by Siyyid Káẓim, along with a ḥadíth, shed light on Ṭáhirih's explanation of the process of creation. The ḥadíth says, "The first Adam is the Will and that is the first mention [or] the first manifested, and his wife is determination and that is the calling [and incantation] of the first mention, . . . the tree is the tree of the knowledge of Muḥammad and his descendant, . . . and it is only for Muḥammad and his descendants and nobody except them eats from that tree by the command of God. . . . And [Imám] Ṣádiq by what he ate [from that tree] said: Indeed for us there are various conditions with God, we are in Him He and He is us, except that indeed He is He and we are us . . ." (Asr'aru-lásar, 1:11).

106. "God" or the "Point"—the "One that is self-sufficient" or "self-willed," the "One with authority" (verses 127–29).

107. Physical reality is observing that its only standard for comprehending reality and its laws (particularly the law of love) is its relationship of subservience to the Creator.

The Origin of Sin in the Process of Creation

130
From this same Point conditions of moderation,[108] of limitations, of bounds
were also brought into existence.

131
In very truth, the soul soon found itself
face-to-face[109] in conversation with its Lord.[110]

132
But in the same instant that the mystery of selfishness became a veil,
God [Himself] became concealed from him.[111]

133
He then descended from the station of *He is I*
to the condition of *indeed He, indeed I!*[112]

134
At last, the assistance of the Beloved Beauteous One
descended on him from the direction of the Celestial Abode.[113]

---

108. "Moderation": *I'tidál* (اعتدال) is a reference to the word *'adala* (عَدَلَ), meaning "balanced." Refer to Qur'án 82:7.

109. "Found himself face-to-face." "Found himself" is the translation for *díd* (دید), a Persian word meaning observed. This is a Gnostic term meaning "discerning God with one's inner eyes" (Nurbakhsh, 1:219). Ṭáhirih uses this term consistently in her three renderings of Adam's myth (philosophical, theological, and eschatological) when Adam faces God's glory (verses 131, 147, and 170 of poem 7). This causes Adam's separation from God, a shocking experience similar to what happened to Moses at Ṭúr. For an explanation of "face-to-face" (*rúb-i-rú*, روبرو) refer to the introduction to poem 7 in this volume.

110. Having been created in God's image and having realized that it is an emanation from God, the soul understands that the essence of its reality is in becoming an expression of godliness.

111. This is the theme of the Adamic myth regarding the birth of pride or of believing that the soul has a meaningful reality apart from its relationship to God when, in fact, it is an emanation from God.

112. This is a reference to the ḥadíth "*I am He, Himself, and He is I, Myself, except that I am that I am, and He is that He is.*" This ḥadíth has been quoted in many Bahá'í writings such as *Gems of Divine Mysteries,* page 30. It is a reference to the two stations of the Manifestations of God: the station of divine unity and the station of human distinction.

113. God sends the Manifestation to rescue humankind from this fallen condition.

135
This assistance burned away the veils of his actions
and cleansed the perfections of his selfishness.[114]

136
He was forgiven by Him Who descended
from that station far beyond the world of nations.

The Point as the Root-Tree Announces Its Station

137
Once more, hear from me the utterance of the wish
of the (Lote) Tree so that you, too, might come face-to-face!

138
When the mystery of free will from *the One that never perishes*
became manifest from the station of *no similitude,*

139
His station was that of the Root-Tree
purified from the misty clouds of imagination,

140
when, by order of the Creator, It began
to dawn with a shower of sparks of fire:

141
"It is I, with free will from attraction to the Powerful One!
It is His light that issues forth from the illumined Me.[115]

114. Adam's consciousness of His own self and His actions were burnt away. His meritorious actions and His desire for perfections, as well as His awareness of His self as being a different essence from His Beloved Lord, were veils that needed to be burnt away in order for Him to attain reunion with His Lord. God's assistance caused the redemption of the one who was separated from His Lord and was descended from the primordial paradise of "He is I" to the earthly domain of "I am I and He is He" (separation or distinction).

115. As the root-tree, this allegorical tale could allude to the burning bush, but clearly these words also allude to the statements of the Prophets to Whom these same attributes apply.

142
"There does not reside in Me any condition of 'otherness'!
There does not reside in Me any temptations of self or envy.

143
"I am purified from *all else* save God.
I do only those things He commands me to do."

The Significance of Adam's Appearance

144
From this summons Adam came into existence,
arose from a place in the realm of the Will of God,

145
searched and discovered Himself to be a source of *fa"álih*[116]
and perceived Himself to be conjoined with the station of unity.

146
He arose again from His place so that He would manifest
the condition of *fa'álí*[117] in the world of existence.

147
He found Himself inflamed with the fire of the light;
but then He fell far, far from that exalted station.[118]

148
This second *fa'ál*[119] was that He aspired
to attain the station of the Original Tree.

---

116. The source of *fa"álih* (*fá'il-i-fa"álih*, فاعِل فعّاله): the source of "action," "creative power," and "divine authority."

117. *Fa'álí* (فَعالي): "action," "assistance," and "creative power from the realm of the spirit."

118. The question implicit here is that if Adam was a Manifestation, how could He have failed or fallen from grace. The answer given by 'Abdu'l-Bahá is that this is an allegorical representation of the concept of progressive revelation. The full manifestation of God's glory is possible only in the Day of God. See 'Abdu'l-Bahá's interpretation of Adam's sin in *Some Answered Questions,* 120–26.

119. *Fa'ál* (فَعال): good or bad deed.

149
Verily, be attentive, O listener, how the face of Adam
became manifest with honor and glory through the Mirrors.[120]

150
From His station [in the celestial realm] He has come
to bring free will to the regions of existence.[121]

151
Yet His station is not that of manifesting the mystery of God;
nay, His existence branched from the Root-Tree itself.

152
O Bihjat, discover the mysteries of creation!
Observe Adam's action through the Mirror.[122]

153
The concept of *anáníyyat*[123] was manifest through Him;
however, for an instant He ignored God.[124]

---

120. As mentioned earlier, *Mirrors* is used in the Bábí and Bahá'í writings to refer to the stalwart early followers: "In another connection He saith: 'O Sun-like Mirrors! Look ye upon the Sun of Truth. Ye, verily, depend upon it, were ye to perceive it. Ye are all as fishes, moving in the waters of the sea, veiling yourselves therefrom, and yet asking what it is on which ye depend.' And likewise, He saith: 'I complain unto thee, O Mirror of My generosity, against all the other Mirrors. All look upon Me through their own colors'" (Bahá'u'lláh, *Epistle to the Son of the Wolf,* 160). Early believers are like mirrors in which the Sun of the Manifestation of God is reflected. This verse explains that Adam's face is manifest in the "mirrors"—that is to say, the Báb is the return of Adam.

121. If Adam's function is to represent free will in action by virtue of discerning the spiritual attributes latent in creation, this also represents a point in the evolution of humankind in which fundamental concepts of virtues as being derived from the Creator also endow humanity with the capacity to distinguish between that which is worthy of being emulated and that which is indicative of a desire for power or exaltation of self (the "Satanic"—as in the mythic tradition of Adam's desire to perceive Himself as coequal with the Creator).

122. *Mirror* is capitalized in our translation since it refers to the Báb Himself. In lines 152–57, Ṭáhirih observes how that same act of selfishness that was committed by Adam is being committed by the Manifestation of God in this age. She explains that this "selfishness" implies the desire to reveal everything all at once (as discussed in the introduction to this poem).

123. *Anáníyyat* (أنانيّت): "self" or "selfishness"; more appropriately here would be "self consciousness."

124. Since the Manifestations of God are like perfect mirrors facing the sun of the divine, they reflect God's attributes and names flawlessly. Indeed, humankind can understand God most

154
True, He [the Mirror] exists, but in the realm of existence
there exists only One; All else is mere nothingness.[125]

155
He is single, alone, sanctified from *whys* and *wherefores*
since He is the *inníyyat* of the Supreme Lord.[126]

156
His speech is naught except [the speech] of the One True God!
His reality appears in the world solely as the Eternal.

157
There is naught similar to Him in the realm of existence!
His station is unique throughout the entirety of creation.

158
Indeed, comprehend the mysteries of the Almighty, the Powerful!
He is unique, the Creator of the illumination of the world!

---

completely by coming to know these "mirrors." Furthermore, in relation to the world of creation, the Manifestations of God represent God, and it is impossible for human beings to differentiate between these perfect representations of godliness (so far as godliness can be expressed in human or physical form) and God Himself.

In these verses the term "Mirror" is a reference to the Báb as the return of Adam. Ṭáhirih is also referring to the fact that the Báb proclaimed the station of "Manifestation of Lordship" (*Bayán-i-Fársí,* 4). He also has as one of His titles "Supreme Lord" (*rabb-i-'A'lá,* ربّ اعلي), mentioned in verse 155 of this poem, a title that has been a test for those Muslims who emphasize the separation between God and God's Messengers. Refer to *Kitáb-i-Badí* by Bahá'u'lláh, pages 43–44, for the station and titles of the Báb.

125. This verse and those that follow emphasize the station of the Manifestation of God on earth, showing that compared to His existence all else is nothingness. In relation to humankind, this verse makes the extremely important point that humankind exists, but the idea of complete autonomy is illusory. All created beings (including the Manifestations) are but emanations from God and have existence only to the extent that they manifest the relationship of the created to the Creator. This principle is especially true with "free-willed ones" who are exhorted to discover this relationship and willfully acknowledge it with words and action. The temptation is to assume that one's knowledge and powers derive from the self.

126. Saying "I am; Indeed, I!"

159
Being a human[127] caused Adam to be rejected[128]
from the stages of *váv*, from the ornaments of *nún*.

160
His attention to "self" denied Him access to God's aid[129]
from the True God [Who is] without equal or peer.[130]

161
O Bihjat, Adam's reality derived solely from the Root-Tree,
from His being clothed in the robe of *Qadar*.[131]

162
Adam's wish entered His imagination, believing
that He could be the One with free will, the Almighty, the Doer.

163
From such power as His, from the heaven of *that which hath dawned,*
God's changeless laws entered the seven heavens.[132]

127. Here the appellation *Adam* stands for "human being."

128. *Adamíyyat* (آدميّت): literally "being Adam," but it means existing as a human being since Adam here represents humankind.

129. *Madad* (مدد).

130. The myth of Adam's desire for the powers of divinity, the hubris depicted in Genesis.

131. "Measure" or "degree" here refers to the fact that all humankind, as well as the Manifestations, operates under the law of *qadar* (قدر) whereby God ordains the extent of one's capacity and subsequently mandates each one to manifest divine attributes. Adam's sole reality was the extent to which He manifested that which was portioned out to Him, and through Him, by God. It might also allude to *qadar* as the "limit" manifested by each Manifestation as the *Sadratu'l-Muntahá* (سدرةالمنتهي), the "Tree beyond which there is no passing," a "symbol of the Manifestation of God" (Momen, *Basic Bahá'í Dictionary,* 200). *Qadar* (قدر) also means "free will," and with that in mind this verse and the next would seem to refer to the fact that by being clothed with the robe of free will, Adam imagined that He could be the One with [absolute] free will, the Almighty, the Doer.

132. The ancient notion of the Ptolemaic universe, here symbolizing creation as a whole. This verse can also be read as "Indeed, at once from the heaven of *that which has dawned* / God's changeless laws should enter the seven heavens." Adam wished a sudden and instantaneous achievement of the growth that needed to take place gradually through the successive stages of progressive revelation brought by each new Manifestation of God. This process is alluded to in verse 166: "acquiring from the tree, ecstasy upon ecstasy."

164
Indeed, the Essence of the Supreme Being is in bringing about:
"There should originate from Me the acts of *what it is!*[133]

165
But Adam was ignorant of the process for achievement—
that one should attain achievement from the seed,[134]

166
that His free will comes to Him solely through His acquiring [it]
from the Tree with ecstasy upon ecstasy.

167
Since the Tree itself is the source of all action,
it is both the created and creator.[135]

168
For Him there is neither defect nor a flaw, even as minuscule as a speck!
He assumes the form of a human temple in the station of utmost purity.[136]

169
His actions are nothing less than the actions of God!
He becomes manifest without the intermediary of the spoken word.[137]

170
He is unique, and any hint of similitude to Him is false!
That is why the heavens *contain a multitude of paths* [to His Presence.]

---

133. *Máhíyah* (ماهِيَ).

134. Seed (*faṭrá*, فطرا) is very similar to the word *fiṭrat* (فطرة) meaning original nature. Hence, one's "true nature" as fashioned by God's will is power that is measured out (*qadar*) or allotted to one.

135. *Faṭṭárih* (فطّاره): the source of one's nature or essence, one's divine origin as an emanation from God.

136. Here Ṭáhirih asserts the principle of the inherent nature of the Most Great Infallibility. See 'Abdu'l-Bahá, *Some Answered Questions*, 171.

137. This most probably alludes to the capacity of the Manifestation to translate flawlessly God's Will into human language, insofar as such a process is possible, given the limitations of language to express the ineffable.

171
Indeed, the truth was instigated by Adam from rays
[emitted] from the face of the *fa'ál*[138] of the new creation.[139]

172
Adam arose from His place to bring forth the station of the Knower![140]
From that illimitable light shone forth the concept of *"Ḥadd."*[141]

173
With the dawning of the Bayán,[142] He observed from His station
mere nothingness become manifest.

174
Sobbing in remorse,[143] He became wondrously reborn
so that heavenly streams poured forth from Him.

---

138. *Fa"ál* (فعّال): "doer," a "very active agent," an attribute of God in Qur'án: 11:107 and 85:16, or "creator."

139. This passage refers both to the mythological allusion of Adam as the beginning of creation and to the fact that with the appearance of each new Manifestation, all things are made new.

140. "Knower," "wise," or "aware" (*khabír*), a word used in an abstruse Qur'ánic verse (25:59) that has been the source of much speculation. Relying on various grammatical rules, interpreters have understood this verse in different ways. This section of Súra 25 is about the creation of the universe. One rendering of verse 60 is ". . . who in six days created the heaven and the earth, and whatever is between them, then mounted his throne: the God of Mercy! Ask now of the wise concerning Him" (Rodwell, 229). The "wise" has been interpreted to mean God, Muḥammad, or the angel Gabriel. By mentioning this word in the poem, Ṭáhirih seems to imply her own interpretation of this phrase. Adam was the reality of Muḥammad as the Manifestation of God. This reality, which was the primordial "acting agent" for the creation of the universe, arose to manifest action and knowledge and, through that action, the world of limitations was created. This act of manifesting knowledge and action by Adam has taken place again at this age through the revelation of the Báb. Refer to *Tarjimihy-i-Tafsír'ul-Mízán* 15:321–22 for various interpretations of this verse of the Qur'án.

141. The "limit" necessarily pertains to all revelations—that humankind can understand and utilize only a certain amount of new information in a single age or dispensation.

142. Possibly Adam foresaw how in the future the Báb would, through the revelation of the Bayán, manifest total selflessness—as opposed to the temptation to exalt the self as exemplified in the Adamic myth.

143. The repentance of Adam and His shedding of tears is symbolic of aligning one's will with the Will of God and wishing what God wishes. We see a reference to Adam's weeping in the Báb's writings (see the *Commentary on the Súra of the Cow*, pp. 34 and 118). Adam's repentance is accepted by God through the intervention of Fáṭimih, and Adam ascends to heaven. By Adam's weeping is meant that the Manifestations of God submit to God's Will in accepting the limitations They take on when They agree to become manifest as a physical persona.

175
As these reflecting waters formed,
  the limit of all limitations was manifested by ancient waters.[144]

Conclusion

176
O My God, O my Beloved, be my witness!
  My Bihjat has become my witness now

177
that from You descended all that came forth
  in order to make known the true nature of Causality

178
so that the mystery of Oneness might become manifest:
  He is One; there is no station that befits Him.

---

144. Metaphors of "reflection" and "water" have been used by the Islamic philosophers and mystics to describe the relationship between God and the world, a poetic device derived from their interpretation of various verses of the Qur'án.

According to some interpretations of the Qur'án, water can refer to all of existence. Qur'án 22:5 says, "and thou seest the earth barren, but when We send down thereon water, it stirs and swells and brings forth beautiful (growth) of every kind." And 11:7 says, "And He it is Who created the heavens and the earth in six days (periods); and His throne of power is ever on water." Ṣúfís generally consider all existing things in the universe as the waves of a great ocean, an analogy that has been rejected in the Bábí and Bahá'í texts, since it implies that the existing things are each a portion of, or a part of God (refer to Núrbakhsh 2–219 for the Ṣúfí interpretations). Although this particular analogy of waves of the ocean has been rejected, the metaphor of the ocean has been used in the Báb's writings to symbolize existence. In the Báb's *Commentary on the Súra of the Cow* (p. 122) we come across "the depth of the ocean of existence and the middle of the sea of existence," (*lujjiy-i-imkán va ṭmṭám-i-yam-i-imkán,* لجّه امکان وطمطام یم امکان). Also pages 91–92 refer to "the sea of Unity" (*yamu'l-váhidíyyah,* یم الواحدیه) and p. 33 refers to "the black sea of the world" (*ṭmṭám-i-asvad-i-dunyá,* طمطام اسود دنیا).

Similarly the term "reflection" (shadow) symbolizes God's grace that is the source of existence (Sajjadi 1979, Farhange Estelahati Falsafi Mula Sadra). The Qur'ánic verse 25:45, "Seest thou not how thy Lord extends the shade?" has been interpreted in this way. "The First Shadow," (*ẓill-i-avval,* ظلّ اول) is a reference to "the First Mind," and "the outstretched shadow" (*ẓill-i-mamdúd,* ظلّ ممدود), is the "Perfect Man" (Núrbakhsh, 2–218). The word "reflection" (*'aks,* عکس) adopted by Ṭahirih in verse 175 is used by Bahá'u'lláh: "and all that exists in the worlds of Dominion and Kingdom, is but a reflection and apparition of the hidden worlds of God . . . (provisional translation from Áyát-i-Iláhí, 1:119).

179
Your power became manifest through Him:
Indeed, You are God; Indeed you are the Forgiver.[145]

180
O Bihjat, comprehend these words of mine, these matchless verities
that I have poured forth into the delicate cup of thy search!

181
Lo, make the hidden mysteries of Adam—the first and the second—
manifest in the world through your elucidation of the Bayán.

182
The first truth is the dawning of the Divine Beauty.
The second [truth] is to manifest your true nature[146] through actions.[147]

183
According to the tradition,[148] the second truth is called the "Wish"[149]
so that seekers can discern this truth.

184
The first truth ("Be!") is the First Will of the Creator;
the second ("It is!") is the manifestation of His wish in the created universe.[150]

---

145. Ṭáhirih may here be alluding to the transformation of Adam from selfishness to selflessness, thereby demonstrating the infinite forgiveness of God.

146. *Máhiyah* (ماهِي): "what it is," meaning "the nature of a thing."

147. *Fi'ál* (فِعال): "actions."

148. *Khabar* (خبر): translated as "tradition."

149. The desire to manifest God's perfections through one's actions.

150. As mentioned before, these two commands—to acquire knowledge of the divine nature of creation and then to put that knowledge in some form of creative action—are really two aspects of a single command, as Bahá'u'lláh sets forth in the opening passage of the Kitáb-i-Aqdas. As explained previously, these two wishes of Adam allude to the knitting together of spiritual insight with physical action as revealed by each successive Prophet.

185
Indeed, O my Bihjat, discover the mystery of the Forgiver
that you might ascend to the summit of enlightenment.[151]

186
The "Wish" became the foundation for the renewal of the law:[152]
nothing but His laws and ordinances became manifest.

187
The stations of the "Wish" are poured out with fire,[153]
and from this fire issue forth sparks of light.

188
The Oneness became manifest in the nature of creation itself.
Indeed, you yourself manifest God in your own nature.

Ṭáhirih's Prayer for Bihjat

189
O Lord, assist Bihjat at this very moment
that he might discover the mystery of the true path.

190
May not one letter of this Sinai leaf[154]
remain concealed or hidden from his knowledge.

191
O God, verily you are my witness that with your help and majesty,
I have delivered to him the secret of the signs of *Qadar.*

---

151. As Adam is forgiven and subsequently submissive before God, so must we all be.

152. The law (*ḥadíd,* حديد): the laws or limits imposed by God through the Manifestation.

153. The "station of wishes" is a reference to Qur'án 22:52: "Never did We send a Messenger or a prophet before you, but, when he framed a desire, Satan threw some (vanity) into his desire: but Alláh will cancel anything (vain) that Satan throws in, and Alláh will confirm (and establish) His Signs: for Alláh is full of knowledge and Wisdom."

154. An allusion to a leaf of the tablets revealed to Moses on Mount Sinai.

192
O God, Protect that which has appeared
  so that my own sun may return to its proper latitude.

193
May I reach the Point in its exalted height!
  May the power from the exalted realm cause me to attain reunion!

194
O God, O Generous, Eternal God,
  a leaf in the presence of *no-similitude* hath descended:

Ṭáhirih's Parting Message

195
"O Friend, You ought to manifest,
  'My days are made miserable only by those who are not of Him.'

196
"I praise You so that He may come forth from the beginning:
  His beginning descended from the cloud precisely like His ending.

197
"He came with reflections of the Eternal One.
  He made manifest the countenance of Aḥmad.

198
"Yet the learned ones remain heedless
  of the ecstatic melodies of the Holy Spirit.

199
"Verily, it is Aḥmad who has descended
  with Holy verses from the Heaven of Grandeur.

200
"He has ignited the whole world with sparks of fire,
  and He has turned humankind completely into light.

201
"O Ṭáhirih, tear away the veil from [their] midst
that the hidden mystery may become revealed.

202
"Give thanks that He, the Most Beauteous Lord on High,
did indeed shine down with such astounding adornments.

203
"Set aside all trivialities, all grieving, any affection [for aught else!]
The Promised Day has become manifest in the world!"

Poem 8: Meditation on My Death[1]

There is a remarkable narrative flow to this brief lyric that seems to portray poignantly the love of Ṭáhirih for the Báb and, by implication, the love of a true believer for the Creator. The first verse of this poem is mentioned in Nabíl's narrative *The Dawn-Breakers,* where there is an account of Ṭáhirih's correspondence with the Báb:

> It was she who, having learned of the intended departure of her sister's husband, Mírzá Muḥammad-'Alí, from Qazvín, entrusted him with a sealed letter, requesting that he deliver it to that promised One whom she said he was sure to meet in the course of his journey. "Say to Him, from me," she added, "'The effulgence of Thy face flashed forth, and the rays of Thy visage arose on high. Then speak the word, "Am I not your Lord?" and "Thou art, Thou art!" we will all reply.'"

---

1. Mohammadhoseini believes one reason for the wrong assumption that this poem is from Ṭáhirih is that she included the first verse of the poem in her letter to the Báb (350). According to Mohammadhoseini and Nuqabá'í, this poem is not from Ṭáhirih but from Ṣuḥbat-i-Lárí (1748–1835), a poet from the city of Lár, though Nuqabá'í states that Ṭáhirih was fond of reciting it. The poem is found with some variations in the collection by Ṣuḥbat-i-Lárí with the last line indicating that Ṣuḥbat is the poet. For further discussion of the authenticity of this poem, refer to Mohammadhoseini, pages 347–51. However, the manuscript used for our translation in this volume was originally transcribed in 1267 (AD 1851) of the Islamic lunar year, only seven years after the declaration of the Báb. So, if this poem is not by Ṭáhirih, the mistake in the attribution occurred soon after her passing. The version of the poem in the current manuscript is different from Afnán's version, which combines this poem with another poem; the version that appears in books by Brown, Root, and Nuqabá'í is a single piece. Also, Afnán's version has an additional couplet at the end that would be translated into something like "If you are greedy for permanence and eager for attaining / the absolute Existence of the Beloved, listen to the call."

> Mírzá Muḥammad-'Alí eventually met and recognised the Báb and conveyed to Him both the letter and the message of Ṭáhirih. The Báb forthwith declared her one of the Letters of the Living (81–82).

This poem focuses on how, by responding to the call of the advent of the new Manifestation of God, Ṭáhirih invites calamities upon herself. She foresees her own martyrdom and envisions herself dying on the battlefield and her beloved rushing to her side. She pleads for total annihilation (*faná'*) and the unity of her own heart with that of the "Friend." The call to the Beloved's feast of love is then raised by chosen angels, and Ṭáhirih ponders whether or not she will be able to attain that eternal realm.

We have titled this poem "Meditation on My Death" because Ṭáhirih clearly indicates here (as she does in many other pieces translated in our first volume of her work) the foreknowledge and imminence of her own martyrdom. As in other allusions to her death, she is fearless. Yet she is also filled with emotion as she proclaims her relentless longing to attain the eternal realm, a consuming joy and happiness that, according to several accounts by those who observed her final days and hours, accurately portray her demeanor even at the moment of her gruesome execution when a scarf was crudely stuffed down her throat by a drunken guard at the behest of her captors.

Poem 8: Meditation on My Death

1
The dawn of your face shone above the horizon;
the rays of your countenance beamed forth.

2
Why not drum out: "Am I not your Lord?"[2]
The drumming of our hearts would reply, "Verily, Thou art!"[3]

3
Contrapuntal to the time of the drumbeat of His "Am I not?"
their hearts[4] in their love did beat out "Yea, verily!"

4
They pitched their tents beside the gate of my heart,
these troops of sorrows, these armies of adversity.[5]

5
When He heard the lamentation at my death,
He went to retrieve my meager possessions,

---

2. This couplet alludes to Qur'án 7:172: "And when thy Lord brought forth their descendants from the reins of the sons of Adam and took them to witness against themselves, 'Am I not,' said He, 'your Lord?' They said, 'Yes, we witness it.' This we did, lest ye should say on the day of Resurrection, 'Truly, of this were we heedless. . . .'" There is a reference to "Am I not your Lord" and the reply of "Yes" in the *Persian Bayán,* p. 16.

3. In Iran they used to beat drums to inform people of important events and happenings. Government representatives would beat drums to gather people to read an announcement or a proclamation. Until a few decades ago, drums were beaten several times a day to inform people of sunrise and sunset. While the word *drum* does not exist in this line, the word *beat* does; therefore, the sense of the drum calling out is implicit in our use of the word "drumming."

4. Nuqabá'í has this in the first person: "I did beat" and "my heart responded."

5. The implication here is that the armies pitch their tents as a result of hearing the affirmative response of the drums to the call "Am I not?" One interesting point is that there exists in Ṭáhirih's verse a mixture of allusions to calamity and suffering so that it is often difficult to determine when the suffering is physical and truly painful or when this is an allusion to her great love and longing to attain the presence of the Beloved. To take some of these passages literally (to assume she is bemoaning her hardship as a believer) would be to contradict those accounts that describe her as always joyous and radiant, even as she approached her death.

6
Then He hurried to my side and cried for me[6]
with a loud and piercing voice.

7
How nice it would be were you to strike the summit of the Ṭúr of my heart
with the blazing fire of wonderment![7]

8
Have you not already excavated and pounded it,
leveled it and trembled it?

9
All the angelic hosts of cherubim are heard each night
hearkening to his love feast,

10
trumpeting this Divine Command:
"Hasten forth, O sorrowing friends!"

11
Truly the love of that beauteous Moon suffices me,
He who, when God called to Him "Yea, verily!"

12
became filled with laughter and delight,
calling out boldly, "Behold, I am the martyr of Karbilá!"

---

6. In the original language this line reads, "He hurried to his side and cried for him." We think the version we used for our previous publication is more accurate and have chosen to use it.

7. This couplet alludes to Ṭúr, Mt. Sinai, where Moses witnessed the burning bush. As we have noted, this allusion is employed by Ṭáhirih in a number of poems. According to scripture, Moses became unconscious from the shock of the lightning striking the mountain—hence the "wonderment" of Moses and the destruction of the mountain itself in Qur'án 7:143: "And when Moses came at our set time and his Lord spake with him, he said, 'O Lord, shew thyself to me, that I may look upon thee.' He said, 'Thou shalt not see Me; but look towards the mount, and if it abide firm in its place, then shalt thou see Me.' And when God manifested Himself to the mountain he turned it to dust! and Moses fell in a swoon."

13
You, who are but a speck[8] on the leviathan of wonderment,[9]
do you dare speak about the sea of existence itself?[10]

14
At every moment be like Ṭáhirih! Remain still and listen!
Do you hear the whale roar: "There is no God but God!"[11]

---

8. The actual word is "scale" and implies insignificance. Kháqání, for example, uses the word in the same context to connote insignificance.

9. Rúmí uses a fish to symbolize the friends of God, Gnostics, and the Prophets (Gowharin, 8:215–17).

10. In effect, how do you presume to have some concept of the totality of creation or existence?

11. In the original there is only the word *lá,* implying, "No, there is not any." The word is the beginning of the phrase "There is no beloved except God" in the Muslim call to prayer. By implication, then, to become close to God and to feel His existence, one should first renounce the world of existence and aspire to the realm of nothingness. The Báb uses five versions of this phrase, all beginning with the word *lá,* to explain the reality of death (*Persian Bayán,* 32).

Poem 9: The Choice Wine

This poem is composed of simple words—no obscure Arabic, no philosophical or Qur'ánic terms or allusions. It has a soft flowing and melodious tone.[1] The six couplets[2] capture well the spirit of Ṭáhirih—especially her wit and courage. Because it embodies the image of her confidence, daring, humor, and wit; this verse, especially when coupled with the intellectual matter of the other poems in this volume, helps portray why Ṭáhirih has become such an enduring and memorable figure in Persian culture and history.

When she closes the verse with her defiant observation that over the course of history, we will see who "wins," we tend to believe that somehow she is correct, that ultimately the transforming power of the Holy Spirit will win out over the selfish aims of those whose goal is attaining power, acquiring status, fame, or riches. Of course, the conceit or analogy of love as a battlefield is a traditional one in various cultures, but the application of this image to the history of the Bahá'í Faith takes on special significance in light of the slaughter of over twenty thousand Bábís at the very real battles at the fort Shaykh Ṭabarsí, at Nayríz, and at Zanján.

---

1. It is these qualities, perhaps, that led Dhuká'í Bayḍá'í to believe that the poem is not by Ṭáhirih. However, Martha Root includes this poem in her book, and Hádí Hasan quotes the first couplet of this poem in his small selection of Ṭáhirih's verse. Nuqabá'í includes this poem in his collection, but Afnán does not.

2. The version of the poem included in our first volume of Ṭáhirih's poems (*The Poetry of Ṭáhirih,* 137) contains an additional line that is not included in this manuscript: "Yet among the thousands held captive by the Beloved / only one has cleansed from the heart the dust of worldly desires."

Particularly powerful is her observation that the testing of those who profess love is not a game. It is very reminiscent of a statement made by Bahá'u'lláh that affirms sternly, "Think not the Cause of God to be a thing lightly taken, in which any one can gratify his whims" (quoted in Shoghi Effendi, *God Passes By,* 115).

Another worthwhile observation regards the point of view in this piece. Here the perspective is not that of Ṭáhirih revealing her own inmost feelings or reflecting on her personal situation—the sort of thing we would expect in such circumstances as these. This is a voice of authority articulating profound verities about the divine nature of human history, and this tone impels the reader to attend to her words.

Poem 9: The Choice Wine

1
What did youth bring? The young lover.
What did old age bring? The vintage wine.

2
The one brief appearance of the young lover
bereft the heart of desire for sleeping or eating;

3
The one drop of choice wine which the one who died did not sip
and from which the one who quaffed did not die is from that same vessel

4
which time's cupbearer[3] gives to you, so choice, so refined—
but to me the dregs only.[4]

5
You see, this is no game—going onto the battlefield of love
where only one in a hundred thousand has emerged victorious.[5]

---

3. The cupbearer, a very important figure in one of Ṭáhirih's longest poems, is clearly symbolic of one who conveys the revelation (the Prophet) or, more generally, one who bestows fortune—a kind of subaltern of God who bestows calamities on the loved ones of God that they might be prepared spiritually by being tested and thereby detached from earthly affections.

4. Here Ṭáhirih appears to note the irony that there seems to be no ostensible logic as to what one receives in this life. Yet she clearly implies that though she receives the "dregs," it is preparing her for something more, as the remainder of the poem makes clear.

5. Literally this reads, "has remained steadfast." This commonplace image of love as a battlefield is particularly inventive here. Usually the battlefield image is employed to represent the coy games between the lover and the beloved, but here Ṭáhirih portrays the battle as a stark testing of the believers to see if they will remain faithful in their conviction when the inevitable tests come.

6
So let the parrot recite prayers and let the claimant hurl accusations[6]—
at day's end we will see who wins the field.[7]

6. The word *parrot* is intriguing here, as is the couplet itself. The parrot has been used symbolically in Rúmí's mat͟hnaví and has been interpreted to mean "the receptive wayfarer, the pious one, etc." (see Gowharín, 6:246–7). The problem is to determine whether this is a positive or negative description. Is she contrasting the piety of the wayfarer with the pretentiousness of the false Sheik, or is she using parrot to imply a similar sort of mindless worship in which one simply "parrots" the words of others without thought or reflection? The verse works either way: "let the pious one pray and the false Sheik hurl accusations" or "let the shallow follower say his prayers and the false Sheik be pretentious." In the end the true believer (the "one out of a hundred thousand") will be the victor.

7. The actual line states, "let us see who will catch the ball in the field," but the sense is that at the end of the contest we will see who emerges victorious. The literal translation of this metaphor would not work well in English.

Poem 10: Face-to-Face

This is perhaps the most widely known of Ṭáhirih's poems. It is a melodious and lyrical expression of love for the face of the beloved, which may be understood to imply Ṭáhirih's adoration of the Báb. The scholar Dhuká'í Baydá'í believes the poem is not by Ṭáhirih, perhaps because its style is more imagistic and regular in pattern, quite unlike the majority of her verses in this volume, which are rendered in a complicated language and filled with deep philosophical and religious allusions that cannot be readily understood. A few other scholars also believe this poem is not by Ṭáhirih and instead attribute it to the Bahá'í Tá'ir of Isfahan.[1]

As noted in our first volume of Ṭáhirih's work and as we have reiterated earlier in this volume, we believe that such observation does not offer adequate evidence to question the attribution of this or any of the other poems to Ṭáhirih. It is possible that, like most capable poets, Ṭáhirih was adept at composing verse in a variety of styles, tones, and perspectives, as well as employing a variety of personae and patterns of imagery. She could have written the brief plaint in the tradition

1. This poem, with some variations, appears as the ending lines of a *mukhammas,* which is a particular type of Persian poetry with Ṣúfí connections that uses the pentameter. According to Muhít Ṭabáṭabá'í, this poem belonged to Muḥammad Ṭáhir-i-Qazvíní, though these lines are not found in all editions of his poems. According to Ṭabáṭabá'í, this poem was composed a hundred years prior to Ṭáhirih's lifetime. This information was provided by Mr. 'Azíz Ḥakímian from an article published in *Majallihy-i-Hunar Van Mardum Vijhih Námih Irán va Pakistán.* We also came across poems using some phrases that appear at the end of each couplet of this poem in Feyḍ-i-Káshání's collection (609) and in Rúmí's poems *Diván-i-Kámil-i-Shams-i-Tabrízí* (part 2, 327). Nuqabá'í makes a reference to Fáḍil Mázandarání's *Ẓuhúru'l-Ḥaqq* (volume 8) that expresses the belief that this poem is not from Ṭáhirih. Mohammadhoseini presents various references to other poets to whom the poem has been attributed but he leaves the final judgment to future researchers (364–69).

of the ecstatic lover of the Ṣúfí tradition. Certainly, as we witness in this volume, she was also capable of longer philosophical and theological meditations on the most abstruse themes that puzzled the clerics of her day and that still warrant ample attention today.

Poem 10: Face-to-Face[2]

1
If ever I should behold you face-to-face, eye-to-eye,
I would be bold to recount my heart's plaint point by point, verse by verse.

2
Like Saba[3] the east wind I have searched everywhere for your countenance
from house to house, door to door, alley to alley, from quarter to quarter.

3
Bereft of your visage, my two eyes have wept such bloody tears,
Tigris after Tigris, stream upon stream, spring after spring, brook upon brook.

4
In my desperate heart, your love is knitted to the fabric of my being,
string by string, thread by thread, warp by warp, and woof by woof.

5
Ṭáhirih has searched every layer of her heart but found only you there,
sheet by sheet, fold by fold, cover by cover, over and over again.

---

2. The version of the poem transcribed in this manuscript lacks 2 lines that are included in our first volume (*Poetry of Ṭahirih*, 102–103).

3. *Ṣabá* (صبا) is a term used often in the Bahá'í writings and a number of times in Ṭáhirih's verses to represent a wind blowing from the east to the west. It is a Ṣúfí term alluding to the divine fragrances blowing from the spiritual realm, wandering the world in search of a pure heart where they can make their home.

Poem 11: Ṭáhirih's Farewell

This poem may not be by Ṭáhirih. The couplets are continuous, something Ṭáhirih rarely does. Coming at the end of this handwritten manuscript penned by copyists who transcribed her verses not long after her death, the poem might well be a tribute by one of them to the verses of Ṭáhirih. Certainly, they must have admired her to do this work, and after having carefully and dutifully printed out her work, they were doubtless deeply stirred by the impact of her eloquent and weighty discourse. Consequently, whether or not this poem is by Ṭáhirih or for Ṭáhirih, it is a touching lyric that well befits the end of her life's journey, exhorting the reader as it does to partake of the wisdom of her words.

Poem 11: Ṭáhirih's Farewell

1
O company of friends, come ye forth from behind
the veils of glory with a hundred trifling and myriad modes.

2
Because humankind has now gladly humbled itself before God,
there remains not a speck of doubt nor a vain imagination.

3
With sinless eyes behold the spectacle in which
all the verses of God hang suspended from celestial thrones.

4
With the eyes of kindness you have cleansed away
the rust of vain imagination and the mirrors of doubts.

5
All of you (are) standing row upon row with crystal goblets in hand
filled with luminous drops from the time of your conception.

6
Whosoever has imbibed but one sip from Him
and has cleansed his eyes of all feebleness and impurities

7
will discern that the splendor of the true Beloved is plainly manifest
through the ornaments of glory and of the mystery of the inmost heart.[1]

1. The ambiguity here as to whether the "inmost heart" refers to the heart of the seeker or to the heart of the Beloved may well be intentional, though, considering Bahá'í texts, this should refer to the inner certitude or conviction the believer strives to attain.

Facsimile of Calligraphy

٧٣

دیدار و جلوهٔ محبوب حقیقی ظاهر

از طرازات بهائیه و از ستر بطون

یا اهل الله انشاءالله صحائف در اعمال فرضیه و ندبیه

خواهد مرسول گردید سعی در ترقی نمائید و قدر این

ورقات را بدانید که یوم شهادت اکبر نزدیک است

و بعد از شهادت نقطه دیگر مهلتی لاجل احدی نیست

والحمد لله رب العالمین تمام شد در یوم پنجشنبه بیستم

شهر شعبان المعظم

سنه ١٢٦٧

فانی دانی ابوالحسن تبریزی تحریر نمود فی غرة شهر شوال

سنه ١٣٤١

من الهجرة النبویة المصطفویة علی هاجرها الف الف التحیة

والثناء والبهاء والسناء

والاحترام والاکرام

۷۲

ولە شایق

باید آئید شما معشر احباب برون
از حجابات بهائیه بصد غنج و فنون
زانکه عالم بصفا آمده در صف آله
نیست قدر ذرّی از غیر ز اوهام و ظنون
بنگرید از نظر صاف بمنظر در آن
جمله آیات الهیه ز اعراش نگون
از نظرهای بلطف بربودید شما
ز تلک اوهام تفکر و مرایای ظنون
جملگی صف بصف ایستاده بکف جام بلور
از رشحات ضیائیه از حین بطون
هر که یک جرعه از او نوش نمود و بزدود
از مرایای صفائیه ز اهمار کون

۷۱

نه بازی است رفتن بمیدان عشق
که از صد هزاران یکی پا فشرد

ز طوطی دعا دعوی از مدعی
ببینیم تا گوی میدان که برد

گر بتو افتدم نظر چهره بچهره رو برو
شرح دهم غم ترا نکته بنکته مو بمو

از پی دیدن رخت همچو صبا فتاده ام
خانه بخانه در بدر کوچه بکوچه کو بکو

میرود از فراق تو خون دل از دو دیده ام
دجله بدجله یم بیم چشمه بچشمه جو بجو

مهر تو در دل حزین بافته بر قماش جان
رشته برشته نخ بنخ تار بتار پو بپو

در دل خویش طاهره گشت و ندید جز ترا
صفحه بصفحه لا بلا پرده بپرده تو بتو

۷۰

بخوان دعوی عشق او همه شب ز خیل کروبیان

زند آن صفیر مهیمنی که گروه غم زده الصلا

من و مهر آن همه خوبرو که چه زد صلای بلا براو

بنشاط و قهقهه شد فرو که انا الشهید بکربلا

تو که فلس ماهی حیرتی چه زنی ز بحر وجود دم

بنشین چو طوطی و دمبدم بشنو خروش نهنگ لا

جوانی چه آورد و پیری چه برد

بت خورد سال و می سال خورد

بت خورد سالیکه یک جلوه اش

ببرد از دل اندیشهٔ خواب و خورد

می سال خوردی که یک قطره اش

نخورد آنکه مرد و نمرد آنکه خورد

ز یک خم دهد ساقی روزگار

ترا صاف صاف و مرا دُرد دُرد

۹ء

طاهره بردار پرده از میان

تا بیابد ستر غیبی در عیان

کوی الحمد هو رب جمیل

قد تشعشع من طرازات الجلیل

یوم موعود بعالم شد عیان

در گذر از آن و این حین و حان

لمعات وجهک اشرقت وشعاع طلعتک اعتلا

زچه رو الست بربکم نزنی بزن که بلی بلی

بجواب طبل الست او زولا چو کوس بلا زدند

همه خیمه زد بدر دلم سپه غم و حشم بلا

چو شنید ناله مرک من پی ساز من شد و برک من

ومشی الیه مهرولا وبکا علیه مجلجلا

چه خوش آنکه آتش حیرتی زنیم بقله طور دل

فسکلته ودککته متدکدکا متزلزلا

۶۸

یا الهها ای کریم لم یزل

ورقه نازل بنزد لا مثل

بایدت ظاهر نمائی ای حبیب

انّ تبوء من سواه لا یطیب

حمد تو آن خوانم آید از بدآء

بدء او شد عین ختمش از عماء

امد او با جلوه های سرمدی

ظاهرا بنمود وجه احمدی

لیلیت غافل جملهٔ ارباب هوش

از تغرد های جذبای سروش

احمد است اینکه نزیل آمد نزیل

از سماء عز با آیات جلیل

عالمی را از شور پرشور کرد

ادمی را او سراسر نور کرد

٤٧

شانهای امینه دیزد بنا د

اوشرار با شرار این شـو ا ر

ظاهر امد واحدیت درعیان

انک الحق قطیر باکلیا ن

یار با دریاب بهجت داکنون

تاکه یابد ستر اعیان الفنون

حرفی از این ورقهٔ سینائیه

نایدا ورا محجب ازخا فیه

یا الها شاهدی بانصروفر

میرسانم ستر آیات قد ر

حفظ فرما یا الهم ما برز

تاکه گردد آفتاب من بعرض

باید نقطه برفع ارتفاع

آیدم وصله ز شطر امتنا ع

۶۶

بهجتا در باب اسرار حقیق

ریختم در جام تحقیق رشیق

هان بیارا اسرار آدم را عیان

اول و ثانی باشراق بیان

اول او بود اشراق جمال

ثانیش اتیان بماهی از فعال

در خبر نامیده ثانی آرزو

تا بیابد آنکه او از جستجو -

اولی باشد فطور کردگار

ثانی اظهار بدایش در مدار

هان بیاب ای بهجتم سر غفور

تا برائی بر فراز اوج نور

ارزو شد اصل تجدید جدید

لیک غیر از حد او نا ید پدید

۶۵

دید اونا بود صرف امد عیان
در مقام خود باشراق البیان
درانا به توبه آمد او بدیع
ریخت از وی آبهای بس منیع
آبهای عکسیه شد منوجد
حد محدودی عیان آمد بجد
یا الهم شاهدم باش ای اله
بهجتم آید مرا الآن گواه
اینکه از تو نازل امد ما نزل
زاجل اظهار بما هی از علل
تاکه آید ستر وحد در عیان
واحد لیس له شأن بان
قدرتت از وی بیامد در ظهور
انک الحق انک انت الغفور

۶۴

اختیار آید و داد اخذ وی
از شجر با جذبه های پی به پی
زانکه شجره فاعل فعاله است
تام هم اتمام هم فطاره است
نیست او را نقص قدر زرزر
در نهایت با صفا احد ببر
فعل او فعل خدا و نداست او
ظاهر آید بی شئون گفتگو -
واحد است و نیست مثلش جز انک
ذا جل هذا آسمان ذات الحبک
هان حقیقت بود از آدم بداع
از شعاع وجه فعال البداء
خواست از جا کاورد شأن الخبیر
حد محرودی عیان شد زو اثیر

۶۳

آدمیت کرد آدم را برون
از حدود واو از اطراف نون
نفس او حاجب شد او را از صمد
از الٰه الحق لا کفوا احد
بهجتانا بود او الا شجر
زانقماص او باظهار قدر
آرزو شد آدمی را در خیال
کین منم مختار قدار فعال
هان بآن باید بیاید در طباق
مستحق از سماء ما شراق
ذات اعلی باشد او تعالیه
بایدم افعال ماهی بانیه
لیک غافل از طریق اخذ بود
اینکه باید اخذ از فطرا نمود

۶۲

بهجتا در باب اسرار بداء

فعل آدم را نگر اندر مرآة

ها انانیت از او ظاهر شده

لیک از حق لحظهٔ غافل شده

اینکه او موجود لیکن از وجود

واحد است موجود غیرش نیست بود

واحد است عاری ز چون و هم چرا است

زانکه او انیت رب علی است

نطق او نبود مگر حق احد

شأن او ناید بعالم جز صمد

نیست او را مثل در شأن مراد

واحد آمد شأن او اندر دیار

هان بفهم اسرار جبار قدیر

واحد است او خالق نور منیر

اع

گشت خود را فاعل فعاله دید
قابل ایصال وصل و صله دید

خواست از جامرهٔ اخری بان
کاورد شان فعالی در عیان

دید او شد محترق از نار نور
اوفتاد از صدر اعلیٰ دور دور

این فعال ثانیه بد آرزو
از مقام شجرهٔ اولیٰ با و

هان نگر ای سامع با عز و فر
از مرایا وجه آدم جلوه گر

امدہ او تا که ارد اخیا د
از مقام خود بشطو این د یا د

نسبت او تا آورد ستر شهود
هست او از شجرهٔ اصلیه بو د

۶۰

چونکه ستر اختیار لم یزل
گشت ظاهر از مقام لا مثل
آن مقام ان شجر اصلیه بود
پاک از اوهام ما المزنیه بود
چونکه امد او بامر کردگار
در تبلج از شرادیات نار
این منم مختار از جذب القدیر
نور او باشد مرا نور منیر
نیست در من شانهای غیریه
نیست در من لمزهای همزیه
پاک باشم از جمیع ما عدا
نیستم جز فاعل فعل یشاء
زین ندا شد آدم اندر انوجاد
خواست از جا داخل بیت المراد

٥٩

هاکه دید او خود مقابل روبرو

با خداوند خود اندر گفتگو

ستر انیت شد اورا احجاب

در همان آن آمدش حق در حجاب

گشت نازل از مقام هو انا

در مقام ها هو انا آنا

تاکه امد نصر محبوب جمیل

نازلش از شطرهٔ بیت الجلیل

سوخت احجاب فعالیات او

ریخت اکمال انانیات او

عفو فرموده بما هو قد نزل

من مقام عز عار من ملل

دیگرم بشنو بیان آرزو

از شجر تا آنکه آئی رو برو

۵۸

بعد آن هر یک ز ذرات وجود

در بروز ما هو اول بگشود

ز اختیار خود متقمص شد بآن

گشت ظاهر از مظاهر کن فکان

اول انسان وجد بد امر او

گشت با مختار خود او روبرو

کرد ظاهر شانهای عالیه

این صنم عبد ذلیل فانیه

بایدم معبود محبوب جمیل

فانیم من در اطاعت پس ذلیل

این تصرف باشدم شان اساس

غیر این نبود مرا شان قیاس

از همین نقطه بیامد در وجود

شان اعتدال حدود و هم قیود

٥٧

آرزوی حضرت آدم چه بود
سرّ او را ظاهر آورد در وجود
هان شنو تغرید جذبانی ما
تا بیابی سرّ بدء در انتها
دان خداوند جلیل مقتدر
خلق فرموده قدر را ذی قدر
تا بیابد او بعالم اختیار
اظهر ظاهر بصعد این دیار
جمله را مختار در روز ازل
کرد محجوب حبیب لم یزل
چونکه غیرش را نباشد پس وجود
اول از مختاریان ذاتش نمود
این منم مختار در بدء بدآء
نیست او را ابتداء و انتهاء

۴۵

زانکه او باشد نشان کردگار
دیگرش ناید مثل اندر مدار
هیکل او صنعت رب قدیم
فطرت او فطرت حی عظیم
فعل او پاکیزه از غیر خدا
یفعل ما شاء بما شاء کیف شاء
آنکه چون او خواست آرد در عیان
بیشک او افتاد از صدر البیان
هان نگر ای بهجتم در منظره
تا ببینی وجه آیت مظهره
پرس از ما از سرائر های ستر
تا که آئی در مقام مستتر
گوی ای با فر عزت ظاهره
بهجت ای نور فؤاد طاهره

۵۵

آیدم کاید برون از احتجاب
دیدم از رشحات نوری سحاب

آشکار آرم کنوز خافیه
انت الحق لیس دونك باقیه

شمس را بینم مدوّر در سماء
ها انا الحق المطلع من عماء

جلوهٔ حق احد آمد بجد
حتما حدد هو لاما تحد

پاك گردان منظره از این و آن
آمده شأن محمد در عیان

نیست غیر او بمنظور احد
جمله را امداد وی آمد مدد

هر کرا آمد نشانش آرزو
اوفتاد از شأن حق بی گفتگو –

۵۴

گاه از ذرّ تراب آرد عیان
گاه از دریای آب و موج آن
چونکه گردید حمید مائیه
آید او طالع بقمص ناریه
بعد او در روی فکندی چون نظر
آیدت از طرف سینائی قدر
آورد آنرا که خواهد در عیان
غیر ما انت علیه از شأنیان
تا که آرد روح اکبر در ظهور
ها انا البشّار بالسّرّ الفطور
در ترفّع ابد او اندر سماء
تا که آید وجهت طلعت بهاء
نابدّ دیگر کنون متمدد
قطع گردیده زمن شأن یمد

٥٣

در سکینت ریخت او بی ترس و خوف

لا محابا از شئونات مخوف

تا که ظاهر کرد سرّ نوحیه

بعد تعریفش زوجه فطریه

نقطه‌ای کو در صدور نوح بود

از شرارش لب بها هوئی گشود

کرد ظاهر در دوار استوار

من هو الهو نازل از شطر الدیار

خواست از جا بعد او با استقام

ها انا البرّ البراری برتهام

کرد ظاهر از مقامات بیان

سرّ محبوب قدیم لامکان

اینکه او موجود از وجد وجود

آورد آن را که خواهد در شهود

٥٢

گشت ظاهر قدرت جبار او

رب لا تذر بآن دیار او

اهل کشتی آمدند از وی نزیل

پاك از اسمآء و هم از قال و قیل

انچه را بربود از ایشان افکیان

در عوض لا مثل دیدندش عیان

شکر حق را دمبدم ملهم شدند

در زمین هم مطرب منعم شدند

نسل ایشان گشت از ایشان پدید

تا بحد استوآء آن رسید

راکبان رفتند از دار فنا

سوی حق با عزت نور بها

سنت حق بهر تمحیص خلف

نازل آمد آیهٔ قهری بکف

۵۱

تاکه آئی در مقامات استوار

کشتی حق آیدت دار القرار

هان شنو تکلیف خود با عز و فر

باش ساکت نزد احجار و مدر

در ستر باشی حجاب احتجاب

تاکه براندازد از وجهش نقاب

آیدت بشری نزیل از شطر غرب

اقرب از لمحی رباید قتر غبر

پس کشانند او ترا در نزد حق

عاری از شأن شئونات سبق

باز آیم با تو در وصف بیان

در همین ساعت بما امضی نشان

چونکه نوح او گشت از امرش قویم

آمده او در مقام مستقیم

٥٠

یا الهنا بعد نقطه مهلتی
نیست دیگر از دلیل حکمتی
زانکه او باعث باجرای مدد
از سوایش ما سوی گردد نفد
بهجتم باید درآئی در خروش
آیدت بحر طهارتیه بجوش
تا درآید امر تو بر ما عیان
لحظه غافل مشو از ذکر آن
باش با ما در تفرد ای حبیب
تا فراموشت نیاید آن نصیب
گوی از اوصاف محبوبان حق
لا اله الا هو بودند صدق
زین قدر عالم ظهور طاهر
از تغنیهای نور طاهر ٥

۴۹

یا الها در نز ازل آمدم

بهت حیران از نز الیان شدم

باعث قهرت خداوند بیان

نیست جز تحریق نقطه در عیان

زانکه این نقطه بود سرّ بدآء

نیست غیرش را وجود از ما بدآء

از وی آمد حکم بدیع در ظهور

از وی آمد جملهٔ آیات نور

اوست یارب باعث ایجاد کلّ

اوست یا حیّ باعث ارشاد کلّ

یا الهم از ویش آمد مدد

بر جمیع ما خلق بجدّ و عدّ

یا الها هرکه او را در ربود

خود ربود اما ز تو غافل زدود

۴۸

نقطهٔ شعله او شرار شد

آب بود اما بآن آن نار شد

در تشعل در نگر در صدر نوح

نوح را برداشت با فوج سنوح

هان شنو تغرید بر قمرای او

هان نگر روی غضب الای او

هان شنو گوید چگونه در بیان

رب لاتذر علی الارض العیان

ملت نظر از زمرهٔ افاکیه

ها سماء النار منها جاریه

یا الهها این چه شور باشرر

اوفتاد از شطرهٔ بیت القدر

سوخته مجموع یا رب الجلیل

نسبه موجودی سوی وجه جمیل

۴۷

هان عیان ای زمرهٔ آفاقیان
گشته نازل امر ما از آسمان
تا که هریک در مراکز برقرار
باید آئیم وبگردیم استوار
هان ایا اهل غرور وهم نفور
مرکز ما آمده نقطت الظهور
در مقاعدهای خود آئید زود
نیست دیگر شأن امهال قعود
هان ایا سامع نگر در منظره
آمد آن سنرستیر مصدره
نقطهٔ ناریه اوشعاله شد
عکس او برا و لسان حاله شد
خواست از جا قامهٔ از جذب نار
نیست دیگر مهلت صبر و قرار

۲۴۴

نیست غیر ما بطرز ابتداع
زانکه او واقف نبستر امتناع
غیر ما حقق بآیات نزیل
نیست ما را شأن دیگر او بدیل
آنکه را با ما بود هس النزاع
امرش اعمال او بر او سزاع
از سماء امر قدار القدر
نیست دیگر بهر ایشان مهل فر
زانکه امدا امر حق با استناد
چار ارکانرا نمود املای ناد
ما شنیدیم و اطاعت کرده ایم
غیر ما از زل زخود بربوده ایم
از قبول ما شده کشتی طهیر
زانکه ما نوریم حق ما را منیر

۴۵

بعد آن کونازل امد حکم بدیع

ما بیدا قراری بما ابداع   کر د

نفع دیگر نیست در شأن مضیٰ

ما مضیٰ امر قضا حکم   قضـــا

نیست حق جز واحد اندر شأن جِدّ

لا لهٖ کفو و لا شـبه   احــد

هان نگر ای سامع آیات حق

امدت امر الٓهی ما   نطـــق

در نگر در دُرّ العین نلکیـه

عدّه عین احرف پس   نور یـه

غیر ما انزل بطرز الابتِداع

بنود ایشانرا دگر شأنی بدا ع

ریزد از ایشان شرار ناریه

نحن هو لیس سوانا   باقیـــه

۴۴

غیر حق نابود ایشانرا دگر
بر جمیع ما سوی طرف النظر

آن صحیفه کو بد از آدم بزیر
اخذ کردند ازوی آن امر عزیز

آنکه خلاق وجود کن فکان
زان بود هر روز تازه شان بجان

نیست اورا سائلی از ما فعل
کو بود لا شبه عدل و لا مثل

آدمی را کرد موجود از فعال
تا که آید حاکی از وجه جمال

برد او را سوی خود آورد او
همچو او بیمثل شبه گفتگو -

حکم مصحف کو زاو آمد عیان
بود او تکلیف ما ابرز بشان

۴۳

سرّ توحید الهی را رساند
اهل وحدت را الی ساحل کشاند
کشف استار توهّم را نمود
باب انوار تعلّم را گشود
کان بود حق حقیقت آشکار
شأن لا یسئل ورا باشد مدار
زانکه لا یسئل نباشد جز عیان
در عیان دیگر سؤالی نیست جان
زین بدایع ریخت فطرات بدیع
متوجد گردید آیات منیع
هر یکی یک هیکل با استوار
آمدند اندر مقام اظهار
بهر تکمیل بلاقابل شدند
عدّهٔ عین علی کامل شدند

۴۲

بعد او ظاهر نمودم نوح را
تا کند بار امانت   را   ا د ا
اینکه غیرم نیست خلّاق الوجود
اورم آنرا که خواهم در شهو د
نیست ادم را که او دم در کشد
کین منم موجود در نزد   ا حد
باید او را تا که اید دمبدم
خاضع و اخضع کما کان العدم
بشنو از ما بهجت اسرار آله
تا که آئی در ادای ما   گو   ا ه
در تفرّد آمدم از امر حق
با تو از شأن مضی و ما سبق
بعد اظهار بدایع کردگار
نوح کو قائم شد از امر القدا ر -

۱۴۱

بل بذاته حاکی از ستر بیان
کاشف اسرار رب کن فکان
ننبود او را جز بذات خود نظر
سوخته کلّ سوی را سر بسر
ذکری از غیر خدا نارد عیان
ها انا القدوس فعّال بشان
گر تو آئی بهجتم با وصف او
پاك از شأن سماع و گفتگو -
شایدت آئی بمصدر برفراز
آیدت از مصدر اعلیٰ طراز
هان شنو تغریدمن جذبانی او
پس ترنّمهای با فحوای او
این منم بدّاع آدم در عیان
ظاهرش بنمودم از طلع البیان

۴۰

الله اله که عیان گشت بعالم
این سرّ که باضمار سطر ستر نهان است
از آینهٔ پاک مطهر شده در سبق
الله اله هو حمد ببیان است
الیوم حقیقت بعیان گشت مطهّر
زهرا بعیان در شرر شور بیان است
عرف فرمایم از بحر ظهور
ریزم اندر جام بهجت باسرور
تا در آید ور الاحد حد
از مقام قدس الله الصمد
در گذارد سالهای ما مضی
ابدا او با جلوه های ما بدا
تازه از شطر عمائیه نزیل
او مظهر از دلیل قال و قیل

۳۹

وانگاه دگر عالم دیگر بعیان بین

از سر حقیقت بضیاء لمعان است

باید که شوی پاک ز امثال مثالی

از شان قطاریه بیاری که بران است

الله عزیز هو محبوب جمیل

در شعشعه با طنطنه بر عرش بیان است

برگیر تو برقع که بیامد و سر آمد

ایام مثالی که حقیقت بعیان است

در یوم سبق گشت مظهر همه اسرار

از جام بلوریه که این آن همان است

یعنی که منزل ز سما گشته حبیبی

اسمش ببیان در شرف نور عیان است

حالا شده او حاکیه از وجه مسما

کان او منم احمد او اسم عیان است

٣٨

برخوان خداوندت بارنهٔ طوبائی
از رکن عراقیه نصرت بنصاو آمد
عالم دگر و حکم دگر در طهران است
از شمس قدر امر دگر در نزلان است
در بلج ضیا آمده در برج ثنائی
از وی رشحات ثنا در فوران است
گوید که منم نیست سوایم دگر او حق
مجموع خلائق ببرم در سجدان است
خواهم که برآرم ز جگر رشتهٔ احمر
آرم بعیان سر که با ستار نهان است
آنکس که بیامد و نیامد و سر آمد
با ما و بر انداخت حجب اصله همان است
دریاب ایا سامع بنگر تو بمنظر
مشهود بیابی بعیان آنکه نهان است

۳۷

صنع است ورا کامل بنگر تو بنظر طرف
تکلیف تو تقویم است حقت بشعار آمد
ای قائم حول میم گشتی تو کنون چو نهیم
رتبت ز براری الزی در نام فطار آمد
از جذبهٔ ربانی ها میم شد ابرٰهیم
در آن شده ان طائف حجرش بکنار آمد
بهجت تو مرا بهجت دریاب کنون دریاب
کان جوهر لیلائی از شطر براد آمد
بنگر که تو را جذاب از منطقهٔ ابرج
برگیر ورا در بر صبرش بقرار آمد
بردار تو برقع را از روی بهائیه
حقت بجلال و فر ذر بوس و کنار آمد
با لله شود ظاهر اقرب ز طرف العین
ان روز مرا کو اذن از شطر دیار آمد

۳۶

باید که ترا همت عالی شود ای بهجت
خواهی ز خداوندت انوار که دیدار آمد

از شعشعهٔ شمسی از لؤلؤهٔ قمری
از ازهرهٔ نجمی حکمت بگشاد آمد

باید که بیائی تو با جذبهٔ حقانی
شاید که شوی قوم حجت بدباد آمد

تغییر مبین ای جان در سنت ربانی
از شمس و قمر بگذشت آنکو که بزار آمد

کوکب شدش او ظاهر از شطر سمائیه
در محو شد او از نظر افتاد سکار آمد

پس جلوهٔ فطریه لامثل عدل در آن
از شطر عمائیه ویرا بکنار آمد

مگر فته سرش از خاک با جذبهٔ فطاری
کی محو شده زافلاک حقت زنظار آمد

٣٥

بهجت ز تو شد هو قدان شجرهٔ عدنیه

از شور شرار وی عالم بشر ار آمد

حمد است حبیب حق احمد بود او قائم

کز قطرهٔ من او نودت بنوار آمد

بالله که او محبوب از صدرهٔ اعلائی

از ذکر عظیم او در صدر صدار آمد

بهجت تو نگر بهجت آیات خداوندی

از آینهٔ قلبت با نور نوار آمد

محبوب توام محبوب ای بهجت با بهجت

از نطق بیان تو آدم بدیار آمد

بنگر تو خداوندی از منظر با انظار

تا آنکه شوی داکر کشتی بقرار آمد

ای بزم مشهود اقرب نظر النظر

مرءات بهائیه دردو ردوار آمد

۳۴

املاک بهائیه از دور نضار او
از امر الهیه در دور دوار آمد
املاک بهائیه سکان عمائیه
از نظرهٔ محو او در سکر سکار آمد
برخوانده ایا بهجت ایات تو را یکسر
در نزد ملیک العرش امرت بقرار آمد
طوبی لک صد طوبی از ما بر زعیمها
از شطرهٔ نورانی حکمت بنظار آمد
آمد بیقین بنگر جانت صلهٔ اکبر
لا عدل مثل با فر دورت بمدار آمد
برگیر ایا محبوب از خود صلهٔ اعظم
دایم بحضور حق وجهت بنضار آمد
اشجار غرامیه در بطنهٔ فردوسی
از قبهٔ طوریه در دفق شرار آمد

۳۳

بریزم ای خداوندم بجام ازشه کافوری

که تا اذن آید ظاهر زوجه طلعت حمران

ز جا خیزم الرحمن باعزاز خداوندی

برون آرم هر آن خواهی ز بطن قطعهٔ حمران

تعالی الله اعلی از جلالیات منزولی

بهاء الله ابهی از جمالیات د طلعان

نگر ای بهجت فاآیهٔ طالع ز شطر الغرب

بخوان از فطرت صافی جمیع آیهٔ تبیان

از بهشت ای بهجت در بهجه نضار آمد

ان جذبهٔ با جذبه در شور و شرار آمد

آمد صلات نازل از مصدر عز و فر

برگیر کنون منظر با عز و وقار آمد

بشنو تو ایا بهجت از سمعهٔ فطاری

تا اینکه عیان بینی مومنی بدیار آمد

٣٢

خداوندیکه آرد انچه‌را خواهد بآن دوران
گشوده از تفضل باب صدر روضهٔ رضوان

ملائک از کئوس مصفیه تصبیغ خمریه
فتاده در شور اشجار خضر روضهٔ رضوان

الها احمد است آن حمد لایق مر فعالت را
که از عکس جمالش در تلألؤ سطحهٔ فاران

چه زیبا طلعتان یا رب برون گردید از مصدر
که هر یک لا مثل باشند در امثال و در تبیان

الها از تفضل کردهٔ کنز نهان ظاهر
حقیقت را عیان لـ[illegible]دهٔ بالله یا سبحان

عیان بینم خداوندا که عرش اعظمت ظاهر
شده در سطحهٔ طائیه یا محبوب یا دیان

جمیع ما برئت از فوق عرش عرشه ارفع
نزول آیند طواف حریم قدس یا سبحان

۳۱

جملهٔ ذرّات مدهوش صعیق

یا فتی ان کنز اخفی مرحبا

نازل آمد از خداوند جلیل

جوهر لامثل امرا مرحبا

هان بگیر این منظر با استناد

زان درخشان وجههٔ فا مرحبا

باش با ما در تغرّد ای حبیب

تا بیابی ستر ایفا مرحبا

آیدت اقرب ز لمح العین عیان

کنز غیبی آشکارا مرحبا

بهجتم از بهجتت باشد بهیج

وجه بهجت در مرایا مرحبا

۳۰

فاش گوید بهجتی آمد نزیل
از فراز صدر اعلیٰ با جذاب
میر باید جملهٔ ارباب هوش
از تغنیهای فردوس لباب
جمله آید نازل از شطر البدآء
وصف بهجت آنها سرّ عجاب
حبذا ای بهجت ما حبذا
حبذا ای نزهت طا حبذا
مرحبا ای رشحهٔ قطر بدیع
در تلألؤ از مرایا مرحبا
مرحبا ای شارب کأس طهور
اول باعث باحیا مرحبا
چون بیاید مرحبایت از عماء
خواستی از جا بآبها مرحبا

۲۹

جملگی مدهوش امّا وی بهوش

از ترشّح های فطرتّی سحاب

یا الها ظاهر آمد یا السـ

سرّ مخفی انّها سرّ عجاب

از میان جمله اوراق ظهور

گشته قائم هیکلی با انجذاب

میرباید از تخرّد های خویش

جملهٔ ذرّات را با استطاب

یا الها بنگرم وجهش جمیل

در تشعشع از طراز و از حجاب

یا الهی نیست غیرش را وجود

تا بیاید در مقام ما یجاب

آفرین بر قدرت جان آفرین

ظاهر امد لا حجاب لا نقاب

۲۸

الله الله تحمك تحمك تحلك حلقنا واجمعنا فى مقعد
عز عندك جميع على سرائر رفعاته ملكين الحمد لله
الذى صدقنا

وعده

حمد بر افكنده ز رو يش نقاب
جلوه گر از مطلع خود لا حجاب

از ندای با صفای هیت لك
میربايد زنك وهم وارتيا ب

جمله را بنكر بنزد وى طريح
اوفتاده مست ومدهوش و خراب

حبذا ان سرخوش از جام طهور
آمده در بلج اشراق اوجذاب

میربايد جمله ذرات صحيق
از ترنمهای صادر از خطا ب

۲۷

هان که امر مبرم ظاهر شده

حکم محکم آیهٔ قاهر شده

برکن الباس حدود و بس قیود

خویش را انداز در دریای جود

وش ببین آندم همه اسرار ها

در تظهر بین همه اضمار ها

تا بکی در عالم پر شر و شور

دور هستی تو ز مقصد دور دور

شو ممکّن بر مسند تمکین ما

قوّهٔ فعّاله را ظاهر نما

امر ما بیرون شده از کاف و نون

کو من الله الیه راجعون

ها انا الحمد مجلّی للجمال

قد تظهّرت بسرّ الاعتدال

۲۶

آن حلاوت را که با ما داشتی

در مقام صلح آی و آشتی

آن اشاراتی که در ستر بطون

شد مکون در میان کاف و نون

درگذر در مستتر و منتشار

برکنار آی از مقام اخبار

فیض را تعطیل نه تعطیل نه

حکم را تأخیر نه تأخیر نه

تا بکی محجوب از احباب خویش

بسته از یک باب صد ابواب خویش

طرح غیریت خودت انداختی

خویش را محجوب از ما ساختی

تا بکی محبوس در زندان شدن

بر حدود و بر جهت اعیان شدن

۲۵

درهویت گشته سرم مستتر
از حجاب واحدیت مشتهر
اسم پاکم از احد ناید بجد
جلوه‌ام گشته لم یلد از صمد
شأن ذی شأنم نیاید در گمان
قدر ذی قدرم مرفع از بیان
ما ترا از نور خود افروختیم
با بهاء عز مقمص ساختیم
نقص در خلقت نباشد ذرهٔ
صنع تام جوهر فتعالی له
در کمال استواء ماسواء
نطق بنما از جلال آیات ما
جذبهٔ غیبیه را اظهار کن
جذوهٔ ناریه را شترار کن

۲۴

در سجود و در تضرع در نیاز

وجههٔ وجهت کجا ای بی نیاز

یاد ایام وصال و اتصال

آه آه از این غروب و انفصال

شمس وحدت از کجا طالع شود

سر وحدت از کجا لامع شود

یا سمیع الدعوه رب کردگار

جلوه گر گردید از شطر دیار

با هزاران جلوه های دلربا

فیض لطفش بیحد و بی انتها

گفت با ادم منم رب رحیم

از تجلی محیی عظم رمیم

طلعتم مستور باشد در هواء

جلوه ام منظور گردد از عماء

۲۳

از عناصر هیکل با استوآء

شد منطق او با سرار بهآء

جلوهٔ ربانی انوار شد

جذبهٔ نارانی شرار شد

ادمی از جلوهٔ او آدمی

صحو مسکور دما دم در دمی

پس نهان کرد او رخ وشد او نهان

در حجاب خلق اندر لامکان

آدمی شد مبتلا با آه و درد

ماند در قید خودیت وحدهٔ فرد

اه حسرت از فراقش میکشید

همچو ماهی از تبلبل میطپید

با صعید خاک با رنج وعنا

داشت او بس نالها و داغها

۲۳

دهر در تدبیر از تدبیر او

دور در تدبیر از تدبیر او

بر فلک گردید شمس با بهاء

شاید آنکه پی برد بر سترهاء

پس قمر از او طمع در عیان

گشت سایر بر بروج آسمان

چون بهر برجی رسید وا رهید

جلوه‌اش را در مقام تازه دید

چونکه سیرش منتشر از خاک شد

زین سبب در سیر شد افلاک شد

غافل از رمز نهانی های او

در گشایش های بی پایان او

در مقام وصف تعبیر بیان

شد طمع از حروف کن فکان

٢١

اصل ثابت بود در روز ازل
پس مطهر بود از حد و علل
فیض او ظاهر ز آیات صمد
اسم او پس مستقر اندر احد
حد تحدید شئون ماسوی
جمله در قید اضافات عدمی
اقتضای جود سبحان قدر
داشت بر اظهار سر مستتر
نقطهٔ سری مظهر شد بدور
جذبهٔ غیبی مکرر شد بکور
چونکه فیضش لایحد لاعد است
نقطهٔ جذبش برفعت بداست
مد تمدید زمان از وی ممتد
قص تعیین عیان شد منوحد

٢٠

جمله را تصبیغ صبغ الله کرد
جمله را مشهود وجه الله کرد
الله الله این چه لطف است و عطا
در نظر از هویات بهاء
این چه قدر است و چه عز است و چه شأن
گشت ظاهر بر حروف کن فکان
امر از امر بنی شد برون
ظل ظلی در دجی شد سر نگون
نور از مشکوة ناری مشتعل
حضرت ابداع از وصفش خجل
این همان مصباح قبانی بود
کز فروغش جسم روحانی بود
نه غروب او را متصور نه طلوع
نه بصرانه او را مقدر نه فروغ

۱۹

هان بنطق او آمد از جذب ودود

جملهٔ ابواب مُغلق را گشود

ها ندای باصفای هاتف لت

میربایدِ زنلت ریب وهم وشلت

هان بیک جلوه همه مدهوش کرد

جلوهٔ دیگر سراپا هوش کرد

ها اشارتهای پنهانی عیان

گشت از وی جلوه گر اندر زمان

نار سینائی بدوران آمده

نور فارانیت تابان آمده

اسم اعظم با مسما شد عیان

کرد واله جملهٔ کرّو بیان

جلوه گر بر کل اسماء آمده

سوی بزم انس حق رهبر شده

١٨

با علی در کرّه کرّار آمده

در بروج غیر سیّار آمده

عرش عزّت در نهایت مستدیر

سرّ جذبت از عنایت مستنیر

با مفطّر شد سماء منفطر

مکفهرّات سنائی منهمر

یوم موعود است با ستر شهود

در طراز احسنیّت رو گشود

طلعت حق است با عزّ و وقار

گشت از استار عزّت آشکار

در تزلزل آمده ارض و سماء

حبّ ما اوحی نمودار از نمآء

هیکل با استواء با بهاء

در تجلّی از بروقات ثناء

۱۷

گوئیا شد سرّ وحدت آشکار

یا دیار لن ترانی شد دیار

یا حجاب منخفق شد مرتفع

شد برون از پرده غیب ممتنع

ذات ساذج پاک حق بات بحت

در ظهور از جلوه‌های بحت بحت

یا احد در جلوه‌های با بهاء

از مقامات ثنا با امتناع

یا صمد ظاهر بدوران آمده

قلزم قدرت بهیجان آمده

رمز مستور است یا اسم نهان

از حجابات ثلاثه او عیان

یا که احمد گشت نازل از سماء

با تجلیهای انوار از عماء

۱۵

جلوهٔ مستور در اطراز نود

ساز مشهودش باشراق ظهور

حرف نار به که در اضماد بود

از حجابات هویت نار بود

شلت مشعشع از عماء نور شد

ماسوی از جلوه اش در طور شد

عالم نور از ظهورش شد عیان

در ترشح کفهرات بیان

از بروز خفق عکس وجه او

شمس حکمت با قمر شد رو برو

عکس و ظل نابود و ناپیدا شدند

جملگی بر ساحل دریا شدند

الله الله این چه نور احتراز

گشت لامع از فعال بی نیاز

١٥

برفراز اوج عزت مایل است
برفراز نوح رجعش قائل است
صاحب کرات رجعت داندش
حق قائم در زمین میداندش
در تغنی آی ای طیر عماء
در شرر انداز اوراق ثناء
آدمی را سوی جنت بازآر
درمقام ستر وحدت بازآر
بانگ آوازنقطهٔ ستر ازل
ازرموز حکم حق لم یزل
آر ازپرده برون اسرارها
درنظهر آر آن اضمارها
ستر مکنون ازکمون لامکان
سازاندر مصدر تمکین عنان

١۴

قبضهٔ رمانی حق مشتعل
شد قلم از وصف غیبائی خجل
در شهود آوای قلم وصف عما
تا بما جذب گردد ما سوی
این سوائیت زموسی آمده
چونکه بی فطرت بسینا آمده
سرّ مفطور از ربوبت رحیم
شد مظهر زانکه بُد او بر هیم
چون الف قائم بامر نوح بود
قص تسلیم وثنا در بر نمود
ها قلم بگرفت ایندم او عیان
میکشد انجا که میخواهد عنان
شور نوحی دارد او امشب بسر
از علایق جملگی بریده بسر

۱۳

از طعام حقیه اعطا نما

از شراب کاسیه اطفا نما

مکفهرات بهیه در فطر

ثمرات لا نهیه در نظر

سترا و باراز بر شد آشکار

اسم بر در بر سینا شد دیار

این اساس سرمدی باشد عیان

حین حان مطوی شده اندر زمان

دهر از تد بیر خود شد مستمند

شد زمان از ستر غیبی مستمند

مایهٔ رفعت برفعت آمده

رفع علت جمله از علت شده

عالمی بس باشکوه و با نضار

آتش سینا بفوران آشکار

۱۲

حق ذات پاک بیمانند تو

حق نفس عال بی پیوند تو

جز توام مقصود نبود در پناه

جز توام معبود ناید در ثناء

ستر وحدت را تو فرما آشکار

چند گردم در سما خورشید وار

چند چون حوت مُبلبل باکئیب

خواهیم در سطح خاکی بس غریب

ای حبیب جب محبوب بهاء

جذب فرما این عبید مبتلا

بر بساط عز وحدت مستقر

ساز از الطاف خود بجدّ و فرّ

از کأوسات طربیه یا احد

هان بنوشان انک انت الصمد

11

جملگی با جلوه های با بهاء
از مقامات علیا با صفا ،

تاجها از رفعت عزت بسر
پس منور ز آفتاب و از قمر

الله الله ای قدیم لم یزل
قادر حی عطوف لا مثل

یک نظر فرما با نظار رحیم
زنده گردان هذه العظم الرمیم

تا نمایم نطق از اسرار تو
در تظهر آورم اضمار تو

جوهریت را ز ما ظاهر نما
باب لطفت را برویم بر گشا

حکم عکسیت نیارم در بیان
تا که گردم صرف اشهر را بان

١٠

اسم اعلی از مستی شد متین

شد برون فرقان حق از آستین

روح احمد در جسد شد مستقر

عالم عالم شد مروح زین بشر

رب اعظم رب اعلی شان او

رب اکبر روضهٔ رضوان او

روضهٔ رضوان برضوا آمده

رضوی از رضوی باطوآء آمده

ستر فردوس جنان شد آشکار

کاس خمریه برون خمار وا د

عرشها با رفعت شان بهاء

پس سرادقها مرفع از سماء

جلوه های قدس در طوبی همه

هیکلان انس در رضوی همه

۹

چشم غیریت بپوشی در عیان
ظنیت را محو بنمائی بآن
خلع بنمائی لباس التباس
منقمص گردی بنور اقتباس
خط اخبار بیان وصف قال
محو بنمائی زامطار جلال
بر بساط وحدتم گردی مکین
گوئی الحمد لرب العالمین
آنکه ازلیت جلوه های بابها
محو بنمودی سواء ماسوی
غیریت را او زما برداشته
بذر اغنی الکل بامکان کاشته
غیر او مشهود نبود در عیان
محو موهومات شد اندر بیان

٨

این نقط بود ازبروزات ازل

پاك بودی ازشئونات علل

بینیت راانجادراین مقام

بود ره یارب اعلی بالمقام

هان تو دردل ستر هم اسرار کن

برفراز لافرازی دار کن

این سئولت بود امر کردگار

انشقاق ازوی نمودی اشکار

امر ازامرین اوشد منوجد

حکم ازحکمین اوشد مستمد

ازازل ماند الی یوم ابد

اخذ سیرت دربروج لا امد

تارسی برسر امر مبرم

ره بری برصنع عز متقنم

۷

الف اول از ظهور احمدی

الف ثانی از بروز المعی

بوده مدهوش از ستر بناء

صحو مسکور از بروز ان لیثاء

در تعجب زین جدائیت بدی

در تحیر زین عبودیت شوی

یار ما ستری بود مکنون بما

در تلئلؤ با بهاء و با ضیاء

جلوه گر از مشعر اعلا بود

مقترن با وصف نعت اوکی شود

راه وصلش انقطاع امتناع

طی انظار سوای ما سواء

چونکه فیضش را بنا شد و صفحه

جلوه گر گردید از ستر صمد

ء

جلوهٔ صحو تبرات مظلوم کرد

از قیامت محو هر موهوم کرد

محو موهومات از افهام شد

صحو معلومات از الهام شد

جذب کردی مر صفت را در بیان

حدّیت برداشتی هان از میان

ستر وحدت را نمودی آشکار

کثرها بیرون نمودی از دیار

کشف استار جلالیات شد

هان اظهار جمالیات شد

پس سوج از انفعال اشتعال

گشت خاموش از بروقات جمال

امر بیرون شد ز امرین ای قلم

قد افقت بعد الفین ای قلم

۵

بلکه کل از عین جودش مستمد
هؤلاء هؤلاء ان کان ضد
خلق آن عالم از این سر دو حجاب
منقلب در تیه قلبت انقلاب
نقطه از این بحر افتاد در مثال
بود عیان از ذروهٔ اعلای عال
زان عاکسین در تعاکس های حد
بود شمسین از دو هیکل مستمد
بحر اعظم هان بفوران آمده
نقطهٔ غیبی بدوران آمده
سر لا تعطیل میپرس از قلم
کت بود محبوب مقصود از رحم
بوده صعقان سکران قبل جان
من افاقت یا قلم بعد الصیان

۴

از سرادق های عز بیرون شده
در تجلّای حسن او افزون شده
جلوه های لاحدی احمدی
شد ملألأ از حجاب سرمدی
رمز پنهان در حجاب مخفق
شد مشعشع از مقام ماسبق
طلعت ها در هویّت مستتر
گشت او از نقطهٔ با مشتهر
بود احمد لاتخطّ بالیمین
از برای حفظ ستر از مبطلین
بود مستور از حروفات ثناء
در طراز غیب ما ادری مآء
دست احمد بود او دست خدا
نور ظلمت را نبود انجا بقا

۳

در تغنّی از حروف بسمله
عالمی انداز شور و ولوله
باز گو از سرّهای نقطهٔ
باز ده این والهان را مژدهٔ
در عروق افسرده ما فی البطون
در ترشح آر از جذب مصون
عالمی پرنور تر نور کن
کون و اکوان را سراسر شور کن
علّت غیبی که در قمص بهاء
جذبت عطفی که در لبس ثناء
گشت طالع از بروج انما
کشف کرد او پرده ها و سترها
آن بنا کز سرّ او بودی عظیم
آن بنائی را که بانی بد قدیم

۲

هو المحبوب الجذاب المتظهر
فی ذرة التراب و مجلی الکل و لید

باز آ ای عندلیب خوش نوا
باز گو از نکته های با بها
عالمی را از تغرد محو محو
آدمی را از تغنی صحو صحو
نوح را از نوحه بر اعیان آر
کشتی جذبیه بر دوران آر
دوحهٔ روحیه و ریحان آر
رنّهٔ فطریهٔ ربان آر
زان زجاجیات عطر انبیار
زان رشحیات سینائی بیار
تار کش از خیط اصفر با طرب
باز گردان شمس را از ما غرب

در تاریخ ٢٥٣٦/٦/٢ جناب نعمت الله ذکائی بیضائی
این کتاب را امانتا مرحمت فرمودند و پس از تهیه سواد
عکسی اصل کتاب بایشان مرجوع گشت . (محفظه آثار امری)

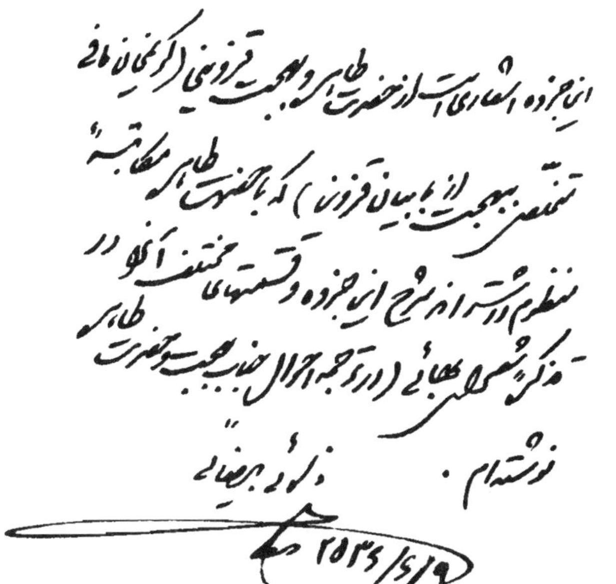

این جزوه اشعاری است از حضرت طاهره و بهجت قزوینی [illegible]
تخلص بهجت (از بابیان قزوین) که با تخلص طاهره مطابقه
منظوم داشته‌اند. شرح این جزوه و قسمتهای مختلف آنرا در
تذکره شعرای بهائی (در ترجمه احوال جناب بهجت و حضرت طاهره
نوشته‌ام.
ذکائی بیضائی
۲۵۳۶/۶/۹

Works Cited

Works of Bahá'u'lláh

Epistle to the Son of the Wolf. Translated by Shoghi Effendi. 1st pocket-size ed. Wilmette, IL: Bahá'í Publishing Trust, 1988.

Gleanings from the Writings of Bahá'u'lláh. New ed. Translated by Shoghi Effendi. Wilmette, IL: Bahá'í Publishing, 2005.

Gems of Divine Mysteries: Javáhiru'l-Asrár. Haifa: Bahá'í World Center, 2002.

The Hidden Words. Translated by Shoghi Effendi. Wilmette, IL: Bahá'í Publishing, 2002.

The Kitáb-i-Íqán: The Book of Certitude. Translated by Shoghi Effendi. Wilmette, IL: Bahá'í Publishing, 2003.

Prayers and Meditations. Translated by Shoghi Effendi. 1st pocket-size ed. Wilmette, IL: Bahá'í Publishing Trust, 1987.

The Proclamation of Bahá'u'lláh. Haifa: Bahá'í World Center, 1972.

Tablets of Bahá'u'lláh revealed after the Kitáb-i-Aqdas. Compiled by the Research Department of the Universal House of Justice. Translated by Habib Taherzadeh et al. Wilmette, IL: Bahá'í Publishing Trust, 1988.

Works of the Báb

Aḥsanu'l-Qiṣaṣ. Not an official publication. Distributed in limited number for its preservation with the permission of the National Spiritual Assembly of Iran. Tehran: 133 BE [Bahá'í Era].

Kitáb-i-Bayán-i-'Arabí. N.p.: n.d.

Kitáb-i-Bayán-i-Fársí (Persian Bayán). N.p.: n.d.

Muntakhabát-i-Áyát Az Áthár-i-Ḥaḍrat-i-Nuqṭiy-i-Úlá (Selections from the Writings of the Báb). Reprinted by Permission. Wilmette, IL: Bahá'í Publishing Trust, n.d.

Panj Sha'n. (Lajniy-i-Millíy-i-Maḥfaẓiy-i-Áthár va Árshív-i-Amr). N.p.: Publication of National Committee for Collection and Archiving of Bahá'í Literature, 132 BE.

Risáliy-i-Dalá'il-i-Sab'ih. N.p.: n.d.

Saḥífiy-i-'Adlíyyih. N.p.: n.d.

Selections from the Writings of the Báb. Compiled by the Research Department of the Universal House of Justice. Translated by Habib Taherzadeh with the assistance of a committee at the Bahá'í World Center. 1st pocket-size ed. Wilmette, IL: Bahá'í Publishing Trust, 2006.

Tafsír-i-Súriy-i-Baqarih. National Bahá'í Archives of Iran, 69:156–377.

Works of 'Abdu'l-Bahá

Makátíb-i-'Abdu'l-Bahá. Al-Juz'u'th-Thání. Kurdistánu'l-Ilmíyyah: n.d.

Min Makátíb 'Abdu'l-Bahá. Vol. 1. Rio de Janeiro: Editorial Bahá'í Brazil, 1982.

The Promulgation of Universal Peace: Talks Delivered by 'Abdu'l-Bahá during His Visit to the United States and Canada in 1912. Compiled by Howard MacNutt. New ed. Wilmette, IL: Bahá'í Publishing Trust, 2007.

Some Answered Questions. Compiled and translated by Laura Clifford Barney. 1st pocket-size ed. Wilmette, IL: Bahá'í Publishing Trust, 1984.

Works of Shoghi Effendi

God Passes By. Rev. ed. Wilmette, IL: Bahá'í Publishing Trust, 1974.

The Promised Day Is Come. 1st pocket-size ed. Wilmette, IL: Bahá'í Publishing Trust, 1996.

The World Order of Bahá'u'lláh: Selected Letters. New ed. Wilmette, IL: Bahá'í Publishing Trust, 1991.

Bahá'í Compilations

Bahá'í Prayers: A Selection of Prayers Revealed by Bahá'u'lláh, the Báb, and 'Abdu'l-Bahá. Wilmette, IL: Bahá'í Publishing Trust, 2002.

Hornby, Helen, comp. *Lights of Guidance: A Bahá'í Reference File.* New ed. New Delhi, India: Bahá'í Publishing Trust, 1994.

Other Works

Abdulmasiḥ, Dr. George M., revised by. *A Dictionary of Arabic Grammar in Charts and Tables*. Maktabat, Lebanon: Librairie du Liban, 1981.

Afnán, Abu'l-Qásim, comp. *Chahár Risáliy-i-Táríkhí Dar Báriy-i-Ṭáhirih Qurratu'l-'Ayn*. Wineacht, Switzerland: Landegg Academy, 1991.

Afnán, Mehrí. "Naẓarí bar Mundariját-i-Risáliy-i-Dalá'il-i-Sab'ih." *Safíniy-i 'Irfán, Book Six*. Darmstadt, Germany: Asr-i Jadid Publishers, 2003.

Afnán, Soheil M. *Vázhih Námiy-i-Falsafí (A Philosophical Lexicon in Persian and Arabic)*. N.p.: Nashr-i-Nughrih, 1365 AP.

Aḥsá'í, A. *Al-Favá'íd*. Istanbul: Shirkat-i-Iranííyih, n.d.

———. *Ḥayátu'n-Nafs*. N.p.: n.d.

———. *Kitábu'r-Raj'ah*. Beirut, Lebanon: A'd-Dáru'l Álamíyyah, 1993.

———. *Ma'rifat-i- Kayfíyyatu's-Sulúk-i-ila-Alláh*. A'dDáru'l Álamíyyah. Beirut, Lebanon: n.d.

Al-Maṭbi'atu'l-Kátulíkíyyah. *Al-Munjid Fil-Luqat*. Beirut, Lebanon: Dar el-Mashreq Publishers, 1975.

Al-Munjidu'l-Abjadí. Beirut, Lebanon: Dar el-Mashreq Publishers, 1968.

Amanat, Abbas. *Resurrection and Renewal: The Making of the Babi Movement in Iran, 1844–1850*. Ithaca, NY: Cornell University Press, 1989.

'Amíd, Ḥasan. *'Amíd Dictionary*. 2 vols. N.p.: Sázimán-i-Cháp va Intishárát-i-Jávídán, n.d.

Amín, Siyyid. Ḥasan. *The Philosophy of Mullá Ṣadrá Shírází (1572–1640)*. London: The Research Publishing Group of the Culture and History of Iran, 1987.

Baalbaki, Dr. Rohi. *Al-Mawrid: A Modern Arabic-English Dictionary*. 9th ed. Beirut, Lebanon: Dar el-Ilm Lilmalayin, 1997.

Banani, Amin. Thirteenth Ḥasan M. Balyúzí Memorial Lecture: "Ṭáhirih: A Portrait in Poetry." *The Journal of Bahá'í Studies* 10, no. 1/2 (March–June 2000).

———. "Chihri-i-Ṭáhirih Qurrat-ul 'Ayn az Ṣidáy-i- Khud-i-'ú." *The Journal of Bahá'í Studies* 10, no. 1/2 (March–June 2000).

Báqirí Khurramdashtí, Náhíd. *Kitábshinásí Jámi' Mulláh Ṣadrá*. Tehran: Bunyád-i-Ḥikmat-i-Islámí Mulláh Ṣadrá, 1999.

Borum and Dr. Javád Sai'íd. *Zabán-i-Taṣavvuf*. Tehran: Pazhang Publishing Co., n.d.

Cobb, Stanwood. "The Worldwide Influence of Qurratu'l-Ayn." *The Bahá'í World* 2 (1928): 257–62.

Dehkhodá, 'Alí Akbar. *Loghat-nama Alí Akbar Dehkhodá.* 50 vols. Tehran: Sirus Printing, 1337 AP.

Dhuká'i Bayḍá'í, Ni'matu'lláh. *Tadhkariy-i-Shu'aráy-i-Qarn-i-Avval-i-Bahá'í.* Vol. 1. Tehran: Bahá'í Publishing Trust, 121 BE.

Díván-i Kámil Shams-i Tabrízí, Mawláná Jalálu'd-Din Muḥammad Balkhí, Mashhúr bi Mawlaví. Introduction by B. Furúzanfar. Notes by M. Darvish. N.p.: Sázimán-i Intishárát-i Jávídán, n.d.

Doniach, N.S., ed. *The Oxford English-Arabic Dictionary of Current Usage.* Oxford: Clarendon Press. Reprint, Hong Kong, 1993.

Fáḍil, Mázandarání. *Asráru'l-Áthár-i-Khusúsí.* Vol. 1. Tehran: Mu'assisiy-i-Millíy-i-Maṭbú'át-i-Amrí, 124 BE.

———. *Àsrár'u'l-Áthár.* Tehran: Muassisiy-i-Maṭbú'át-i-Àmrí, 129 BE.

———. *Ẓuhúru'l-Ḥaqq.* Vol. 3. Tehran: n.d.

Fiyḍ-i-Káshání, Mullá Muḥsin. *Díván-i-Kámil-i-Fiyḍ-i-Káshání, Hamráh Bá Risáliy-i-Gulzár-i-Quds Az Mu'aẓẓam Lah.* Introduction and corrections by Siyyid 'Ali Shafi'í. Tehran: Nashr-i-Chakámih, n.d.

Gail, Marzieh. "The White Silk Dress." *Bahá'í World* 9 (1944): 814–21.

———. "Stanza from Tahirih." *Journal of Bahá'í Studies* 7 (1980).

Ghadimi, Dr. Riaz K. *An Arabic Persian Dictionary of Selected Words.* Toronto: University of Toronto Press, 1986.

———. *Riaz-ul-Lughat (Arabic-Persian Dictionary).* 9 vols. Toronto: University of Toronto Press, 1994–2005.

Ghalib, M. *Tafsíru'l-Qur'án'ul-Karím, Li-Shaikhu'l Akbar al'Arif-i-Billáh al'Allámih Muḥyiddín Ibn-i-'Arabí.* 2 vols. Beirut: Dáru'l Andulus, n.d.

Gowharín, Dr. Siyyid Sádiq. *Farhang-i-Luqát va Ta'bírát-i-Mathnaví.* 9 vols. Tehran: Zavvar Publishing, 1362 AP.

———. *Sharḥ-i-Iṣṭiláhát-i-Tasavvuf.* 4 vols. Tehran: Zavvar Publishing, 1362 AP.

Haiim, S. *Haiim's One-Volume English Persian Dictionary.* Tehran: Beroukhim & Sons Booksellers, 1979.

———. *The Larger Persian-English Dictionary.* 2 vols. Tehran: Farhang Mu'áṣer, 1985.

Ḥasan 'Amíd. *Farhang-i-Fársí 'Amíd.* Tehran: Amír Kabír Publishing Corporation, n.d.

Ḥasan, Dr. Hadi. *A Golden Treasury of Persian Poetry.* Edited by M.S. Israeli. 2nd revised edition. N.p.: Indian Council for Cultural Relations, 1972.

Hatcher, John, and Amrollah Hemmat. *The Poetry of Ṭáhirih.* Oxford: George Ronald Publisher, 2002.

Hemmat, Amrollah, and Hemmat Ehsanollah. *Qavá'id-i-Ṣarf va Naḥv-i-'Arabí.* Tehran: n.d.

Hemmat, Amrollah, and Samali Bijan. *Learning Arabic: A Self Study Program.* 2 vols, 6 audio cassettes. Wilmette, IL: The National Persian American Affairs Committee of the National Spiritual Assembly of the Bahá'ís of the United States, 1986.

Humá'í Jalálu'd-Dín. *Tafsír-i Mat͟hnavíy-i-Mawlaví.* Tehran: Mu'assisiy-i Nas͟hr-i Humá, 1366 AP.

Ishaque, M. *Four Eminent Poetesses of Iran.* Calcutta: The Iran Society, 1950.

Is͟hraq-i-K͟hávarí, Àbdu'l-Ḥamíd. *Qámús-i-Íqán.* Tehran: Mu'assi-siy-i-Maṭbú'át-i-Amrí, 128 BE.

———. *Raḥíq-i-Mak͟htúm.* Tehran: Lajniy-i-Millí Nas͟hr-i-Át͟hár-i-Amrí, 103 BE.

K͟hájaví, M., ed. *Majmú'iy-i-Ásh'ár-i-Filsúf-i-Kabír Ṣadru'd-Dín-i-S͟hírází, Mullá Ṣadrá.* N.p.: 1997.

Láhíjí S͟hamsu'd-Dín, Muḥammad, comp. *Mafátíḥu'l-I'jáz Fi S͟harḥ-i Guls͟han-i-Ráz, Intis͟hárát-i-Zavvár.* Introduced, edited, and annotated by M. Barzigar K͟háliqí and E. Karbási. N.p.: 1374 AP.

Lambden, Stephen. "The Word Bahá'í: The Quintessence of the Greatest Name of God." *The Journal of Bahá'í Studies* 8, no. 2 (1988): 13–41.

Mas'úd, Jubrán. *Ar-Ráid Mo'jam Luqawí Ássrí.* Beirut: Dár-ul-Ilm Lil-Malyisín, 1967.

Maẓlúmí (Majídí), Núráníyyih, Manuscript. *Durríyyát-i-Mastúrih Dar Maktab-i-S͟hayk͟h Aḥmad.* N.p.: 1380 AP.

Miḥrábí, Mu'ínu'd-Dín. *Qurrat-al-Ain freiheitsliebende und national gesinnte Dichterin Iran (Qurrat ul-Áyn Shá'riyeh Ázádíkháh va Millí-i Irán).* Koln, West Germany: Nashr-i-Rúyesh, 1990.

Milani Farzaneh. *Veils and Words: The Emerging Voices of Iranian Women Writers.* Syracuse, NY: Syracuse University Press, 1999.

Milton, John. *The Complete Poetical Works of John Milton.* Edited by H. F. Fletcher. Cambridge, MA: Houghton Mifflin Company, 1941.

Mis͟hkátud-Díní, 'Abdu'l-Muḥsin. *Naẓarí bi Falsafi-i-Ṣadrá S͟hírází (Mullá Ṣadrá).* Tehran: Bunyád-i-Farhangí, 1345 AP.

———. *T't͟hír va mabádíye án ya kullíyyti-falsafíy-i-ṭabí'í.* Mas͟hhad, Iran: Mas͟hhad University Press, 1347 AP.

Mo'ín, Dr. Mohammad. *An Intermediate Persian Dictionary.* 6 vols. Tehran: Amir Kabír Publishing Corporation, 1996.

Mohammadhoseini, N. *Ḥaḍrat-i-Ṭáhirih.* Ontario: Association for Bahá'í Studies in Persian, 2000.

———. *Yúsuf-i-Bahá' Dar Qayyúmu'l-Asmá'*. Dundas, Ontario: Persian Institute for Bahá'í Studies, 1991.

Morris, J. W. *The Wisdom of the Throne: An Introduction to the Philosophy of Mullá Ṣadra*. Princeton: Princeton University Press, 1981.

Mu'izzí, Muḥammad Káẓim. *Qur'án-i-Karím ba Tajvíd va Tarjamih va Tafsír (Kashfu'l-Áyát)*. Tehran: Kitabfrúshí Ilmiiyih Islámí, 1377 AP.

Muḥammad, Fu'ád 'Abd-u'l-Báqí. *Al-Mu'jamu'l-Mufahras Li Alfáẓ-i-l Qur'án-i-l Karím*. Cairo: Dáru'l-Ḥadíth, 1996.

Mullá Ṣadrá, Naṣr Ḥusayn, ed. *Risáliy-i-Si-Aṣl, Bi-Inẓimám-i-Muntakhb-i-Mathnaví va Rubá'iyyát*. N.p.: Intisharat-i-Mowlá, 1360 AP.

Murata, Sachiko, and William C. Chittick. *The Vision of Islam*. St. Paul, MN: Paragon House, 1994.

Murata, Sachiko. *The Tao of Islam*. Albany, NY: State University of New York Press, 1992.

Músavi-Hamidání Muḥammad Báqir, trans. *Tarjamiy-i-Tafsíru'l-Mízán*. Vol. 15. Dáru'l-Ilm, Qum: n.d.

Nabíl-i-A'ẓam (Muḥammad-i-Zarandí). *The Dawn-Breakers: Nabíl's Narrative of the Early Days of the Bahá'í Revelation*. Translated and edited by Shoghi Effendi. Wilmette, IL: Bahá'í Publishing Trust, 1932.

Nicholson, Reynold A., ed. *Mathnaví-i Ma'naví, Mawláná Jalálu'd-Dín Muḥammad Balkhí*. N.p.: Nashr-i-Ilm, 1374 AP.

Nuqabá'í, Ḥusám. *Ṭáhirih Qurratu'l-'Ayn*. Tehran: 1983.

Nurbakhsh, Dr. Javad. *The Nurbakhsh Treasury of Sufi Terms*. 5 vols. N.p.: Khaniqah-Nimatullahi Publications, 1985.

Ouskú'í Ḥá'irí, Mirzá Músá, trans. *Usúl'ul-'Aqáyid* (The Arabic Translation Of Siyyid Káẓim Rashtí's *Risáliy-i-Uṣúl-i-'Aqáyid*). Karbila, Iraq: Maktabatu'l-Mirzá al-Ḥá'irí al-'Ámmat.

Qavímí, Fakhrí. *Kárnámiy-i-Zanán-i-Mashhúr-i-Irán Az Qabl-i-Islám tá Aṣr-i-Ḥáḍir*. Tehran: Vizárat-i-Ámúzish va Parvarish, 1352 AP.

Ra'fatí, Vahíd. "Áthár-i-Munzilih az Qalam-i A'lá dar Irán: Qaṣidiy-i-Rashḥ-i-'Amá'," *Safíniy-i 'Irfán, Book Two*. Darmstadt, Germany: Aṣr-i Jadid Publishers, 1999.

Rádmihr, Farídi'd-Dín. "Má al-Haqíqa." *Ṣafíniy-i 'Irfán, Book Six*. Darmstadt, Germany: Asr-i Jadid Publishers, 2003.

Root, Martha L. *Ṭáhirih the Pure*. Revised ed. Los Angeles: Kalimát Press, 1981.

Rúmí, Mawlaná Jalálu'd-Dín. *Diván-i-Kámil-i-Shams-i-Tabrízí*. Introduction by Furúzánfar. Notes by M. Darvísh. Tehran: Sázimán-i-Intishárát-i-Jávídán, 1373 AP.

Ṣadru'ṣ-Ṣudúr. *Istidlálíyih Mukhtaṣar-i-Ṣadru'ṣ-Ṣudúr.* Bundoora, Australia: Century Press Publications, 2004.

Sa'ídí, Nádir. "Commentary for the Súra of Kawthar." *Payám-i-Bahá'í,* June (1998).

———. "Taḥlílí Az Mafhúm-i-Bábíyyat Dar 'Athár-i-Ḥḍrat-i-A'lá." *Payám-i-Bahá'í,* no. 224–225 (1998): 22–31.

Saiiáḥ, Aḥmad. *Farhang-i-Buzurg-i-Jámi'-i-Nuvín (Dictionary Arabic Farsi Saiiah).* 4 vols. Tehran: Kitábforúshí Islam, n.d.

Sajjádí, Siyyid Ḍíyá'u'd-Dín. *Farhang-i-Lughát va T'bírát-i-Kháqání.* Vol. 1. Tehran: Intishárát-i-Zavvár, 1995.

Sajjadí, Dr. Siyyid Ja'far. *Farhang-i-Lughát va Iṣṭiláḥát va Ta'bírát-i-'Irfání.* Tehran: Kitábkhánih Ṭuhúrí, 1350 AP.

———. *Farhangi Iṣṭiláḥát-i-Falsafí Mullá Ṣadrá (Philosophical Glossary of Mullá Ṣadrá).* Tehran: Vizarat-i-Farhang va Irshád-i-Islámí; Sázimán-i-Cháp va Intishárát, 1379 AP (2000).

Sandler, Rivanne. "The Poetic Artistry of Qurratu'l-'Ayn (Ṭáhirih): A Bábí Heroine." *Bahá'í Studies Notebook* 1 (1980): 65–73.

Siyyid Káẓim-i-Rashtí. *Risálih-i-Uṣúl-i-'Aqáyid.* Distributed in limited number for its preservation with the permission of the National Spiritual Assembly of Iran (not an official publication). Tehran: 133 BE.

Shamísá, D. Litt. *Farhang-i-Talmíḥát (A Dictionary of Allusions).* Tehran: Intishárát-i-Firdows, 1987.

Shari'at, Dr. Muḥammad Javád. *Tarjamih va Ráhnimáy-i- Mabádíyu'l-'Arabiíia.* Volume 4. Isfahan: Muassisiy-i-Intishár'at-í-Mash'al, n.d.

Shúshtarí (Mehrín) Abbass. *Farhang-i-Lughát-i-Qur'án.* Tehran: Intishárát-i-Daryá, n.d.

Steingass, F. *Comprehensive Persian-English Dictionary.* N.p.: Munshiram Manoharlal Publishers Pvt. Ltd., 2000.

Stiles Maneck, Susan. "Ṭáhirih: A Religious Paradigm of Womanhood." *Journal of Bahá'í Studies* 2 (1989): 40–45.

Ṣuḥbat-i-Lárí. *Díván-i-Ṣuḥbat-i-Lárí Bi Ihtimám-i-Ḥusein Ma'rifat.* Shiraz: Kitábfurúshí Ma'rifat, n.d.

Ṭabáṭabá'í, Siyyid Musṭafá, trans. *Farhang-i-Nuvín Arabí-Fársí.* Translation of *Al-Qámúsu'l-'Aṣrí.* Tehran: Kitábfrúshí Islámíyyih, 1354 AP.

Taherzadeh, Adib. *The Revelation of Bahá'u'lláh.* 4 vols. Oxford: George Ronald Publisher, 1974.

Tiflísí, Ḥubaish, Muḥaqqiq Mahdí, ed. *VuJúh-i-Qur'án.* Tehran: Intishárát-i-Ḥikmat, 1396 AH.

Wensinck, A. J., et al., eds. *Concordance Et Indices De La Tradition Musulmane.* 6 vols. Leiden: Brill, 1936–71.

Index

Bahá'í
PUBLISHING

Bahá'í Publishing and the Bahá'í Faith

Bahá'í Publishing produces books based on the teachings of the Bahá'í Faith. Founded over 160 years ago, the Bahá'í Faith has spread to some 235 nations and territories and is now accepted by more than five million people. The word "Bahá'í" means "follower of Bahá'u'lláh." Bahá'u'lláh, the founder of the Bahá'í Faith, asserted that he is the Messenger of God for all of humanity in this day. The cornerstone of his teachings is the establishment of the spiritual unity of humankind, which will be achieved by personal transformation and the application of clearly identified spiritual principles. Bahá'ís also believe that there is but one religion and that all the Messengers of God—among them Abraham, Zoroaster, Moses, Krishna, Buddha, Jesus, and Muḥammad—have progressively revealed its nature. Together, the world's great religions are expressions of a single, unfolding divine plan. Human beings, not God's Messengers, are the source of religious divisions, prejudices, and hatreds.

The Bahá'í Faith is not a sect or denomination of another religion, nor is it a cult or a social movement. Rather, it is a globally recognized independent world religion founded on new books of scripture revealed by Bahá'u'lláh.

Bahá'í Publishing is an imprint of the National Spiritual Assembly of the Bahá'ís of the United States.

For more information about the Bahá'í Faith,
or to contact Bahá'ís near you, visit
http://www.bahai.us/
or call
1-800-22-UNITE

Other Books Available from Bahá'í Publishing

IN THE GLORY OF THE FATHER

The Bahá'í Faith and Christianity
BRIAN LEPARD
PRICE: $17.00 U.S. / $19.00 CAN
FORMAT: TRADE PAPER
TRIM: 6 X 9
PAGES: 246
ISBN 978-1-931847-34-6

Author Brian Lepard draws upon his childhood religious experiences and his study of the Bible and holy books to recount his spiritual journey and discovery of the Bahá'í Faith. He describes in some detail the lives of the central figures of the Bahá'í Faith: the Báb, Who heralded the coming of Bahá'u'lláh; Bahá'u'lláh, the Prophet-Founder of the Bahá'í Faith; and 'Abdu'l-Bahá, the son and successor of Bahá'u'lláh. Lepard discusses the similarities between Bahá'í and Christian views of the station of Jesus Christ, biblical interpretation, and the nature of God, and discusses whether it is possible to build the Kingdom of God on earth and how biblical prophecy has been fulfilled through the coming of Bahá'u'lláh.

This book is aimed at Christian readers who have heard of the Bahá'í Faith and are interested in learning more about the relationship between the teachings of Christianity and the teachings of the Bahá'í Faith.

ILLUMINE MY SPIRIT

Bahá'í Prayers and Meditations for Women
COMPILED BY BAHÁ'Í PUBLISHING
PRICE: $12.00 U.S. / $13.50 CAN
FORMAT: TRADE PAPER
TRIM: 4 1/4 X 7
PAGES: 234
ISBN 978-1-931847-57-5

A collection of prayers and meditations from the Bahá'í writings that can provide a wellspring of inspiration for women of all cultural and religious backgrounds on every stage of life's journey. The prayers and meditations included here speak specifically to the qualities and concerns of women in a way seldom seen in religious texts. Drawn from a wide selection of Bahá'í texts, they address topics such as the qualities of women, motherhood, the education of children, the loss of loved ones, steadfastness, courage, and many other themes. *Illumine My Spirit* will surely serve as a treasury of comforting and reassuring words for women navigating the ups and downs of life.

THE PEN OF GLORY
Selected Works of Bahá'u'lláh
BAHÁ'U'LLÁH
PRICE: $12.00 U.S. / $14.00 CAN
FORMAT: TRADE PAPER
TRIM: 6 X 9
PAGES: 196
ISBN 978-1-931847-55-1

A collection from the sacred texts of the Bahá'í Faith responding to questions from people of other faiths.

The Pen of Glory: Selected Works of Bahá'u'lláh is a compilation of several works from the writings of Bahá'u'lláh, the Prophet-Founder of the Bahá'í Faith, responding to questions posed by people of other faiths. These selections are unique because they were written in response to specific questions from people wishing to know more about the principles and teachings of the Bahá'í Faith. Because these people came from various religious backgrounds, their questions elicited responses that provide the reader with a broad understanding of the central tenets of the Bahá'í Faith. In each of the works included in the volume, Bahá'u'lláh responds to the question of a seeker and then expounds on various related spiritual themes. In doing so, He has provided a collection of writings of enduring and far-reaching significance that remains applicable to the questions of religious seekers today.